Signifying Loss

Signifying Loss

Toward a Poetics of Narrative Mourning

Nouri Gana

Lewisburg
Bucknell University Press

Published by Bucknell University Press
Copublished by The Rowman & Littlefield Publishing Group, Inc.
4501 Forbes Boulevard, Suite 200, Lanham, Maryland 20706
www.rowman.com

16 Carlisle Street, London W1D 3BT, United Kingdom

First paperback edition 2014

British Library Cataloguing in Publication Information Available

Library of Congress Cataloging-in-Publication Data

The hardback edition of this book was previously cataloged by the Library of Congress as follows:

Signifying loss : toward a poetics of narrative mourning / Nouri Gana
p. cm.
Includes bibliographical references and index.
1. Loss (Psychology) in literature 2. Grief in literature. 3. Grief—Political aspects.
4. Psychoanalysis and literature. 5. Signifying (Rhetoric) I. Title
PN56.L58 G36 2011
809/.93353—dc22

2010023549

ISBN 978-1-61148-034-4 (cloth)
ISBN 978-1-61148-578-3 (pbk.)
ISBN 978-1-61148-035-1 (electronic)

TM

In loving memory of my father, Ali Gana

La vraie fidélité, dans le domaine de la pensée, n'est pas la fidélité aux solutions, mais la fidélité *aux problemes.*

In the realm of thought, true faithfulness is not faithfulness to solutions but *to problems.*

—Mikkel Borch-Jacobsen

Contents

Preface: The Poetics of Mourning

This book argues that signifying loss is crucial to adjusting to a persistently mutating and alienating reality and, simultaneously, to carrying out sociopolitical changes. In a world marked by the swift and sanitized infliction of loss and suffering, especially as a result of the insidious banalization of global warfare and everyday violence, it is less obviously ironic, but all the more alarming that homeopathic, communal, national, and transnational mourning practices have either withered, or, worse, turned into consumable spectacles, administered differentially along color and culture lines. A sustained critical engagement of our mourning practices—or lack of them thereof—is never more to be desired than at a time when, from an excess of commodity fetishism and disaster capitalism, the cumulative effects of global and local atrocities have come not only to wreak havoc in our psychic apparatuses and diminish our capacity to integrate catastrophic loss into intelligible narratives of individual and collective history, but also to ratify the racial and geopolitical differentials on the grounds of which grievability and humanity are constructed, valued, allocated, or withheld.

Whether in our conscious or unconscious desensitization to, engagement in, or divestment from mourning practices, humanity seems to be at stake. How come that mourning is devalued and valued at one and the same time? Has mourning really declined or has it changed? By remapping the configurations of mourning across modernist, postmodernist, and postcolonial Anglophone, Francophone, and Arabophone literatures (James Joyce, Jamaica Kincaid, Tahar Ben Jelloun, and Elias Khoury), as well as at the intersection between psychoanalysis, deconstruction, and comparative postcolonialism (Sigmund Freud, Jacques Derrida, Henry Staten, Gayatri Spivak, and Franz Fanon), *Signifying Loss* demonstrates the ways in which the social and public decline and devaluation of mourning practices have, in turn, given rise to a heterogeneous array of discursive and narrative practices of signifying private and collective grief and grievances. It is ironic that the one concrete-universal and common sociocultural means par excellence—mourning—of adjusting to change has itself proven susceptible to change in accord with socioeconomic and technoscientific permutations. In no small measure, this irony points, I believe, to a theoretical impasse in current theories of mourning between the injunction to mourn the early Freudian model of therapeutic mourning and the demand for an ethics of impossible or interminable mourning practices.

Given the long established and organic relationship between mourning and poetry—particularly insofar as the Western tradition of elegiac poetry and the poetic genre of *marthiya* (i.e., elegy) in the Arabic literary tradition are concerned—it is not surprising that this relation has expanded, with the rise of the novel and the urbanization of social life, into other literary genres, especially prose fiction. Following the rise of psychoanalysis and the breakup and dispersal of community into the carefully discriminated spheres of the private and the public, mourning has withdrawn into the recesses of the individual psyche, become a role without an actor, and given rise to what Peter Homans calls in a felicitous phrase, "mourning without mourning practices."[1] It might be the case, then, that the literary and narrative work of mourning is part and parcel of this new practice of mourning without mourning practices. Yet, it might equally, if not exceedingly, be the case that mourning practices have not, in fact, declined; rather, they have come to be regulated differently and in, among others, a form—the novel, or narrative prose fiction writ large—that is conducive to figuring the oft-immaterial and unquantifiable, private and public injuries and experiences of loss that ripple through, produce, and reproduce the conditions of possibility of modernity, postmodernity, and postcoloniality.[2]

The purpose of *Signifying Loss* is twofold: first, to produce a sustained comparative and critical engagement with the narrative configurations of mourning across modernist, postcolonial, and contemporary prose fiction; second, to study the implications of the narrative confluence between mourning and literary tropes, or figures, by discerning both the potencies and limits of such a confluence for an ethically and politically responsible practice of mourning. My title, *Signifying Loss,* has a double thrust that structures the book as a whole. First, I examine how loss is signified (i.e., figured and inscribed) in prose fiction. Second, I explore the critical, political, and ethical significance (i.e., import and valences) of such signifying. Insofar as the first purpose is concerned, I elaborate a narrative poetics—indeed, a tropologics—of mourning that stresses the importance of tropes to studying the dynamics of narrative fiction and mourning (particularly prosopopoeia, which I associate with mourning; catachresis, which I associate with melancholia, and chiasmus, which I associate with trauma). Insofar as the second purpose is concerned, I develop an ethico-political theory of mournership in which the experienceability of mourning becomes no less crucial to rethinking subjectivity and community than the by-now normative claims to inconsolability. Given that loss has become easily politicizable, it is important to develop a situated and flexible theory of mourning, capable of adjusting to diverse contexts—that is, contexts that would, for instance, entail a call for mournability at times and for inconsolability at others. In short, I call for the formulation of geopolitical and differential tactics of mourning and mournability rather than for a clear cut strategy of inconsolability.

Studies that stress the importance of mourning in illuminating narrative modernism have only recently started to emerge. Whereas they had previously been limited to a number of articles on such canonical figures as Virginia Woolf, James Joyce, and William Faulkner, among others, we now have several good books and edited collections by, to name only a notable few, Jahan Ramazani, Henry Staten, Alessia Ricciardi, R. Clifton Spargo, Patricia Rae, Jonathan Flatley, and Seth Moglen. For a period dominated by two major wars, however, needless to say that there is still more to be done for us to fathom the foundational or originative affinities between modernism and mourning. Similarly, in postcolonial studies—and with the exception of recent works by Bhaskar Sarkar, Sam Durrant, Paul Gilroy, Ranjana Khanna, among others—the lack of studies that make use of the insights of the various theories of mourning in reading postcolonial narrative fiction is somewhat puzzling, all the more so in a field in which the theoretical and fictional interrogation of the colonial past continues to be a foundational and enduring preoccupation. What is even more startling, however, is that there has not been any sustained work at the juncture between contemporary Arabic literature, which hovers at the margins of the unbendingly Anglophone postcolonial studies, and the recent theoretical work on mourning and melancholia despite the many palpable convulsions and decolonial wars that have marked and continue to mark Arab contemporaneity.

I would be remiss not to point out, though, that when I first started working on *Signifying Loss* in the early years of this decade, only a few pioneering studies on the question of mourning were available—at any rate, nothing of the sort that would have predicted the overnight proliferation of works on mourning and literature, and particularly on mourning and elegy, which we currently have at our disposal in the twilight of this decade. While indebted to the valuable scholarship on elegy, this book will not, however, include a discussion of poetry, or elegy, partly because there are more studies on mourning in relation to elegy than on mourning in relation to prose fiction, and partly because I find the connection between elegy and mourning a bit predictable,[3] even while I agree that modernist elegies frustrate this predictability and—far from fulfilling mourning and compensating for the loss which occasions them—betray what Jahan Ramazani suggestively calls "melancholic mourning," a form of mourning that, paradoxically, "tends not to achieve but to resist consolation."[4] It is partly because I find the ability of poetry to withhold consolation in the aftermath of catastrophe not easily generalizeable to other more direct modes of writing that I devote this study to exploring its applicability or transferability to prose fiction.

It bears mentioning here that Theodor Adorno must have been made aware of the capacity of poetry to suspend the fulfillment of the work of mourning—

and to "[express] in negative form the impulse which inspires committed literature"—before he hastened to amend his initially undifferentiated ban on "poetry" and restrict it to "*lyric* poetry."[5] Given the rhetorical fecundity and indirect address of poetry, which must have prompted Adorno's amendment of his initial ban, I find Slavoj Žižek's recent proposition to further amend Adorno's dictum rather in tune with the overall rationale of *Signifying Loss:* "Adorno's famous saying, it seems, needs correction: it is not poetry that is impossible after Auschwitz, but rather prose. Realistic prose fails, where poetic evocation of the unbearable atmosphere of a camp succeeds. That is to say, when Adorno declares poetry impossible (or, rather, barbaric) after Auschwitz, this impossibility is an enabling impossibility: poetry is always, by definition, 'about' something that cannot be addressed directly, only alluded to."[6] True, because of its desire for form, coherency and credulity, prose fiction (the novel, in particular) might not necessarily be the ideal indirect mode of expression in the aftermath of catastrophe. Žižek is worried that rather than extracting its inner form from the chaotic reality outside of it, the novel risks neutralizing the very discontinuity of that reality into the all too neat unfolding of its form. Hence, it fails there where poetry would normally succeed. In other words, while the impossibility of poetry is enabling, that of prose is disempowering and deadening.

Signifying Loss seeks not only to examine how narrative prose fiction has addressed this challenge which has put its very raison d'être into question, but also to bear witness to its attempt to transform its formal disempowerment into a basis for empowerment and narrative departure. I read the politics of the literary texts under examination in tandem with sustained analyses of their form in order to develop a poetics of narrative mourning. I find the politics of narrative mourning in the aftermath of disastrous losses indissociable from deliberate investments in form. *Signifying Loss* gradually hammers home this conclusion throughout its constitutive chapters until it becomes patently clear in the final chapter on Elias Khoury's fragmentary novel of the Lebanese civil war, *City Gates, Abwāb al-madīna.*

I became cognizant of the necessity and urgency of formulating what I call a *poetics of narrative mourning* for a number of reasons. For the sake of brevity, I will mention only the two most obvious ones. First, if Freud insists that mourning is a "work" (*die arbeit,* or precisely, *die Trauerarbeit*) and if Derrida further insists that "all work is also the work of mourning" (*que tout travail est aussi travail du deuil*),[7] I think it is incumbent upon literary critics and theorists alike to ask, preparatory to anything else, the following question: How does this "work" *work* in relation to literature? Or, more precisely, how does this "work" *work its way into* narrative fiction? There is a performative dynamic at work here: narrative is the signifying field of mourning and simultaneously the effect or product of the very work of mourning it signifies. Second, not only does the bulk of literary criticism produced on the question of mourning in relation to literature (on pastoral and modern elegy, in particular) reflect on the subject almost exclusively from a thematic viewpoint, but even the more recent and theoretically sophisticated studies which speak overtly about a "spectropoetics," or about, significantly enough, a "poetics of mourning" tend to reduce "poetics" to "thematics," and miss, therefore, the opportunity to explore the narrative function of tropes in signifying mourning.[8] Rather than discerning the intrinsically anomic and dynamic narrative plot of tropes, Ricciardi's and Watkin's studies, for instance, arrest extrinsically the inner dynamicity and versatility of tropes in the pragmatics of consolation or nonconsolation. Yet, the very nature of tropes, if read closely, as I do, troubles ideas of consolation and/or nonconsolation.

In my treatment of *poetics,* I neither use the term as an empty gesture that points toward or instantaneously freezes it into thematic concerns and considerations, nor do I use it in a strictly traditional Aristotelian sense, much less in a narratological and poststructuralist sense, where it denotes systematically how meaning is formally produced through the delineation of types of narrative and their conventions, etc. By poetics—as in poetics of narrative mourning—I mean broadly (to evoke and conceptualize) the passage from suffering *to* signifying loss. This is an unruly passage that cannot be fully systematized at a micropoetic level. What muddies the waters is that mourning itself is from a macropoetic viewpoint a trope or figure of reading narrative ends and the inevitable entanglements between story and plot. The texts I study, however, variably stage and perform a convergence, a confluence of sorts, or an overlap between the rhetorical and psychoaffective dynamics of mourning. "Ultimately, we may dream," following Peter Brooks, "of a convergence between psychoanalysis and literary criticism because we sense that there ought to be a correspondence between literary and psychic dynamics."[9] In no small measure, *Signifying Loss* maps those dynamics.

I am interested in the figures that figure forth the problematic of mourning in narrative prose fiction, the figures that shape and are simultaneously shaped by what they shape. Generally, these are figures of speech that were not dear to the New Critics but that were nevertheless resurrected and reconceptualized by, among others, Paul de Man, J. Hillis Miller, and Hayden White. For instance, in light of the poetics of narrative mourning I elaborate and put forward in this study, prosopopoeia (i.e., personification, apostrophe) figures as the master trope of mourning while catachresis (i.e., the figure of contextual abuse of, or improper, word use) and chiasmus (i.e., the figure of repetition and reversibility) as the master tropes of, respectively, melancholia and trauma. There are, of course, other supplementary tropes that hover in the gravitational pull of each of these master tropes; these include not only prolepsis, metaphor and aporia, but also allegory and metonymy. Occasionally, in the unfolding of the process of signifying mourning, prosopopoeia would spiral or swerve into prolepsis and back, catachresis into metaphor, chiasmus into aporia, etc., creating a relentlessly transformational and generative poetics rather than a systematic and constraining one—a poetics that allegorizes what it seeks to express.

I make no claim to covering all aspects of this poetics of narrative mourning, much less to addressing the potentially playful combinations, convergences, or divergences, etc., that this triadic tropological conception of signifying loss could form with other tropes. What is important about a poetics of narrative mourning is that each of these tropes becomes as much a figure of reading as an organizing principle of narrative. Hence, they open up narrative to multiple operations, including inversion, reversion, diversion, repetition, reversibility, etc., and produce in the process diverse effects which range from epiphany and empathy—or what I call empiphany—to mourning, melancholia and inconsolability. For instance, by drawing on Paul de Man's definition of prosopopoeia as a symmetrically structured trope of personifying the dead and simultaneously petrifying the living, I explore the ways in which the narrative plot or dialectic of prosopopoeia can be aligned with Freud's theory of mourning as a piecemeal process of remembering and severing the ties with the dead. Yet, my reading of prosopopoeia in relation to Joyce's *Dubliners* shows how the trope's power to incite mourning falls short of delivering anything close to either the promise of consolation or the threat of petrification. I follow the same logic throughout the book, bringing into intimate collision the unruliness of literary tropes *and* the energetics of narrative desire while making and remaking the unlikely conjunction between close reading and literary mourning practices.

Apart from Joyce's *Dubliners* and *Ulysses,* most of my literary examples are taken from postcolonial literature. The self exiled Joyce himself has by now been routinely placed in the postcolonial field (given that Ireland was under British rule at the turn of the twentieth century when Joyce started writing). Similarly, the self-exiled Kincaid grew up in her native Antigua during the last days of British colonialism before she moved to the United States at age sixteen. Almost the same could be said about Ben Jelloun who left his postcolonial Morocco in his late twenties and settled in Paris. Khoury grew up in postcolonial Lebanon, fought in the civil war, and has always maintained strong ties to Lebanon and the Arab world in general even though he left Beirut to hold several teaching positions in the United States. These authors are by no means the only ones that I might have written about in relation to elaborating a poetics of narrative mourning. Many others come to mind immediately (e.g., Virginia Woolf, William Faulkner, J. M. Coetzee, Wilson Harris, Ghassan Kanafani, Ahlam Mosteghanemi, Rachid al-Daif, etc.) if my goal were indeed to multiply the evidence and write an inventory or a survey of narratives of mourning rather than elaborate a poetics in which what matters is how it works in specific texts rather than how generalizeable it is to other texts, for it surely is generalizeable to other works once due particularizations and distinctions are belabored.

Joyce, Kincaid, Ben Jelloun, and Khoury offer enough range and continuities in order for me to elaborate a poetics of narrative mourning while simultaneously attending to the geopolitical significance at work in each specific text under examination, be it Joyce's *Dubliners* and Kincaid's *My Brother* or Ben Jelloun's *The Last Friend* and Khoury's *City Gates.* Moreover, Joyce, Kincaid, Ben Jelloun, and Khoury straddle traditionally separate fields: modernism, postmodernism, and postcolonialism. Whether in terms of style, form or content of their work, each of these authors could be approached as a modernist, a postmodernist, or a postcolonialist at one and the same time. Not that these fields mean the same thing but that they share similarities that cut across their disciplinary boundaries. Preeminent among these stands the preoccupation with signifying loss. In addition, in one way or another, these authors can be considered in the words of Edward Said as "rooted exiles."[10] Even though they variably strayed away from their homelands, they have relentlessly been preoccupied with the sociopolitical actualities of their places of birth, respectively, Ireland, Antigua, Morocco, and Lebanon. While I offer both particularized and comparative readings of these authors, I make no claims to any verifiable contacts or exchanges between or among them, except perhaps to conjecture that the latter three must have read Joyce.

Derrida, who read both Freud and Joyce, is the animating figure of this book even though his brand of deconstructive mourning practices is the target of much of my criticism. The issue, in short, is that Derrida makes mourning paradoxically singular yet structural, impossible yet recursive, and excessive yet recessive. The effect is, as I argue, overwhelmingly ethical yet politically undifferentiated. One final note on the chapters included in this book: given our understandably chaotic experience of reading, I have made sure that each of the chapters is written in such a way that it can be read independently from the chapter that precedes it. This entails that some minor repetitions of the theoretical frames of the argument have been unavoidable, particularly in the case of Freud, the initiator of discursive mourning practices.

Acknowledgments

Signifying Loss emerges out of a doctoral dissertation completed in 2004 at the University of Montreal, Quebec. I am particularly grateful to Eric Savoy and Walter Moser for their guidance, generosity, and encouragement. Walter Moser has taught me to think otherwise *and* with modesty. Eric Savoy has taught me to read playfully *and* with rigor. Patricia Rae prompted me to think politics *and* form together. I thank my other dissertation committee members for their questions, comments, and feedback: Heike Härting, Amaryll Chanady, and Andrew John Miller, who passed away on September 4, 2009, and is sadly missed. Peter Hewlett has been an astute interlocutor *and* a formidable skeptic, almost cynical at times *but* for good reasons.

At Queen's University, Kingston, Ontario, where I spent two years as a Social Science and Humanities Research Council of Canada Postdoctoral Fellow, I am deeply indebted to my wonderful colleagues at the Department of English. I thank Asha Varadharajan for her intellectual mentorship. Adnan Husain has been enthusiastically supportive of my work and offered more than critical feedback: friendship. Chris Bongie, Margaret Pappano, and Ariel Salzmann have been wonderful friends, readers, and cooks.

At UCLA, where this project expanded and took its final shape, I am grateful to my colleagues and students for the many stimulating intellectual interactions and discussions we have entertained over the last three years. I am sure some of the ideas that crystallized in my mind during these intellectual encounters must have found their way into this book in ways that I can neither tell nor enumerate. For providing a sense of intellectual belonging, I am particularly thankful to Ali Behdad, Michael Cooperson, Michael Fishbein, Eleanor Kaufman, Katherine King, Kathleen L. Komar, Efraín Kristal, Kirstie McClure, Ismail K. Poonawala, Kenneth Reinhard, Ross Shideler, Shu-mei Shih, and Susan Slyomovics. For their helpful feedback, I thank Michelle Clayton, Gil Hochberg, and Aamir R. Mufti.

For their long term financial support of my doctoral studies in Canada, I thank both La Mission Universitaire de Tunisie à Montréal and the Social Sciences and Humanities Research Council of Canada.

I thank Greg Clingham at Bucknell University Press for endorsing this project and the anonymous readers for their feedback. I also want to thank the staff and editors at Associated University Presses and Rowman & Littlefield for their patience and diligence.

Finally, I thank all the members of my family for their support of my decision to pursue my studies in Canada. I am very thankful to Reem for her courage to join me in Los Angeles and for her love and support at the last stages of this project. My father, Ali Gana, passed away on January 8, 2000, at a time when this project was in an early formative stage. I dedicate this book to his memory.

Some of the material in this book has been previously published. I should like to thank publishers and editors for their editorial suggestions and permissions to reprint material from, among others:

James Joyce Quarterly, for permission to print in chapter 3 a revised version of "The Vicissitudes of Melancholia in Freud and Joyce," *James Joyce Quarterly* 44.1 (2007): 95–109.

American Imago, for permission to use in chapter 2 portions of "The Poetics of Mourning: The Tropologic of Prosopopoeia in Joyce's "The Dead," *American Imago* 60.2 (2003): 159–78.

Études Irlandaises, for permission to use in chapter 2 portions of "Horizons of Desire, Horizons of Mourning: Joyce's *Dubliners,*" *Études Irlandaises: Revue Françoise d'Histoire, Civilization et littérature de l' Irlande* 28.1 (2003): 25–43.

Comparative Literature Studies, for permission to print in chapter 6 a revised and expanded version of "Formless Form: Elias Khoury's *City Gates* and the Poetics of Trauma," *Comparative Literature Studies* 47.4 (2010): 504–532.

Signifying Loss

1

Thresholds of Mourning: Freud and After

Go out of mourning first.
—Joyce, *Ulysses*

THUS SPAKE JAMES JOYCE—IN THE IMPERATIVE![1] THE ORDER IS SIMPLE. IT asks us to go out of mourning, to move out of mourning and into something else that it holds in reserve or keeps in store for us until we have met the demand of leaving mourning behind. Preparatory to anything else, we are required to go out of mourning. What follows, what is about to unfold—really, the condition of its very unfolding—hinges on the fulfillment of the task we are assigned. Joyce's categorical imperative, we begin to realize, is also a *promise* of something else, of something better that is about to happen to us. A world of possibility seems to be awaiting us were we to go out of mourning. Joyce's injunction is quite explicit about this world of possibility awaiting us, since we are asked not to go out of mourning as such, but precisely to go out of mourning *first.* Herein lurks the kernel of the promise: in the conditionality and primacy of the categorical imperative over any other suchlike imperatives.

Whether there are other imperatives or not, going out of mourning is preeminent among them. In the beginning, there is mourning, and there is mourning to begin with. Mourning is the condition of beginning, yet going out of it is the condition of what will follow, of the very unfolding of what will follow. The promise of what will follow is identical with the condition of its unfolding. Going out of mourning, we begin to grasp, is also both the promise and the condition of what will follow. In fact, what will follow—the promise of which going out of mourning is the condition—is nothing but the state of *being out of mourning.* Going out of mourning is then the condition and the promise of being out of mourning.

Because it is essentially aphoristic, Joyce's sententious imperative exceeds hermeneutic mastery (if by hermeneutic mastery we mean the establishment of an essential or core meaning encoded in the order given to us). It exceeds hermeneutic mastery even while it preaches psychoaffective mastery or emotional closure tout court. For, were going out of mourning a naturally occurring phenomenon, it would have hardly become an imperative, much less a condition for a promise to come. In other words, the logic of the imperative itself is inhabited by the skepticism, if not despair, over the unobtainability of what it seeks. Joyce's imperative is, moreover, uttered by Leopold Bloom in the bosom of Hades, and, more accurately, at Glasnevin Cemetery, at Paddy Dignam's funeral—the axis around which revolves the "Hades" episode of *Ulysses.* Set thus, within an ostensibly charged site of mourning, the imperative becomes doubtlessly all the more cogent and urgent. Yet the more urgent the imperative becomes, the more uncertain its implementation appears to be. It is this fear of unfeasibility—really, the fear of the failure of implementation—that lingers behind, at the very back of the intransigent nature of the command. The command is therefore preceded, if not conditioned, by the anticipation or expectancy of incompletion or failure.

The amount of emphasis laid on the command implies, however, something else, something that has to do with the nature or "business" of mourning itself: particularly, that "mourning" is a stumbling block, a crucible—a trial of the utmost difficulty. So powerful a commandment—*Go out of mourning first*—signals that we are indeed presented with an equally powerful challenge. No longer are we merely *ordered* to go out of mourning, but we are precisely *challenged* to do so. If going out of mourning is to be framed as a challenge, does this mean that it is *beyond* our means to meet that challenge?

To the extent that *Go out of mourning first* is understood as an order or imperative, it implies that it is within our capacity to act upon or accomplish it with a certain amount of success; to the extent that it is understood as a challenge, however, it implies that it is both within *and* in excess of our capacity to accomplish it. It can be argued, I suppose, that whether going out of mourning is an order or a challenge, the promise remains the same—the hypothetical state of being out of mourning. At first glance, one might react to a challenge in the same fashion one might react to an order, yet it is oftentimes the case that to meet a challenge one has to push to the limits of one's means; moreover, one is oftentimes *deprived* of the means to meet the challenge. One is, perhaps, deprived of the means of going out of mourning as soon as one enters (into) mourning. In other words, the very fact of being *in* mourning might imply that one is *unable* to go out of it, that all of one's psychic resources are engaged in mourning, such that there is no energy left in store to enable the passage out of mourning; were one able to go out of mourning, one would not probably have entered (into) it in the first place. Or is it, rather, that one deliberately enters into and tarries with the process of mourning, resisting in the meanwhile any incentive or challenge to go out of it? Can one then stop at the threshold, refuse or decide not to enter into mourning? For why should one, after all, enter into something out of which one is soon required or challenged to exit? How do we enter (into) mourning? Why do we linger in mourning or refuse to go out of it? What is mourning?

The Work of Mourning

> I wasn't even sure that I fully understood my own central concept of 'mourning.' I was taking it from Freud, but he didn't understand it either.
> —Geoffrey Galt Harpham, "The Business of Mourning"

In his epochal, metapsychological essay, "Mourning and Melancholia" (1917), Freud contends that mourning is, like melancholia, a *reaction* to loss. I will come to the question of melancholia's oppositional distinction to mourning in due course; suffice it now to stress that Freud associates it with the obstruction or sabotage of the "normal affect" of mourning.[2] The loss for which mourning is the reaction does not solely involve the death of a beloved person (or object-cathexis), but it can also involve the demise of a number of abstract ideas, ideals, polities, or human rights, such as civic liberty and freedom of expression or democracy, as well as the loss of an era, a political regime, an economic system, a historical movement, a homeland to settler colonialism, a culture or a language to the forces of globalization, and so on. Whatever the loss may be, the appropriate emotional response, Freud argues, is mourning. Depending on the scale or magnitude of each suffered loss as well as on the psychic wherewithal of each mourner, the duration of mourning will vary, sometimes significantly, but it is not expected, on the whole, to go beyond "a certain lapse of time."[3] The processive stepping or progress of mourning toward its resolution is in keeping with the irreversible forward movement of time. Mourning is then an economy of emotional response to a painful loss that counts on the passage of time in order for it to carry out its reparative work. It is not for nothing that Freud refers to this contingent emotional economy as a *work of mourning* (*Trauerarbeit*). Yet, what exactly is the task that the work of mourning is said to carry out?

To make some headway into this difficult question, let us first examine Freud's elaborate answer at some length:

> Reality-testing has shown that the loved object no longer exists, and it proceeds to demand that all libido shall be withdrawn from its attachment to that object. This demand arouses understandable opposition—it is a matter of general observation that people never willingly abandon a libidinal position, not even, indeed, when a substitute is already beckoning at them. This opposition can be so intense that a turning away from reality takes place and a clinging to the object through a medium of hallucinatory wishful psychosis. Normally, respect for reality gains the day. Nevertheless its orders cannot be obeyed at once. They are carried out bit by bit, at great expense of time and cathectic energy, and in the meantime the existence of the lost object is psychically prolonged.[4]

Perhaps it is too premature to concur with Geoffrey Galt Harpham, in the above epigraph, that Freud did not really understand what mourning is; after all, I make no claims to understanding what it is either.[5] Let us willingly suspend our impulse to make sense of mourning in an attempt to host—in accordance with the laws of hospitality relevant to critical thinking—Freud's core definition.[6] To begin with, I think Freud's argument is predicated upon the *reconciliatory* process that the work of mourning initiates (and presumably fulfills), not only with regard to the lost object but also with regard to the decrees of reality—the literal "hard rock" against which the mourner's fantasies of recovering the object are shattered. Here, the conciliatory is consolatory. But, since Stephen Dedalus insists that "[w]here there is a reconciliation . . . there must have been first a sundering,"[7] what kind of sundering, one might ask, does the loss of the object result in?

It is commonly argued in psychoanalytic theory—and in object relations theory, in particular[8]—that subjectivity is a relational enterprise. I will treat this point in some detail later when I discuss the question of identification; suffice it for the moment to stress that love-objects serve to accommodate libidinal investments and to maintain psychic balance. Once a love-object is lost, it can no longer fulfill its former function—the reception and mediation of libido. Unless the (mourning) subject proceeds to withdraw and reinvest his or her libidinal energy in a new object, his or her ego is left bereaved and burdened with surplus libidinal energy circling in the void, and, not infrequently, channeled into aggressive conduct in the private or public sphere. When lost and no longer in sight, any given love-object can *theoretically* be compromised in the service of acquiring a new one; the ego becomes, once the withdrawal and displacement of libido is accomplished, no longer debilitated by the enormous suffering incurred in the wake of the loss of the object but quite invigorated and adjusted to the world of reality again. Freud states, "Why this compromise by which the command of reality is carried out piecemeal should be so extraordinarily painful is not at all easy to explain in terms of economics. It is remarkable that this painful unpleasure is taken as a matter of course by us. The fact is, however, that when the work of mourning is completed the ego becomes free and uninhibited again."[9] The loss of the object comes, in point of fact, to sunder an otherwise originary capacity or freedom of choosing and picking up objects of desire. To regain this freedom of attaching to other objects must come then, at least theoretically, at the expense of the loyalty to the lost object(s). The reconciliatory work of mourning can be understood as nothing less than an incitement to and a normalization of the praxis of disloyalty.

Furthermore, the reconciliation with reality—or the exercise of reality-testing about which Freud speaks—is, as it were, an attempt at exorcising the estrangement effect produced by the loss of the object. The mourner attempts to make reality his *own* again after having been *alienated* from it by the loss of his or her loved object. In this sense, the work of mourning is a "genuinely hermeneutical" process of refamiliarization with an unchanging but repressed reality—*unchanging* because it has always involved loss and dying; *repressed* because the reality of death and loss would hardly have been painted by the libidinal adventurer at the time of libidinal approach and attachment.[10] The refamiliarization with reality implies, perhaps inherently, the refamiliarization with the technique of repression of the knowledge of death and mortality involved in the search for new objects. In other words, while the loss of a love-object and mourning might culminate in an illuminating and epiphanic experience (in that they open up the mourner or survivor, for instance, to the irreducible otherness of the object of desire), the completion of the work of mourning implies the premeditated forgetting or nescience of the harsh knowledge earned via the experience of mourning: it reinstates precisely the illusion of life and the repression of death.[11]

There is one additional feature of the reconciliatory feat that the work of mourning performs that I would like to address here. One of the aims of the work of mourning, as described by Freud, is the severance of the libidinal relations from the lost object. While it is not clear whether the work of severance leads to the acquisition of a new object or whether the acquisition of a new object leads to the completion of the work of severance, "There are," as Freud argues elsewhere, "nearly always residual phenomena, a partial hanging-back" to earlier libidinal fixations and to lost love objects.[12] In order for the work of severance to be thorough and complete, it has to be founded on a sound basis. This sound basis is nothing other than the cornerstone of psychoanalytic treatment writ large—remembering. Accordingly, "[e]ach single one of the memories and expectations in which the libido is bound to the object is brought up and hypercathected, and detachment of the libido is accomplished in respect of it."[13] I cannot here illustrate sufficiently the incommensurable activities of hypercathecting and detaching,[14] but I will demonstrate throughout the main chapters of the book the constant slippage of hypercathecting-detachment into recathecting-attachment: far from being a means of completing the work of severance and mourning, hypercathecting and remembering become the *conservational* forces of the work of mourning beyond a certain lapse of time.

By and large, Freud's *Trauerarbeit* does not seem to me to work *at* anything except at its *own* dissolution. The work of mourning is the means whereby mourning can be achieved, yet it is simultaneously the product of the very mourning it seeks to overcome, fulfill, or alleviate. Going *out* of mourning then necessitates going *through* mourning, which implies, in turn, that going *through* mourning cannot be experienced unless as an instance of going *out* of mourning. Mourning is the arrow and the target, *la flèche et la cible.* The end of mourning is the end of mourning. Nothing else can call for the dissolution of a work in the name of its completion. In Freud's conception, mourning cannot be experienced as such, let alone maintained or sustained. No tarrying with it, period! For mourning is a work that is always at work in view of its own exhaustion and resolution. No wonder, then, that by the end of the "Hades" episode, Bloom heaves a sigh of relief as he leaves the cemetery: "Back to the world again. Enough of this place."[15] It is as if Bloom indeed implies that it is prohibited to be stationed in mourning.[16] The temporality of mourning itself is delimited and calculated: "Good Hamlet, cast thy nightly color off," Gertrude urges her son.[17] Between a sense of *getting into it* or *going out of it* and a feeling of having *had enough of it,* mourning, as a transformational and generative force of subjectivity—and of self-refashioning and reinventing communal ties and collectivities—is lost to us, or left largely unexplored.

One broad aim of *Signifying Loss* is to offer a corrective to Freud's insistence—at least, insofar as "Mourning and Melancholia" is concerned—on the temporal constraints and therapeutic aims of mourning. A more deliberatively relational and sociopolitical conception of mourning seems to me conducive not only to framing ways of relating to lost others, to the past, and to history writ large, but also to rethinking the present and the future by contemplating how the experience of mourning can become a threshold moment of solidarity and community building, particularly in the wake of the Great War and the decolonization struggles in the first half of the twentieth century, both of which can be seen, respectively, as the midwives of modernist and postcolonial literatures and cultures. Narrative becomes by the same token—and insofar as it directs our unshrinking attention to the experience of mourning it stages—a function of sociocultural formations and transformations of intelligibility, collectivity, and subjectivity. This brings me to the other aspect of the broad aim of *Signifying Loss:* to loosen the therapeutic grip of Freudian psychoanalysis on the concept of mourning. Relations are built in mourning, not in response to it, even though the contingencies and dynamics of response remain crucial to envisioning and initiating sociopolitical and subjective transformations. Only when mourning has been repressed or willed away does its protean return become harrowing and unbearable. The imperative *Go out of mourning first* would mean, were it to be understood literally, nothing less than a further repression of an otherwise indispensable constituent of relations at large. By urging the mourner to reinvest in a new object, Freud's brand of modernist therapeutics does not, in my view, proffer us with more than a momentary solution to the inevitable recurrence of mourning, except perhaps the benefit of the experience itself in refashioning the self.[18] For as soon as one reinvests one's cathectic energy in a new object, one simply paves the way to another outbreak of mourning. We begin to grasp that mourning has, in many respects, less to do with the loss of the object per se than with the movement of desire as such.

MOURNING AND THE CIRCLE OF DESIRE

> As soon as desire is something felt by a mortal being for a mortal being, eros (as desire-in-general) will always be to some degree agitated by the anticipation of loss.
>
> —Henry Staten, *Eros in Mourning*

In "Remembering, Repeating and Working-Through" (1914), Freud tells us how precarious the work of remembering is, not because it preys on flashes of memory, on slips of forgetting, as it were, but because remembering what had been kept in abeyance may only lead to the intensification of the illness rather than to its gradual cure. On this score, it is worth noting that the "bit by bit" tempo of remembering and hypercathecting can lead to the intensification and conservation of mourning rather than to its dissipation. It is not that Freud is unaware of the fault lines of his postulations, but, perhaps, he is only too aware of the portion of truth in each of them to attempt to resolve their tensions. In fact, Freud's awareness of the precarious nature of the analytics of remembering is such that he has recourse to *Gerede,* to idle talk, that is, in order to overstep the collapse of his theoretical premises: "one can easily console the patient," Freud observes, "by pointing out that [the intensifications of his illness] are only necessary and temporary aggravations and that one cannot overcome an enemy who is absent or not within range."[19] Only pure sophistry can reside comfortably in such conspicuous contradictions. On the one hand, Freud would comfort his patient by insisting on the *temporality* of the aggravations; on the other, he would point out the precise opposite: that the originator of his or her sufferings had left the field of battle and could therefore no longer be wrestled to the ground. It is in this light that I will attempt to understand Freud's insistence on the temporality of mourning and his parallel prescription of libidinal reinvestment. It seems to me that the temporality of mourning becomes untenable as soon as it becomes an impetus for new libidinal expeditions.

In his brilliant study, *Eros in Mourning,* Henry Staten argues that "[as] soon as desire is something felt by a mortal being for a mortal being, eros (as desire-in-general) will always be to some degree agitated by the anticipation of loss—an anticipation that operates even with regard to what is not yet possessed."[20] Far from being a reaction to object-loss, mourning runs the gamut of love relations from libidinal approach through attachment to the loss of the love-object.[21] Mourning is the unconscious of desire; it is wired to the circuit of desire for new objects but does not become manifest—in a cultural and phenomenological sense—only following the loss of the object of desire.[22] In the spirit of deconstruction, and *pace* Freud, Staten understands mourning not as a reaction to loss or as a process of healing from loss, but in terms of a dialectic that structures every move in the formation of object-relations. Furthermore, at the core of this "dialectic of mourning" are not only the moments of libidinal approach, attachment, and loss, but also the very concomitant "strategies of deferral, avoidance, or transcendence that arise in response to the threat of loss—strategies by which the self is 'economized' against the libidinal expenditure involved in mourning."[23]

Anchored in desire, the work of mourning cannot possibly overcome the ruptures of libidinal relations, much less by inciting the mourner to strike into yet another libidinal adventure. Here lies the ultimate irony of Freud's economy of libidinal exchange, of withdrawal and reinvestment of libido, of which mourning is the driving force. What Freud offers us, in other words, is not a final resolution of the problem of mourning but a blueprint for its perpetuation, for it does not matter whether or not one divests his libido from a lost object-cathexis and reinvests it into another, if one were to realize the inextricably bound relationship between desire and mourning. The movement of desire is structured by mourning; the movement out of mourning is predicated upon the redistribution of desire. This is the circle of desire and of mourning: the road out of mourning is precisely the road leading back into it. Insofar as going out of mourning is keyed to desire—to the *transferal* of libidinal energy into yet another mortal object—it is a perpetual *referral* back to mourning. The ultimate irony of Freud's conception of going out of mourning through the exit door of desire is that it turns into a recessive mise en abyme, begetting the very problem it seeks to solve. Instead of overcoming mourning, it multiplies and therefore perpetuates it.

Attentive to the reiterative circularity of eros and mourning and wearied of scenes of unseasonable grief, Platonism, Stoicism, and Christianity, among others, joined forces to create and disseminate a prophylactic theory of managing mortal eros via the implementation of an economics of idealization and transcendence. This is squarely, according to Henry Staten, the gist of the trajectory that the whole Western tradition has followed in its hitherto contested relation to eros. If all desire has mourning at its horizon, the more radical solution than the one with which Freud proffers us would proceed by the containment of desire rather than by the reactionary management of mourning, for it is always too late to work through mourning once desire has found route to the object. Since desire for a mortal object is, by definition, tipped toward mourning, only by winnowing out desire or nipping eros in the bud can the possibility of transcending grief become tenable.

Lacan's contention—"That the one unbearable dimension of possible human experience is not the experience of one's death, which no one has, but the experience of the death of another"[24]—can be located in reference/contradistinction to the Stoic tradition of philosophical wisdom. In Lacan, this unbearable dimension of death refers to the "hole in the real" left by the loss of the object—a hole that, while it "sets the signifier in motion," cannot possibly be filled, since the signifier that designates it can be "purchased only with your own flesh and your own blood," that is, only through (the mourner's) bodily dissolution or death tout court.[25] In the Roman Stoic tradition of philosophy, it is precisely this eventuality of the mourner's bodily dissolution, this memento mori effect, so to speak, that motivates the very project of transcendence, "of learning how to extract one's libidinal substance from the mortal or losable objects in which it could be trapped."[26] This practice of anticipatory withdrawal of libido from the mortal objects is a diurnal ascesis among the Roman Stoics. In *Enchiridion,* Epictetus describes this ascesis with remarkable clarity: "In every thing which pleases the soul, or supplies a want, or is loved, remember to add this to the (description, notion); what is the nature of each thing, beginning from the smallest? If you love an earthen vessel, say it is an earthen vessel which you love; for when it has been broken, you will not be disturbed. If you are kissing your child or wife, say that it is a human being whom you are kissing, for when the wife or child dies, you will not be disturbed."[27] This might seem, of course, easier said than done, yet the inevitable mortality of the object is thought to be made less of a shock if it is diurnally painted and anticipated or called upon to mediate and check libidinal investments. While there are obvious differences between, for instance, the Stoic emphasis on autosufficiency and self-regulation and the Christian insistence on God's grace, the fulcrum of the Platonic-Stoic-Christian argument is, according to Staten, the mastery or attenuation of the otherwise runaway force of eros prior to object-loss. For it is vigorously ordained that "no object that may be lost is to be loved in an unmeasured fashion—that only a limited or conditional libidinal flow toward such objects is to be allowed, such that the self remains ready and able to retract its substance from the object before the unmasterable violence of mourning might assail it."[28]

By means of an "economized" engagement with several variations on two "archetexts," Homer's *Iliad* and the Gospel of John, Staten's *Eros in Mourning* delivers a compelling remapping of the idealizing-transcendentalizing and religio-philosophical Western tradition of policing and controlling desire. The subsequent chapters of Staten's book—which range from studies of the troubadour song, Shakespeare's *Hamlet,* Milton's *Paradise Lost,* and Conrad's *Heart of Darkness* to Lacan's *Seminars*—lay bare the sedimentations and residues of this tradition of regulating desire in the Western literary and philosophical trajectory from Shakespeare through to Lacan. Taking my lead from Staten, in chapter 2 I will trace the sedimentations of this idealizing-transcendentalizing tradition in an early modernist collection of short stories, Joyce's *Dubliners.* My aim is not to show that the modernist subject is inconsolable—a view that has so far dominated the study of the modernist elegy (e.g., Jahan Ramazani, Clifton Spargo, and Patricia Rae) and, to a lesser extent, the novels of James Joyce, Virginia Woolf and Marcel Proust (e.g., Karen E. Smythe, Tammy Clewell, and Alessia Ricciardi)—but to inquire whether the modernist subject *ever* experiences mourning in the first place. Not infrequently, inconsolability in the modernist horizon is a sign of deferral rather than divestment from the promise of mourning. For one thing, inconsolability is not in excess of narrative form, whose surge for closure frustrates and even corrodes the refusal to mourn that modernist narratives are said to perform and advocate. For another, inconsolability is irreducible to an attitude against mourning; it is a refusal of mourning as much as it can be a refusal of that very refusal (before it turns into dogma). My point about inconsolability will become clear when I relate mourning to desire; suffice it to say now that inconsolability is indeed mourning by other means. At any rate, inconsolability might be sustainable only in its chiastic oscillation with the search for consolation, but what interests me in relation to Joyce's *Dubliners* is not whether Joyce's protagonists refuse to mourn but whether mourning has unfolded as an experience in the first place.

More important by far, my aim is to reach a better grasp of the nexus of desire and mourning, not by engaging it solely from a thematic perspective, but also from a poetic one—by discerning the ways in which mourning and desire are recon*figured* in narrative. While Staten's *Eros in Mourning* offers the groundwork for a new poetics, which we can confidently call a *poetics of mourning,* it does not articulate the tropological architecture of *narrative mourning.* I therefore start the elaboration of a poetics of narrative mourning by attempting to theorize the passage from suffering mourning to signifying it—*signifying* in the composite sense of tropologically figuring and hermeneutically grasping mourning. I concentrate on discerning connections between tropes and affects and demonstrate the ways in which prosopopoeia (i.e., the figure of personification) can be seen as the master trope of narrative mourning. By drawing on Paul de Man, in particular, I examine the ways in which the narrative plot of prosopopoeia can be aligned to Freud's theory of mourning so as to allow the formulation of a *therapoetics of mourning,* that is, a poetics in which the consolatory valences of prosopopoeia (i.e., the conferment of voice and face on the dead) are conducive to the fulfillment of the work of mourning. But, my reading of prosopopoeia in relation to Joyce's *Dubliners* shows how the trope's power to incite mourning is not necessarily coupled by the power to enforce, or deliver consolation. My analysis is critical of previous facile interpretations of prosopopoeia (J. Hillis Miller, Paul Ricoeur, and others) which have combined to inspire Karen Smythe, for instance, to conclude that, "What is at stake in the modernistic fiction-elegies exemplified by the work of Woolf and Joyce is the ability of the aesthetic to console structurally or tropologically."[29]

In contradistinction to the ideology of transcendence, the tropologic of prosopopoeia confronts the (mourning) subject with both the knowledge of desire (as is the case, for instance, with James Duffy in "A Painful Case") and the acknowledgment of mourning (as in the case of Gabriel Conroy in "The Dead"). Prosopopoeia—understood as a dialectic of personification and reification (Paul de Man)—results not only in the collapse of the ideology of transcendence of mortal eros, but also in the face-to-face rendezvous with the other (the lost object), which I deem of "empiphanic" proportions (a dynamic of interpersonal/collaborative empathy and inward/cognitive epiphany) in that it opens up the mourning subject not only to the irreducible alterity of the deceased but also to the *actuality* of death, loss, and mourning. Yet the *reconciliatory* force of prosopopoeia with mortal eros is by no means *consolatory.* It leaves the mourner with the same old demand for mourning that he or she can neither fulfill nor disregard. It becomes patently clear that neither the strategy of transcendence of eros nor the Freudian strategy of redistribution of libido is commensurate with the Joycean imperative—*Go out of mourning first.* It seems that the desire for the mortal object outwits the ideology of anticipatory transcendence and finds, albeit through detours, a route to the object even in a postmortem fashion, as is the case with James Duffy in relation to Emily Sinico; by the same token, the desire for a lost object might persist not only in the face of the loss of that object but also despite the acquisition of a new object, as is the case with Gretta in relation to Michael Furey (i.e., her lost love-object) and Gabriel Conroy (i.e., her new love-object).

The outcome of the transcendence or embrace of mortal eros is the same: desire survives the loss of the object. In this respect, the contribution of Freud's conception of mourning consists, I think, in opening up the possibility for the mourning subject to hijack this lingering desire for the lost object and lavish it on a new object. Freud's economics of mourning is, after all, an economics of managing surplus libido, libido that cannot presumably be directed any longer toward the lost object. To mourn is to tame a desire that has not been sated but interrupted. It is not for nothing that Freud deems the withdrawal of libido from the lost object as key to the success of the work of mourning. Yet this is the crux of the problem: not that the withdrawal of libido from the lost object is oftentimes thwarted, but that such withdrawal does not indeed seem to be possible, for the locus of the lost object of love is not always *external* but becomes exceedingly *internal* to the structure of the ego; the withdrawal of libido would be possible if the lost object were indeed situated outside the ego. The further afield we look, the more cognizant we become of the challenging nature of Joyce's imperative—*Go out of mourning first.* Now, after having seen the ways in which this challenge has to do with the circular logic of desire and mourning, it becomes necessary to address the topography of the lost object in relation to the architecture of the ego. It will become clear, once I have rounded out my discussion, that the lost object cannot be objectified (i.e., distanced from the ego), since it must have always—and as soon as it has been approached and cathected—assumed a place in the geography of the ego. The (lost) object is no longer, to put it in a more Derridean fashion, that of which the ego can speak, but precisely that from within which the ego speaks.

The Quandary of Identification

> Some of the things that one is unwilling to give up, because they give pleasure, are nevertheless not ego but object; and some sufferings that one seeks to expel turn out to be inseparable from the ego in virtue of their internal origin.
>
> —Freud, *Civilization and Its Discontents*

In *Civilization and Its Discontents,* Freud pursues a nowadays much-discussed Hegelian theme: happiness. Disenchanted and pessimistic, as he generally is, Freud contends that "Unhappiness is much less difficult to experience."[30] Freud singles out three hurdles in front of happiness: bodily decay, the external world, and, above all, "relations to other men."[31] While I do not intend to pursue the topic of happiness at length herein, there is no gainsaying the fact that the movement out of mourning is indeed a function of the pursuit of happiness. Yet, as characteristic of his overall philosophical logic, Freud always starts by entertaining and propounding psychoanalytic pronouncements prior to moving on to show how untenable they eventually are. The fulfillment of the work of mourning is Freud's solution to the outbreak of grief following the loss of a love-object. Yet this solution is most often unsuccessful, not solely because of individual incompetence, but because of the structure of the psyche itself. One can reproduce verbatim Freud's view of the impossibility of happiness and locate it in reference to the impossibility of mourning: "when we consider how unsuccessful we have been in precisely this field of prevention of suffering, a suspicion dawns on us that here, too, a piece of unconquerable nature may lie behind—this time a piece of our own psychical constitution."[32]

How is it that when one is asked to mourn, one, is in point of fact, asked to expel something that is nevertheless interior to the ego? An answer to this question necessitates a reflection on the layers of identification as the motor force of identity formation. Throughout his work, Freud continually reformulated his theory of identification: whether by invoking the formation or the dissolution of the Oedipus complex, Freud constantly tried to inventory a new language to articulate the enigma of identification more fully and more thoroughly. In "On Narcissism" (1914), for instance, he traces back the development of the process of identification to the emergence of "autoeroticism," which he later dubs as "ego-libido" or "primary narcissism."[33] The first form of identification appears in the veneer of a primary narcissism, of an ego-libido, part of which is later transferred into an "object-libido"—the mother or father. Freud had not produced a full account of the transition from ego-libido to object-libido, but, in "Inhibitions, Symptoms and Anxiety" (1926), such a transition is described in terms of a different experience of pain. In a passage that is reminiscent of *Beyond the Pleasure Principle,* Freud states that this transition is first initiated by the intermittent absences of the mother—absences that are not experienced on a physical plane but on a mental one: "The transition from physical pain to mental pain corresponds," Freud concludes, "to a change from narcissistic cathexis to object-cathexis."[34] This distinction between the two experiences of pain is of paramount importance insofar as it reaffirms the psychogenic—and therefore more problematic—character of mourning.

Identification can therefore be first defined as the expression of an "emotional tie" with another person—most common, one of the parents or both of them.[35] This identification soon sparks the emergence of the Oedipus complex—a confused state of identification and libidinal attachment, in which a male child would confound libidinal object-cathexis (directed toward the mother) with desexualized object-cathexis (directed normally toward the father) and find himself therefore locked with his father in an oedipal struggle that ends with an intensified identification with his oedipal rival and a regressive identification with his mother. It is beyond the scope of this inquiry to delve into the "gender trouble" that the oedipal struggle creates; it suffices to stress, however, the wedge that the dissolution of the oedipal complex installs between two types of identification: the one with the father (mimetic) and the one with the mother (identificatory).[36]

What is important to bear in mind here is that identification is at the origin of the Oedipus complex and, at the same time, the only means of dissolving it through an intensified mimetic identification with the parent of the same gender and a correlative abandonment of identification with the parent of the different gender. We should not fail to note here also that identification, insofar as it serves to dissolve the (originary) identificatory ambivalence of the Oedipus complex, acts in an analogous manner in relation to the work of mourning. In fact, in *The Ego and the Id,* identification is understood as a *function* of the work of mourning, in that it becomes "the sole condition under which the id can give up its objects."[37] If the work of mourning consists in the gradual severance of libidinal ties with the object, identification permits this severance to occur by enabling the interiorization of the lost object. Insofar as identification is—as is the case in "Mourning and Melancholia"[38]—a function of melancholia and insofar as it is now translated as a function of the work of severance, melancholia itself can be seen, in turn, as a function of the work of mourning. In fact, and as Freud also suggests, melancholic identification is a "common" and "typical" process characteristic of both mourning and identity formation.

Freud explains how his exploration of the concept of identification—and, especially, its annexation to the formation and dissolution of the Oedipus complex—allows him to correct his earlier theory of melancholia: "We succeeded in explaining the painful disorder of melancholia by supposing that [in those suffering from it] an object which was lost has been set up again in the ego—that is, that an object-cathexis has been replaced by an identification. *At that time, however, we did not appreciate the full significance of this process and did not know how common and how typical it is.*"[39] While in "Mourning and Melancholia,"

Freud suspected melancholia of a pathological disposition, he seems here to rectify that attitude by demonstrating "how common and how typical" is the melancholic procedure of setting up objects inside the ego. What is even more striking than the alleged typicality of melancholic identification is Freud's discovery of its indispensability for any envisaged completion of the work of mourning: "When it happens that a person has to give up a sexual object, there quite often ensues an alteration of his ego which can only be described as a setting up of the object inside the ego, as it occurs in melancholia; the exact nature of this substitution is as yet unknown to us. It may be that by this *introjection,* which is a kind of *regression* to the mechanism of the oral phase, the ego makes it easier for the object to be given up or renders that process possible. *It may be that this identification is the sole condition under which the id can give up its objects.*"[40] While Freud is concerned with the theorization of the dissolution of the Oedipus complex, his argument is in fact haunted by the concept of mourning for which he had previously been proud to offer a commensurate and readable account. Now it seems that the reverse is possible—that only melancholia can be accounted for with a measure of ease. Yet there is no reason not to believe that Freud's original conception of mourning is still at work here. The transition from the identification with the father and the abandonment of identification with the mother corresponds to the transition that the work of mourning is expected to effect—the identification with a new object and the abandonment of the lost one—except that, in the case of the child, the mother might not be entirely lost.[41]

Only on the condition of the interiorization of the mother—by way of a regression to an oral and cannibalistic phase—can the resolution of the Oedipus complex become possible. In the same vein, the work of mourning cannot be accomplished unless through a melancholic identification with—or internalization/incorporation of—the lost object. Such a strategic identificatory readjustment has warranted Judith Butler to conclude that "melancholic identification permits the loss of the object in the external world precisely because it provides a way to *preserve* the object as part of the ego and, hence, to avert the loss as a complete loss."[42] Butler is here adumbrating the "never-never" theory of "melancholy gender," in which a "double disavowal, a never having loved, and a never having lost" is superimposed on, for instance, an otherwise originary childhood desire for the parent of the different sex.[43] Among other things—namely, the deconstruction of normative heterosexuality as a "foreclosure of homosexuality"—Butler deconstructs the cultural prohibition against incest by inscribing it in the site of "repudiation," "refusal," or "sacrifice of desire" for the parent of the different sex, a desire that remains "ungrieved and ungrievable."[44] While the deconstruction of normative heterosexuality is better theorized than the deconstruction of the cultural prohibition against incest, Butler's argument nonetheless enables my reflection on a broader conception of subjectivity in relation to ungrievable losses, losses that can neither be avowed nor grieved. I do so, however, by discriminating frontally and forcefully between the foundational melancholy practices on which all gender identity is founded and the painfully historical and cultural, deeply disturbing, and oftentimes impossible mourning tasks that the modernist and postcolonial (largely exilic and diasporic) subject is called upon to accomplish.

Rather than dwelling on the prohibition against incest, I ask in chapter 3 whether an adulterous desire, for instance, can be nurtured as well as grieved (when it is lost or frustrated) in a culture that proscribes it altogether. In "A Painful Case," Mrs. Sinico, a married and frustrated wife, pursues a romantic adventure with James Duffy, a loner. When their bond grew strong, and Mrs. Sinico's horizon of desire fused with his, Duffy suddenly broke the relationship, arguing that "every bond is a bond to sorrow." Mrs. Sinico is left with the impossible task of mourning a loss that cannot be accommodated in an Irish Catholic culture that prohibits its inaugurating or originating adulterous desire. That such a loss must remain unspeakable—"ungrieved and ungrievable"—leaves the mourning subject with the uneasy recourse to silence or, as is the case with Mrs. Sinico, to suicide. As I move from chapter 2 to chapter 3, my focus shifts from the *access* to mourning to the *excess* of mourning. Reading Butler reading Freud, I trace the ways in which an ungrievable loss can reach suicidal proportions if rejoined by the guilt of having nurtured an adulterous desire. Mrs. Sinico's suicide is not, however, inconsequential: Joyce subtly reconfigures it in his famous "style of scrupulous meanness" to expose the bankruptcy and cruelty of the sociocultural norms of policing desire and mourning in turn-of-the-century Dublin,[45] for few things are worse than living with a grief that can be neither recognized nor disregarded.

On a slightly different plane than that of Mrs. Sinico, Fr. Flynn, a priest absorbed in the diurnal ascesis of the transcendence of mortal eros, is reborn—after the breaking of his holy vase—into the loss of a desire for grief he had long forsaken and repudiated. Fleshing out and nuancing Freud's theory of melancholic identification by means of Nicolas Abraham and Maria Torok's distinction between introjection and incorporation, I map out the psychoaffective vicissitudes of melancholia into suicide (Mrs. Sinico) and into madness (Fr. Flynn). In their detailing of the tragedies of Fr. Flynn and Emily Sinico, Joyce's stories are unequivocal about the imperative to seize the moment of loss and mourning to press forth sociocultural reform. When in tension with the prescribed strategies of its fulfillment, mourning becomes a political force that forces the reconfiguration of those strategies. Not only is it a mode of adjusting to a changed reality (after the loss of the other), mourning here can be read also as a threshold force of sociocultural change. That a melancholic identification should, however, suddenly swerve into suicide or madness signals (perhaps from a different perspective) the persistence of the violence and ambivalence characteristic of the oedipal rivalry on the pyre of which melancholic identification is established.[46]

The virtue of Freud's theory of melancholic identification is that it not only enables the ego to work through the Oedipus complex and interiorize the object-cathexis it has to abandon, but also prepares the ego to apply the same procedure to subsequent libidinal attachments. The ego evolves on the wreckage of its object-cathexes. Melancholic identification seems to offer the proverbial formula for the success of the work of mourning, that is, for going out of mourning without being inhibited by the fear of having to reenter it again with every act of attachment to a new object. An exploration of this voracious emotion in relation to consumerist society may offer laudable insights into the affective mechanics of consumption. This is not, however, an immediate concern of mine here. In fact, my aim here is not to pursue a consumerist notion of identification but a rather consuming and transformational notion of melancholic identification. The fact that melancholic identification is key to the conservation *and* the abandonment of object-cathexis—that is, to the resolution, in the case of a boy, of the Oedipus complex and to what I call the *mournful-filling* reconciliation (i.e., reconciliation that fulfills the task of mourning) to the loss of the mother as a pursuable libidinal object—leads to the striking supposition that "the character of the ego is," in the words of Freud, "a precipitate of abandoned object-cathexes and that it contains the history of those object-choices."[47] Freud proceeds to lend credence to this supposition by a remarkable amplification of the scope of the ego and of the unidentifiable objects that contribute to its formation: "when the ego forms its super-ego out of the id, it may perhaps only be reviving shapes of former egos and be bringing them to resurrection."[48]

While Freud's earlier theories have been notoriously known (and reproached) for their concentration on the individual, his later writings—from *Totem and Taboo* onwards—testify to the capacity of psychoanalysis to construct a theory of religion (*Moses and Monotheism* and *The Future of an Illusion*) as well as a theory of culture (*Civilization and Its Discontents* and *Group Psychology*), and to move at ease between theorizing the individual and theorizing the collective. I do not intend to discuss the still-rampant resistances to psychoanalysis, not least because psychoanalysis is itself a theory of remains, residues and resistances; perhaps psychoanalysis is in the final analysis nothing but the history of those resistances, resistances whose confrontation in a psychoanalytic fashion has eventually made possible the very evolution of the technique of psychoanalysis (namely, the technique of *Durcharbeiten* or working-through).[49] It is not for nothing that the theory of the ego itself is a theory of remains, a history of what remains (even there where there are no remainders). Freud insists that even while "it is not possible to speak of direct inheritance in the *ego*," the ego nevertheless harbors—under the influence of the inheritable id—"the existences of countless egos."[50]

Freud's description of ego-formation as a function of melancholy identification and of the ego as a "precipitate of abandoned object-cathexes" already places the ego within a community of egos. His further description of the formation of the superego on the pyre of the id's prohibited desires locates the ego in a history to which it is nevertheless belated.[51] The ego is thus not only the precipitate of its abandoned objects, but also the haunted site of "shapes of former egos" whose ghosts are resurrected in the very process of the ego's evolution. The ghostly demarcations of this description cannot be overstressed; what is important to underline, however, is the suspicion that the ego might be inhabited not only by a plethora of residual objects, but also by a crowd of ghosts it cannot fully account for. The gothic underworld of the ego is brought to the fore in Derrida's *Specters of Marx:* "But this Ego, this living individual would itself be inhabited and invaded by its own specter. *It would be constituted by specters of which it becomes the host and which it assembles in the haunted community of a single body.* Ego = ghost."[52]

Perhaps I should now refine the question I asked earlier: how is it that when one is asked to mourn, one is, in point of fact, asked to expel something that is nevertheless interior to the ego? So far, melancholy identification has been advanced as a function of mourning, as a means of giving up the lost object by setting it up inside the ego through the economies of identification and resultant ego-transformation. Yet, given that this operation might also involve the possibility of "reviving shapes of former egos," it ultimately *reopens* the question of mourning. The reopening of this question is provoked, not by the ego's own individual history of melancholy identifications (which might, after all, be indexed and identified), but by the indirect inheritance to which the ego is subjected in the transhistorical and transgenerational trajectory of cumulative and constellating identifications. The reopening of the question of mourning coincides with the surfacing of an inherited and therefore dormant identification: the resurrection of an object that cannot be located within the cathectic and identificatory history of an individual ego. This object is resurrected in the process of the ego's entry into a community of egos characterized by a sharable repertoire of cathectic history. It is when the resurrected object compels the *return* to the history of that object—in order to locate the ego in reference to it and vice versa—that melancholic identification segues into melancholic bafflement, perplexity, and archival uncertainty. Thus, the wedge is installed between the *identification with* and the *identification of* the resurrected object.

In chapter 4, I read Kincaid's (auto/alter/biographical) fiction and nonfiction writings in terms of this interval between the *identification with* and the *identification of* a cathected object (whose loss insists but cannot be codified, because it belongs to an archive of inherited identifications through which the postcolonial subject has nonetheless to muddle, or so is the case in Kincaid's writings). For how do we begin to understand a declarative statement such as this: "My history begins like this: in 1492, Christopher Columbus discovered the New World"?[53] Such a statement implies, in my view, a *claim* to a history of loss—really, to the loss of history itself—that remains nevertheless unlocatable in narrative historiography. The statement invokes a date, a beginning of a presumably traumatic history, yet, in so doing, it betrays the inability to cope with the magnitude of what is invoked. Melancholy identification as a function of mourning pertains to those objects locatable in the cathectic history of the ego, those objects that the ego lived through their loss; in Kincaid, however, it is often the case that the objects invoked or claimed are locatable neither in the cathectic history of the ego nor in the wider history of the community of the egos to which the ego belongs. The demand for the identification of the object insists as long as the identification with it persists. It is not that the identification of the object is a prerequisite to the identification with it, much less that the identification with any given object presupposes its identification, or its epistemological and ontological transparency.

Would the *identification with* the unidentifiable object, however, restore it to identification, and proffer it with the dignity of recognition? One of Kincaid's essays in *My Garden (Book)* is titled "To Name Is to Possess." The main argument of the essay is stated in the title: that knowledge of things proceeds by naming them and that naming them is ultimately a means of possessing them. In Kincaid's fiction and nonfiction alike, we are oftentimes presented with a loss that cannot be repossessed except through the task of naming, only this task cannot be fulfilled because the loss exceeds the catachrestic names in which it is inscribed. In fact, catachrestic designations of the lost object sprawl untidily throughout Kincaid's corpus in response to the demand to identify the site of one's identification. The main purpose of this chapter is to offer an affective poetics of understanding the configurative locus of historical trauma in narrative—how the history of slavery is verbalized, however inadequately, as "the wrong," "the crime," or "what happened" tout court. The impossibility of articulating quite fully, beyond the maddening tropo*logic* of catachresis, the object with which one identifies yet of which one can offer no identification (i.e., no identifiable function or definition) stems, I argue, from the affective temperament of melancholic identification that subsides it.

If the ego of the postcolonial subject is a precipitate of melancholy identifications, which it internalizes but of which it can provide no finite account, then the distance between historical loss and narrative inscription becomes the real measure of Kincaid's affective devastation, resistance, and rage. By drawing on Gayatri Spivak's definition of catachresis as a claim for something for which there is "no historically adequate referent,"[54] I study the melancholic dimension (of identifying with the unidentifiable) of Kincaid's claims to historical loss throughout her writings, and especially in *The Autobiography of My Mother.* My interest here is to show how catachresis functions in Kincaid's work, not as a sign of linguistic abuse—a still-dominant misperception of approaches to catachresis—but as a signal, a stamp or a symptom of the abused. Catachresis is the price that narrative mourning pays for its scramble to signify historical loss; it permits an understanding of the material effect, as well as the signifying impulse of loss as they overlap in language; in other words, catachresis is treated here not only as a symptom of loss and of bearing witness to an inherited experience of loss, but also as the signifying motor-force of loss—a signifying whose political import cannot be overstressed given the enduring hold on the contemporary world scene of the compulsion to repeat and perpetuate atrocities. In this same chapter, I further develop my elaboration of a poetics of narrative mourning by analyzing the many instances in Kincaid in which the melancholic affect is figured forth through the recurrent recourse to catachresis. While in most instances catachresis proves to be indeed a claim for something for which there is "no historically adequate referent," I rethink the trope in terms of the melancholic affective disposition of the postcolonial subject (which is *historically* produced) rather than solely in terms of melancholy identifications (which is *constitutive* of ego-formation at large).[55]

In postcolonial narratives, and particularly in Kincaid's work, to stake a claim for a lost object is to stake a claim for justice, yet the problem is that the identification of the lost object hinders, rather than makes possible, the birth of justice. Justice, if it is to come, has to come from without and not from within the history it seeks to inscribe. This seems the only way of ascertaining that justice is, in the words of Derrida, "removed from the fatality of vengeance."[56] Yet how can narrative (mourning) recuperate and inscribe history at the very moment it attempts to move beyond its mooring clutches? How do we reconcile the demands for inscriptive justice, for right-writing the law, with the demands of incalculable justice—the quasi-messianic justice that belongs to the future-to-come (but certainly not to the history of which it wants to account)? Only when the recuperation and inscription of history is discontinuous with the presentist "putting on trial" of the actors in such a history—and only when narrating colonial history is dissociated with expiation—can we speak of justice as an enabling structure, as a movement beyond history, that is, as an instance, in Derrida's lexicon, of the "incalculability of the gift."[57] The narrative inscription of history (as a lost object) has to emerge from a logic it seeks to surpass. It is at this juncture that one is compelled by Spivak's observation: "Literature contains the element of surprising history."[58]

Raising the Threshold of Mourning

> All work in general works *at mourning.*
> —Derrida, *The Work of Mourning*

Chapter 4 investigates the possibility of situating melancholic identification not only at the level of egoic history, but also at the collective level of history. Kincaid's claim that her history began in 1492 requires that we flesh out the narrow horizon of melancholy identifications with lost object(s) such that it includes both the particular context of individual losses and the broader historical contexts which have, after all, originated in those losses. This is all the more important since individual losses in Kincaid's fiction are constantly understood in terms of the vaster historical perspective in which they are produced. The overture to chapter 4 attempts to show the relevance of Freud's technique of analytic treatment, as exposed in "Remembering, Repeating and Working-Through" (1914), to any theory of narrative mourning, since narrative mourning and analytic treatment are both concerned with the task of tracing back a symptom (of an unlocatable loss) to a historical past—a task that eventuates, as is the case with Freud's case histories, in the *construction* of that past.

I deem it theoretically fruitful, as well as analytically and critically beneficial, to draw an analogy between the dyad of transference-resistance at work in every psychoanalytic situation and its proximate analog at work, at variable depths, in postcolonial narratives. One can, at least provisionally, argue that the open page of the book-to-be occupies, for the postcolonial writer, the same status that the analyst occupies in the eyes of the analysand. The transference and inscription of weighted experiences of colonial legacy are for the postcolonial writer—by virtue of being fraught with uncertainties, anxieties, scruples, inhibitions and so forth—a task as psychically taxing as the transference (dictated by the protocols of the analytic situation) of disquieting memories in the case of the analysand. The analogy is not immaculate since the transference-resistance dyad is, in the case of the postcolonial writer, triangulated by the reader or the addressee while it might remain, in the case of the analysand, buried in the analyst's files unless it is turned into a case history, as in Freud's many case histories. What is important to stress, however, is that the postcolonial writer—by virtue of being the analysand in relation to the narrative demand—might find herself, as if naturally, acting in a way not so dissimilar to that of the analysand in the analytic situation.

Having established the terms of the analogy, I then inquire whether the hurdle of repetition-compulsion so rampant in psychoanalytic treatments is permissible in (postcolonial) narrative mourning. Freud maintains that "[t]he main instrument . . . for curbing the patient's compulsion to repeat and for turning it into a motive for remembering lies in the handling of the transference. *We render the compulsion harmless, and indeed useful, by giving it the right to assert itself in a definite field.*"[59] On this score, if the narrative rendition and inscription of colonial legacy is to grow into something serviceable, it has, perhaps, to host the repetition of insults of colonial history; it has to enact partially the structures of that history; it has, in the words of Hamlet, *to speak daggers but to use none.* Perhaps we should understand Kincaid's narrative acts of aggression, especially in *A Small Place,* in this vein, as ways of channeling the anger fomented by an unreadable history of colonial transgressions.

Drawing on Johannes Fabian's *Time and the Other,* Ali Behdad cogently shows that postcolonial narratives are, by virtue of their belatedness, "exercises in remembering; they bring into consciousness the repressed time of the other."[60] This time of the other can be understood as the unregistered loss of the object of melancholy identification—*history tout court.* They attempt, in other words, to bear witness to the foreclosed and disavowed scene of imperialism. Bearing witness in Kincaid's writings—as much as in Khoury's *City Gates,* as I demonstrate in chapter 6—must then be understood as an attempt to narrate the impossible, that unlocatable time of the other to which we will never be able to bear witness, that which is precisely the site of the "collapse of witnessing."[61] Bearing witness must therefore start from within the impossibility of which it speaks and of which it is an effect. Bearing witness is always thus—the impossible par excellence. It has nothing to do with being on the spot while a traumatic event breaks out or takes place; it has nothing to do with being a witness to this and that—bearing witness must always come after the event. It is a function of telling, of narrating, of reliving and repeating. Narrative mourning is ultimately trained on the impossibility of bearing witness to the wedge that colonialism (Kincaid) and ethnic civil war (Khoury) enter in the individual and collective psyche between his present and his past.

In chapter 5, I reflect further on the impossibility of narrative mourning. More precisely, by bringing into an intimate collision Kincaid's *My Brother,* Derrida's *The Work of Mourning* and Ben Jelloun's provocative novel *The Last Friend,* I attempt to probe and move beyond the ethical limits of narrative mourning. I explore the ways in which narrative mourning following the death of a relative (Kincaid) or a friend (Derrida and Ben Jelloun) may become the uneasy site of an ethical disquiet. If "writing," as Derrida argues in *Cinders,* "denies and recognizes its debt in a single dash," in what way can narrative mourning become possible and impossible at one and the same time?[62]

With Derrida, we reach the point at which we may deliberately have to raise the threshold at which we should start to act on Joyce's command—*Go out of mourning first.* It is no longer a question of going out of mourning, but rather a question of dwelling in mourning. "All work," Derrida contends, "works *at mourning.* In and of itself. Even when it has the power to give birth, even and especially when it plans to bring something to light and let it be seen."[63] Since the work of mourning is already there at work, in every kind of work, not exempting this one, it becomes the impossible to resolve, much less so following the death of a friend or a relative. On the other hand, in recognizing the limits of narrative, we also recognize the limits of the present work, if not its impossibility, given that, according to Derrida, "one should not be able to say anything about the work of mourning, anything about this subject, since it cannot become a theme, only another experience of mourning that comes to work over the one who intends to speak. To speak of mourning or of anything else."[64]

With Derrida's *The Work of Mourning,* we are left to stare blindly at the aura of "impossible mourning" and at the chiastic poetics of aporia which is said to suspend the mourner between two impossible choices—two infidelities: to write and therefore to deny the deceased the right to speak or not to write and to send the deceased from the silence of death to the silence of forgetting, the "worse than death," in Adorno's memorable idiom.[65] We are left to wonder whether an ethics of impossible mourning can proffer us with a modus operandi and whether the practice of impossible mourning is not phantasmagorical in orientations, that is, whether or not it is amenable to everyday practice. The question is precisely whether the very idea of doing away with therapeutic mourning is obtainable, since it tends to affirm rather than subvert the truth about normative mourning. A discourse about the impossibility of mourning must proceed, preparatory to anything else, through mourning, the mourning of mourning itself, that is, the mourning of Freud's idea of curative mourning. Otherwise, how can one ever dream of mourning the very idea of clinical mourning, the idea of possible mourning? In order for the very idea of impossible mourning to be possible, the clinical idea of mourning itself has to remain possible. Does not the idea of an impossible mourning take for granted the idea of possible mourning here? Does not Derrida, in fact, deconstruct Freud and depend on him at the same time? Otherwise, who would be able to mourn Freud's theory of mourning? Who would mourn mourning?

We either have to assume that mourning is impossible—and abstain from exhortations to mourn the old idea of successful mourning in favor of an ethically impossible mourning—or we have to concede that mourning is all there is, and that the idea of impossible mourning itself is built on, if not determined by, the clandestine, thwarted, or unconscious belief that mourning is ultimately the only game in town. While I believe Derrida's idea of impossible mourning is an attempt to deconstruct and to perfect the law of mourning—the law of the human—I would be remiss not to ask again: How can we mourn this idea of (clinical) mourning? How can we mourn mourning? How can we be born into impossible mourning? Is not there—in the very idea of impossible mourning, already located in its very core—a degree of possible mourning? Why, if at all, should this idea of impossible mourning be understood as a spark of affirmation? What does it affirm? I ask these questions because Derrida's ethics of mourning is entirely constructed from the perspective of the mourner/the survivor even while it is intended toward the other/the mournee/the diseased.

I draw on Tahar Ben Jelloun's novel, *The Last Friend,* to move the discussion of mourning from the perspective of the mourner into the perspective of the mournee and to assess in the process the extent to which what works for the mourner might or might not work for the mournee. I ask, how does the mournee mourn? This concluding section of chapter 5 formulates partial answers to this question and examines their political implications and, above all, their challenges to what I call an ethics of mournership, that is, a poetics of relationality between the mourner and deceased, which would henceforth oscillate chiastically between the sometimes dueling perspectives of the mourner and the mournee. While the reflection on the ethics of mournership allows me to bring together all the different threads of the narrative poetics of mournership around aporia, prolepsis and chiasmus, it is important to point out that mourning itself becomes a trope for and a function of narrative. Although there are no simple ways of demarcating the lines at which mourning becomes a trope and those at which it generates its own tropes, my trajectory throughout the book is to continually raise the threshold of my discussion from the micro-poetics of mourning within the economy of narrative to the macro-poetics of mourning in relation to narrative and in relation to the world at large.

The underlying purpose of the various ethical considerations I forge is to elaborate a theory of relations between human beings (between the dead and the living as well as among the living themselves) based on the continuous perfectibility of the sociocultural laws of mourning. In what way, I ask, does mourning inaugurate my relation to and ethical responsibility toward the other? How can mourning the loss of the other become the very law of my relation to him or her and therefore the cornerstone of the formation of the social? In *State of Exception,* Giorgio Agamben suggests that law can "[apply] itself to chaos and to life only on the condition of making itself, in the state of exception, life and living chaos."[66] While throughout his study Agamben is quite unequivocal about the correlation between political unrest and public mourning, he does not think of mourning, for instance, as the law that can apply itself to life and to living chaos. I, therefore, set out to speculate in chapter 6 on whether the law of mourning can be theorized in such a way as to structure our relations to others and to fill the legal vacancy left by the break of those relations.

Chapter 6 focuses on Elias Khoury's experimental novel, *City Gates,* written during the Lebanese civil war (1975–90). I make use of this novel, which is an allegory of trauma, to round up my discussion of the poetics of narrative mourning and to press home the transformational and generative aspects of mourning, not only for rereading modernist and postcolonial narratives but also for rethinking our very contemporaneity. Several tropes come into play in the signifying process of trauma, including allegory and metonymy, but chiasmus emerges as the master trope of the traumatic narrative of *City Gates.* The novel chiastically vacillates between the *return to* and the *return of* the traumatic event, between the insistence and inaccessibility of trauma, and between identification and disidentification, as well as between traumatic ties and exilic lines of flight. A potential survivor of the 1976 siege and massacre of Palestinians in the refugee camp of Tal al-Zaʿtar in the suburbs of Beirut, the protagonist of the novel, referred to simply as "the man and the stranger," holds on to the traumatic event, "preventing it from slipping back into its proper chronological place in the past, and relives it over and over again in the compulsive musings of the day and the seething dreams of night. The moment becomes a season, the event becomes a condition."[67]

While my reading of *City Gates* will entail that I draw eclectically on trauma studies—particularly on the contributions of Cathy Caruth, Dori Laub and Ernst van Alphen—I remain especially focused on the poetic and critical valences of narrative, the ways in which narrative articulates and/or blocks the transformative power of mourning, draws out and enacts posttraumatic stress disorder as a form of political and human crisis, and positions and implicates the reader as a witness to or accomplice in acts of painful recall. Because it unfolds as an allegorical performative of trauma, Khoury's novel tends toward fragmentariness, formlessness and plotlessness. In the very same way that trauma demands and defies witness, the stranger's story also demands and defies witness. *City Gates* becomes an allegory of trauma as much as an allegory of its own crisis to tell the story it sets out to tell. Chiasmus becomes the master trope of the traumatic and traumatizing narrative, relentlessly spiralling into unreconciled oscillations between articulacy and inarticulacy, inadequacy and excess, and form and formlessness. The sustained experimentation and fragmentariness becomes in the final analysis a price willingly paid for Khoury to highlight the *form* of the story—its chiastic and traumatic poetics—by making it *conspicuous* in its very inaccessibility (in very much the same manner as the trauma it wants to articulate, to tie and untie). Yet, it is precisely this very failure to tell the story which becomes exemplary: it permits trauma to circulate as a story precisely because of the void at its structural rib, in spite of it. An unlikely conjunction emerges between the tendency of trauma to traumatize and to build ties, trauma ties.

A close reading of the novel makes it possible to compare the communal ties formed by the workings of trauma to what might be called *critical distance at close range:* it is precisely the exilic ties that develop between the estranged protagonist and the city—as well as the community of refugees, or exiles that surround him—that transform the traumatic condition into a vantage point from which to ponder the value of drifting away from social bonds in order to rediscover one's interdependencies, intersubjectivity and communal ties. Khoury's *City Gates* prompts us to take seriously Kai Erikson's rhetorical questions: "To what extent may one conclude that the communal dimension of trauma is one of its distinctive clinical signatures? And to what extent does it make sense to conclude that the traumatized view of the world conveys a wisdom that ought to be heard in its own terms?"[68] An answer to these questions must pass through an interpretive rediscovery of mourning not only as a generative, transformational experience but also as a law of sociocultural intelligibility, communal ties, and narrative enterprises writ large. Any such communal, global, or transnational ties must reckon with what Butler characterizes as our "primary vulnerability to others" and acknowledge therefore the mutual rather than dueling vulnerabilities at the basis of the social writ large.[69]

I credit all the texts under examination not only for staging (through their tactful prolongation of the act of reading and sustained experimentation on style and language) modalities of affective and communal recognition and solidarity, but also for their tacit call for acknowledging the socio- and ethico-political potencies of contemplating and engaging with the psychoaffective question of mourning. The argument of *Signifying Loss* proceeds along two ultimately complementary trajectories—deploying narrative fiction to intervene in the ethical turn in current mourning theory from Freud to Derrida and deploying theories of mourning to offer fresh readings of an eclectic number of works by Joyce, Kincaid, Ben Jelloun, and Khoury; the existent critical studies on each of these authors have so far neglected the importance of the theories of mourning in illuminating the complexities and the latent ties between modernist and postcolonial cultural, intellectual, and literary turns. Hence, in the same manner that my reading of Joyce opens up inroads into a rethinking and recasting of modernist narratives through the lenses of mourning theory, my reading of Kincaid, Ben Jelloun, and Khoury shows how the whole field of postcolonial studies might benefit from a critical deployment of the insights of psychoanalytic and deconstructive theories of mourning. Similarly, my juxtaposition of Freud's and Derrida's theories of mourning is intended to push the limits of current mourning theory beyond the standstill rhetoric of "impossible mourning" without diminishing the ethico-political concerns that cluster thick around Freud's original imperative to mourn.

The demand for mourning remains a vital element of our psychic life despite or perhaps because of the sometimes misguided calls for inconsolability that can wittingly or unwittingly end up condoning certain forms of violence and retaliation, as has been the case following the airborne attacks on the World Trade Center in New York and the Pentagon in Virginia on September 11, 2001. An ethics of mournership should, however, enable us to recast widely the ties of identification, empathy and empiphany, and to do so in an uncoerced and uncoercive fashion (such that it would amount to doing what comes naturally).[70] Clearly, the critical potential of mourning and melancholia hinges on the suddenness, and therefore the spontaneity, occasioned by these powerful affects. The imperative to mourn and the reverse imperative to withhold mourning both feel, and in the very same way, abusive, let alone conducive to the free and unadulterated expression of critique. If I rethink mourning here in a continuum between mourning and melancholia, I do so more in the sense of an unresolved chiastic oscillation, a negative dialectic of sorts, between the demand for mourning, inherent in narrative form itself, and the elusiveness of mourning as a search for emotional closure. Thus, mourning is the transformational generative experience of being stranded somewhere along a continuum or inside an unresolved chiastic oscillation between mourning and melancholia or between the demand for consolation and the insistence of inconsolability. In no small measure, this is also the poetics of narrative mourning.

2
Horizons of Desire, Horizons of Mourning: Joyce's *Dubliners*

> Mourning is the horizon of all desire.
>
> —Henry Staten, *Eros in Mourning*

> One mourns less for what was than for what can no longer happen now.
>
> —Hans-Jost Frey, *Interruptions*

Eros in Dublin

In a compelling article titled "*Dubliners* and the Art of Losing," John Gordon maps variations on Joyce's literary appropriation of a strange Irish habit that consists of converting accidental absences into engineered subtractions and simple lacks into suffered losses. But while Gordon glosses over the more sedimented cultural twin of such a habit (i.e., the tendency to defuse historically specific losses into constitutive or structural absences) and attributes the alleged habit generally to a kind of hermeneutics broken loose from its historical moorage, I would rather ascribe it to the workings of a fully fledged psychic apparatus, set in motion largely by a post-famine cultural history of successive experiences of loss. The conversion of absences into identifiable historical losses testifies to the progress of the communitywide work of mourning.[1] Rather than remapping the literary inscriptions of such a complex history—a task accomplished differently by many scholars such as David Lloyd, Seamus Deane, and Declan Kiberd[2]—my interest in this chapter branches out into a far more modest yet necessary direction: to lay bare, through a close examination of a number of characters from *Dubliners,* the inscriptions of patterns of psychic engagement with loss not at the collective but at the individual levels of history. There are, of course, significant overlaps between the management of loss at the collective and the individual levels: working through individual losses hinges considerably on a collective expression of solidarity such that the examination of the individual patterns of containing loss can teach us a great deal about the functioning or malfunctioning of the larger cultural paradigm of mourning. More important by far, the ways in which mourning is managed at the individual level not only reproduces the socio-cultural norms of mourning practices, but also constitutes the threshold moment of scrutinizing and ultimately refashioning those norms.[3]

The *Dubliners* collection presents us with an impressive array or panoply of characters who handle loss quite differently. The difference lies primarily in the *psychoaffective* response a given loss generates. In "The Sisters," for instance, while Fr. Flynn is deeply aggrieved by the breaking of his chalice, the boy narrator seems hardly saddened by the death of Fr. Flynn himself. Eveline, Mrs. Sinico, and Gretta, on the one hand, and James Duffy and Gabriel Conroy, on the other, offer a number of interesting variations on such an antithetical model of affective response to loss, established at the very outset of the collection. In sum, the difference between these two types of characters lies in whether or not a given loss arouses in them, if at all, the appropriate (i.e., expected) emotional response.[4]

Since Freud's normative bifurcation of the affects generated by loss into "Mourning and Melancholia" (1917), the tendency has been to pry apart the affect of mourning from that of melancholia. To refresh our memory of the key characteristics of mourning in psychoanalysis and to provide theoretical anchorage for the argument that will follow, I would like to rehash a few ideas that were discussed earlier. For Freud, mourning, like melancholia, originates in loss; but while mourning is thought to liberate the mourner from the tyranny of the lost object, melancholia instantiates nothing but a submission to such a tyranny. Freud describes the task that "the work of mourning" (*Trauerarbeit*) performs as follows: "Reality-testing has shown that the loved object no longer exists, and it proceeds to demand that all libido shall be withdrawn from its attachment to that object."[5] Although this description sounds prima facie no more than a temporal mechanical operation of *withdrawal* and *displacement* of cathexes, bespeaking our ineluctable implication within a quasi global system of libidinal circulation and exchange, Freud cautions us that the path of the work of mourning toward fulfillment might be easily stalled by the mourner's unwitting attachment to or fixation on the lost love-object.

For Freud, then, it is incumbent upon the survivor of loss (loss of any sort: an object, a thing, an ideal, an abstraction, etc.) to consciously proceed by *working through* (*Durcharbeiten*) the libidinal wreckage that the loss of the love-object results in. Such a process of working through is expected to be painful, energy-consuming, and long or short depending primarily on the mourner's self-conscious *will* to attain mastery over a situation to which he or she was forced to submit. This is all the more so given that "people," as Freud rightly conjectures, "never willingly abandon a libidinal position, not even, indeed, when a substitute is already beckoning to them."[6] However, Freud reassures us that, "normally, respect for reality gains the day" and when the "piecemeal" and bit-by-bit work of mourning is completed, "the ego becomes free and uninhibited again."[7] In other words, the ego has to resignedly come to the conclusion that it has no alternative but to masterfully prostrate (such is the oxymoronic measure of helplessness) itself before the irrevocable verdict of reality, to let itself be commanded by it in the hope that its libidinal cathexes might eventually be reoriented toward and reinvested in a new love-object. That hope might, however, be nuanced by a struggle of two ambivalent and contending forces—"the one seeks to detach the libido from the object, the other to maintain this position of the libido against the assault"—a struggle that takes place in the unconscious and whose path to consciousness is, Freud maintains steadfastly, "blocked."[8] This struggle coincides with the onset of melancholia, which Freud suspects—at least in "Mourning and Melancholia" —of a pathological disposition.

Seeking to offer primarily a reading that traces the *therapoetic inscriptions* of mourning in *Dubliners*—that is, the ways in which the therapeutic process of mourning is figuratively staged by narrative tropes—I will carve out my argument in the hinge between the emergence of eros, the suffering of loss, and the onset of mourning. By invoking the work of Freud and Henry Staten, to which I will come later, I will analyze what in a number of characters in *Dubliners* emerges as a constitutive inability to carry out the double bind of withdrawal and displacement of libido following the loss of a love-object. Such an inability lies at the borderline between melancholia—including its narcissistic excesses, or recesses—and the strategies of managing mortal eros in general. In *Dubliners,* and perhaps because of the embattled colonial setting of turn-of-the-century Ireland, which weighed heavily on Irish self-esteem, narcissism is only occasionally presented as a regression into a primary oral phase *à la Freudienne,* but it oftentimes takes the form, as it will become clear in due course, of a self-regulated, Spartan strategy of libidinal investment, masterfully exemplified by James Duffy and Gabriel Conroy.

While taking their lead from Sándor Ferenczi, Nicolas Abraham, and Maria Torok expound in *The Shell and the Kernel* a theory of mourning that remains deeply indebted to Freud's system of affective bifurcation: they associate "introjection" with successful mourning and "incorporation" with an unsuccessful mourning, or with what Torok had originally called, "the illness of mourning."[9] Introjection, understood as a process of egoic broadening and expansion, amounts to Freud's version of an achieved mourning, which is nothing but the accomplishment of the process of withdrawal and displacement of cathexes. Furthermore, although attentive to conceptual nuances, their conceptualization of incorporation as the fantasy of ingesting the lost love-object is by and large very much similar to Freud's melancholia, understood as the ambivalent but sustained struggle in the ego between the forces that want to abandon the lost love-object and the other forces that want to incorporate it within the ego by devouring it.[10]

Tempting as it is, this particular system of affective bifurcation is not the norm in *Dubliners.* In this collection, Joyce hardly presents us with characters who can exemplify Freud's or Abraham and Torok's respective conceptions of *Trauerarbeit* and introjection. In fact, no significant character in *Dubliners* can be said to have effectively reached the affective closure afforded by the work of mourning, not even the boy of "Araby," whose sense of shame by the end of the story intensifies, thus wreaking havoc in his erstwhile, well-integrated psychic balance. Imbibing from a Homeric and pre-Platonic culture, as well as from a Platonic-Stoic-Christian tradition, Joyce discreetly cloaks *Dubliners* in the veneer of the two traditions, both at one and the same time. On the one hand, we are presented with such characters as Fr. Flynn, Eveline, Mrs. Sinico, and Gretta, who variably fall prey to the unbridled outbreaks of grief actuated by the loss of their love-objects. Such characters are always viscerally prompted to react to a loss that must have always taken them by surprise. Their libidinal attachments to the objects of their desires are unconditional, unreserved, and unseasoned. Such characters are, to use Henry Staten's words, "not yet sedimented with the strategies of idealization and transcendence"[11]—that is, they are not yet equipped by those priceless buoys that keep the sufferer of loss afloat within the otherwise overwhelming storms of grief. On the other hand, we are presented with unmournful, unfeeling, and intellectually triumphant characters, such as James Duffy and Gabriel Conroy, both of whom are prefigured early in the collection by the boy-narrator of "The Sisters" and the boy-narrator of "Araby."

In *Eros in Mourning* (1995), a wide-ranging book that in my estimation has not received the attention it deserves in recent studies of modernism and mourning, Henry Staten manages successfully to isolate, at least technically, two major loci of mourning in the Western history of dealing with desire. The first is the moment of illimitable grief, which, through a focalized reflection on the *Iliad* and particularly on Achilles' controversial relations to Briseis and Patroklosin, he situates in Homeric times. Achilles, Staten argues, is driven into a maze of endless mourning because of his originary blindness to the mortality of the objects of his desire. Contrary to Freud, Staten does not treat mourning simply qua a process of reparation, much less qua a reaction to loss. Like Derrida in his *Mémoires for Paul de Man* and *The Work of Mourning,* among others, Staten understands mourning, it bears repeating, as a *dialectic* permeating the very incipient structure of libidinal attachment.[12] Every desire is therefore shadowed by the mortality of the object of desire, and really by the ineluctable modality of mourning *constitutive of every object-relation.*

Such an uncompromising state of affairs makes the libidinal adventurer think twice before squandering his or her entire libido on a mortal object. Such is not the case, however, Staten argues, with Achilles, who loves with a force second only to the force with which he mourns once his object-libido is lost. According to Staten, Platonism, Stoicism, and Christianity have joined forces in the creation and dissemination of a more economic theory of object-relations. Staten identifies such a collaborative project as the second moment in the

Western tradition of engaging with desire. Attentive to the mortality of all love-objects, the fulcrum on which such a cumulative theory turned has ab initio been strategies of idealization and transcendence of mortal objects: "The fundamental terms of classical problematic of eros are simple...one may love mutable, contingent beings *as such,* in which case one is subject to limitless mourning; or one may love such being as a step on the way to the true, ultimate, and unfailing object of love, in which case mourning is mastered or at least mitigated by a movement of transcendence."[13]

Although Joyce "reemplots" these two philosophico-religious models of libidinal economy within the texture of *Dubliners,*[14] he does not show a preference for either; quite the contrary, he suggests that both models serve only to foster the paralysis endemic to most Dubliners under British colonial occupation. Bearing these theoretical concerns in mind—and by laying bare the affective behavior of a selected number of characters in *Dubliners*—I will study the *narrative poetics* of such libidinal economies of mourning and discern Joyce's subtle critique of their cultural sedimentations in the service of rediscovering mourning in its transformational, generative dimensions. In their deftly crafted figurative juxtaposition of loss and death, Joyce's stories force on the reader not only the urgency of acknowledging mourning, but also the timely necessity of submitting and exposing oneself to its transformational work/effects. Mixing formal with theoretical and critical lines of inquiry in a dynamic relation of complementariness, I will first establish prosopopoeia as the master trope of narrative mourning and then address the critical and transformational valences of mourning.

The Therapoetics of Prosopopoeia

Both Eveline and Gretta have witnessed at different stages in their lives the inadvertent and powerful returns of the phantoms of the past. Eveline was on the threshold of agreeing to submit to the enthralling call of eros, and she almost eloped with Frank to Buenos Aires. Such a would-be runaway marriage demands that she compromise her home, including all the familiar objects "from which she had never dreamt of being divided."[15] Moreover, it demands that she suspend sine die a hitherto effective vehicle of channeling mortal eros: her identification with Blessed Margaret Mary Alacoque, whose promises remind her of her own promise to her mother to keep the family together. From the outset, Eveline is unsettled by the underpinning tensions between the available strategies of transcendence with which she is domestically equipped and the blandishments of apotheosizing mortal eros with Frank in his faraway home in Buenos Aires. Given that at the end of the story Eveline is overridden by the hold of the past and by the strategies of transcendence burrowing into her whole being, Donald Torchiana concluded that Eveline "highlights in

Joyce's Dublin a *misguided* young woman who *denies* the sacredness of the heart, largely because of her devotion to the Order of the Sacred Heart that lies behind the *pious pretense* of Irish family life."[16]

Although, when caught in almost the same situation, Nora Barnacle did eventually elope with Joyce, I do not think that what is at stake at the story's end is the bankrupt piety of Irish family life, much less Eveline's denial of the sacredness of the heart. Such a conclusion would, in the words of Margot Norris, "reductively polariz[e] and simplif[y] choices that are far more inscrutable and complex."[17] The invisible forces of memory, legacy, and promise—which constitute the fulcrum upon which the plot of the story turns—are irreducible to a mere depreciation of love in favor of mere pretentious piety. Indeed, very much like Gretta in "The Dead," from the very beginning of her tale Eveline is set within a structure of conjuration of the past, of old times, of the dead, and of the departed until the sudden playing of a street organ prompts her virtually to exhume her mother, her voice, and her promise. The trope that is often related to such a mental ascesis, or exercise, is known as prosopopoeia. Paul de Man understands prosopopoeia in terms of a Hegelian dialectic of personification and reification, in which making the dead speak "implies by the same token that the living are struck dumb, frozen in their own death."[18] The exhumation of the dead, in other words, implodes veritably into the petrification of the living.

De Man's conceptualization of prosopopoeia as a composite trope involving not only the *personification* of the dead but also the simultaneous *reification* of the living is conducive to a psychoanalytical reflection on the nature and possibility of remembering and mourning in the context of *Dubliners.* Predicated on the praxis of remembering, the trope seems to set in motion the reparative and therapeutic process of mourning and survival such that one might be warranted to speak, at least provisionally, of a *therapoetics of prosopopoeia.*[19] Yet the trope is also inhabited by the threat of undermining the very restorative and consolatory task it incites and sets out to accomplish. First, I will explore the psychic and emotional effect of prosopopoeia on the characters who—lured by its quasi-magical conjuration and restitution of the dead as well as by the fantasy of reuniting with them—fall prey to the trope's pretension to cure, and are thus victimized by its fundamental impotency. On this score, I demonstrate the protean affective turmoil in which the performative reach of prosopopoeia leaves Eveline, Gretta, Gabriel, and James Duffy. While Eveline and Gretta are jolted by the prosopopoeic conjuration of the dead, Duffy and Gabriel are unsettled by an empathic involvement with Mrs. Sinico's and Gretta's tragedies respectively. Second, I will argue that the prosopopoeic moment of remembering and mourning overlaps, in the case of Duffy and Gabriel, with the moment of empathy and epiphany—in short, with their transformation and ascendance into maturity. Simultaneously, I will pave the way to conclude that the figure of prosopopoeia in Joyce's stories operates in such an entropic fashion as to thwart the fulfillment not only of the Freudian work of mourning, but especially of the de Manian prophecy that "the living are struck dumb, frozen in their own death." I contend that "A Painful Case" and "The Dead" orchestrate with remarkable clarity the impotence of the tropologic, which, while conjuring and decreeing a certain vision of the end, leaves the subject (i.e., Duffy and Gabriel) held in *automourning,* suspended in a present without potentiality: past the end, yet at the same time bereft of it.

The opening paragraph of "Eveline" sets in motion a gradual process of amassing images that figure forth the de Manian moment of prosopopoeic reversal. The evening that invades the avenue is in fact the figurative harbinger of the ubiquitous shadow of the past, which will further subdue the already prostrate head of Eveline. Bit by bit, Eveline grows from a passive consumer of the odor of dusty cretonne ("Her head was leaned against the window curtains and *in her nostrils was* the odor of dusty cretonne")[20] into an active inhaler ("Her time was running out but she continued to sit by the window, leaning her head against the window curtain, *inhaling* the odor of dusty cretonne").[21] By implication, Eveline evolves from a detached and machinic distillation of past childhood, forgone memories, and departed friends into a more active and elaborate engagement with the past. The reactivation of the past gains momentum when Eveline hears a street organ playing. In the very same manner, Gretta's already operative conjurative process of her past childhood romance with Michael Furey ("I'd love to see Galway again,"[22] she confides to her husband, pressing him to accept Miss Ivors's invitation to the Aran Isles) intensifies when she listens to a chance singing of *The Lass of Aughrim* by Bartell D'Arcy.

Both the street organ playing and the chance singing of "The Lass of Aughrim" act as prosopopoeic motor forces. Once these two archconjurations in both stories occur, the prosopopoeic dialectic speeds irresistibly toward its ineluctable reificatory reversal. By virtue of its retrospective logic, prosopopoeia, as defined by de Man, is technically conducive to a *therapoetic* process of remembering and working through the past. However, in the case of Eveline and Gretta, it is more fitting to say that it has served mainly to *spectralize* both the living and the dead. Eveline is hostage to rather than host of the ghostly voice that shouts unintelligibly within her: "Derevaun Seraun! Derevaun Seraun."[23] In the same manner, Gretta is marbleized by the sudden reemergence of the voice that screams within her that it "did not want to live;"[24] hence the incommensurability located at the very heart of the "conjure-and-dispel" double bind of clinical transcendence expounded by Freud. Although attentive to the potential "hypercathecting" operative in every prosopopoeic practice of conjuration and remembering, Freud nonetheless maintains that that should only be seen as a step toward the thorough detachment of libido from the lost object. "Each single one of the memories and expectations in which the libido is bound to the object is," Freud expounds, "brought up and *hypercathected,* and *detachment* of the libido is accomplished in respect to it."[25] Yet, hypercathecting serves, in the context of *Dubliners,* as the launching pad for the ultimate prosopopoeic reversal: the petrification of the living.

Small wonder, then, that Eveline and Gretta are reduced to the deathliness of disembodied presences! Transfixed into motionlessness, Eveline stares blindly, eyes-wide-shut, at Frank rushing beyond the barrier while she "clutch[es] the iron in frenzy" before she loosens her grip and "set[s] her white face to him, passive, like a helpless animal," giving him "no sign of love or farewell or recognition."[26] Likewise, after listening to a chance singing of the song that Michael Furey used to sing to her during their long walks in the countryside, Gretta becomes so divested of herself and possessed by Michael's image that her husband did not hesitate to drag her down to the deadness of a "symbol," a "picture"—an abstraction and an image.

Upon listening to the musical performance by Bartell D'Arcy, Gretta has become the site of a perturbing and unsettling memory such that Gabriel himself, still unable to attend to her crisis, nails her down to the alleged deadness of a "picture": "There was grace and mystery in her attitude as if she were a symbol of something. He asked himself what is a woman standing on the stairs in the shadow, listening to distant music, a symbol of. If he were a painter he would paint her in that attitude . . . *Distant Music* he would call the picture if he were a painter."[27] At his stage, Gabriel is unaware of the meaning of such a perplexing abstraction of his wife. Yet what I find strikingly ironic in this passage is Gabriel's unwitting imaginative involvement in the very activity native to the dialectic of prosopopoeic reversal—the act of defacing and disfiguring the living. That Gabriel should abstract Gretta means at least that Gretta, as a living entity, is possessed by another nonliving entity, by an absent being—by a revenant. This passage then captures a concrete prosopopoeic dialectic, an achieved prosopopoeia, in which the conferment of face upon the faceless (Michael) engenders a symmetrical stripping of face from Gretta. Prosopopoeia clearly has the animating force not only of defictionalizing the faceless but also of fictionalizing the living face. But Gretta is as oblivious to her abstraction as Gabriel is unaware of its full significance. Meanwhile, the reader has, while giving free play to this imaginative flight, part and parcel of any interpretive enterprise, to bear in mind that prosopopoeia is, as Michel Riffaterre explains, a fiction that, "[f]ar from inviting visualization, let alone sensory perception," presupposes an "animating," "mock" force whereupon "no real personification need take place."[28] I am therefore by no means suggesting, as will be better illustrated later, that Gretta is literally dead, much less that Michael is really back from the dead; nor am I suggesting that the signifying force of prosopopoeia demands that the animated entity (Michael Furey) be fictitiously embodied by a certain ghostly revenant, let alone by a *visible* ghostly revenant.

The return of the prosopopoeically animated Other occurs not so much in narrative space as in narrative time, within and through the (de)contracting consciousness of Gretta. This return becomes visible only as an effect brought to bear on the mourning subject: the visibility of the invisible Michael correlates with the invisibility of the visible Gretta, to whom Aunt Julia declares, "—O, good-night, Gretta, I didn't see you."[29] Although Michael Furey does not really come back in the manner of the ghost of Hamlet's father demanding that he be remembered and honored, he emerges not only as an undying flame, a voice whose words do not die, but also as an eye, seen while unseen: "I implored of him to go home at once and told him he would get his death in the rain. But he said he did not want to live. *I can see his eyes as well as well!* He was standing at the end of the wall where there was a tree."[30] That Eveline and Gretta become, to borrow a word from *Ulysses,* so "wrapt" (i.e., rapt/wrapped) in/by the past is the outcome not only of the prosopopoeic rupture they undergo but of their *uneconomized* libidinal expenditures after the prosopopoeic outbreak.[31] The dialectic of prosopopoeic reversal, to which they have submitted, originates in their active conjuration and hypercathecting of the dead, without which the reificatory reversal would never have taken place. At length, seduced by the trope's magical conjuration and restitution of the dead and by the promise of reuniting with them, Eveline and Gretta find themselves, while locked in the trope's uncompromising logic, unable to undergo the threat of death that, de Man insists, inhabits prosopopoeia. It follows then that prosopopoeia is actually inhabited by a fundamental performative impotence that decrees but fails to fulfill the end. Exposed to the prosopopoeic trap, Eveline and Gretta are suspended in the aridity of a present without potentiality: marbleized and statuified. Hence, there is more to their tragedies than a "misguided" denial of the sacredness of the heart, as Donald Torchiana would have us believe.[32]

The affective turmoil that Eveline and Gretta experience is, it bears repeating, largely precipitated by the malfunction of their systems of libidinal management following the prosopopoeic resurfacing of their love-objects. Surely, they have *rehearsed* their positions in relation to the objects of their libidinal attachments (i.e., Eveline is on the threshold of marriage, and Gretta is already married), but they have variably failed to achieve the affective closure afforded by the Freudian brand of mourning—a closure that would presumably shield them against the incidental sparkers (such as distant music) of grief. Yet pointing out their failure of arriving at this protective affective closure does not by any means imply that such a closure is after all possible. Mourning presents itself primarily as a demand for affective closure, yet the demand cannot be understood separately from the countervailing force of desire.

Once loss occurs, it must have been always already too late to avoid the overwhelming spiral of desire and mourning. Indeed, eros seems so central to the emergence of life that the affective closure of the work of mourning is but a rebirth of eros, a beginning of another cycle. Even the more libidinally economized characters such as James Duffy and Gabriel Conroy prove, I will argue, vulnerable to the intractable detours of eros in the route to fulfillment, and, by implication, to the latent structure of grief inextricably bound to it. Although arrayed in more rigorous prophylactic structures of *affective foreclosure* aimed at nipping eros in the bud, James Duffy and Gabriel Conroy undergo nonetheless, a prosopopoeic experience that forces them not only to approximate *empathically* Mrs. Sinico's and Gretta's crises respectively, but especially to recognize *empiphanically* their fundamental loneliness (James Duffy) and ineluctable mortality (Gabriel). They undergo, in other words, what I call an *empiphany:* a transactive dynamics of recognizing the irreducible otherness of eros at the very moment of its manifestation—a mysteriously tied knot between empathy and epiphany, or recognition and cognition. To better understand the radical nature of this empiphanic moment, this moment of merging and generative transformation, let me first shed some light on the myths and beliefs of the former selves of James Duffy and Gabriel Conroy. It is, after all, in the detailing of the subtle transformations that these two characters undergo in their struggle with mourning that Joyce's stories become of particular relevance to a critique of the sedimentations of the transcendentalizing impulse in turn-of-the-century Irish culture as well as of today's desensitized and spectacular mourning practices.

EMPIPHANY

Before their empiphanic awakening, both James Duffy and Gabriel Conroy deploy an ideology of transcendence that, while tentatively alive to the inevitability of affective ties, is either deliberately exiled from them (Duffy in relation to Emily), or murderously overappropriative of their otherness (Gabriel in relation to Gretta). Although Duffy might not be influenced by Platonizing Christianity, he comes very much under the influence of a Stoic-Platonic tradition that articulates a fundamental schism between the mortality of the flesh and the immortality of the idea. Much to the detriment of eros—the driving force of psychic life—I think that Duffy's maxim, "[e]very bond is a bond to sorrow,"[33] attests undoubtedly to the immortality of the idea. This maxim is, in fact, the most profound statement in *Dubliners* about the aporetic nature of object-relations. Many Joycean scholars have been, however, seduced by the irresistible temptation to indict Duffy for having disdained love. In this regard, Philip Herring, for instance, was able to ascertain—even though the very title of his book is Joyce's *Uncertainty Principle*—that by the story's end, "James Duffy is *punished* by a deep longing for the love and the human contact he had earlier prided himself on disdaining."[34] Such a conclusion is, in my view, insensitive to the serious questions Duffy's maxim raises. It, moreover, passes over in silence not only Duffy's attempt to rehearse his libidinal investments (i.e., his libidinal approach to Emily Sinico and his simultaneous suspension of such nonsymbolic investiture), but also his eventual empiphanic realization that he is *lonely.* At length, Herring seems to imply that if Duffy were to reciprocate Emily's libidinal overtures, he would have been sheltered from the pain, suffering, and loneliness that are, nonetheless, constitutive, as Duffy's maxim rightly suggests, of eros (in Dublin).

By cautioning us that every bond is a bond to sorrow, Duffy suspends us between the demands of eros and the ineluctable modality of mourning, "the horizon of all desire," in the words of Staten.[35] And only through the sublimation of eros can the rising horizon of mourning begin to shrink. By means of an *exilic attachment* to Emily Sinico, Duffy attempts to avoid both eros and mourning. He rehearses an economics of libidinal expenditure that would both preempt the pangs of eros and shelter him from the outbreak of grief. Indeed, Duffy wants to shore up a life in the hinge between philosophy and music, between friendship and love, between libidinal transcendence and libidinal investiture. Many are the references that figure forth this attempt to mediate or glide chiastically between these two virtually incommensurable demands. Although he acknowledges, for instance, the crude presence of his body, he keeps it in constant check. More important by far, by *inscribing* and simultaneously *withholding* his self in his odd "autobiographical habit,"[36] he paradoxically seeks to take a line of flight that enables him to evade the very activity (i.e., writing) in which he is involved. Little wonder, then, that he stops at the threshold of writing and on the verge of articulation, and all he manages to pen are nothing more than disparate sentences on a sheaf of papers. His poetics of libidinal economy unfolds on the borderline between the desire to inscribe his self autobiographically and the symmetrical transcendentalizing imperative to veil and impersonalize. He thus oscillates chiastically between self-exaltation and self-denunciation, between self-love and self-denial, and really between the temptations of eros and the mortifications of grief.

Such a poetics, which is sensu stricto a poetics of the threshold, would intensify by an unbridled prosopopoeic outbreak of grief. Like Gabriel, Duffy grows from a practitioner of negative conjuration of the dead Emily into a practitioner of empathic approximation of her experience. At one point, he seems, in an obviously Freudian aside, to reduce Emily Sinico to pure, unpunctuated eros—"to one of the wrecks on which civilization has been reared."[37] And he feels a particular need for sublimation, and for civilization, on whose suburbs he has nevertheless hitherto lived. Moreover, he perceives Emily's death as veiling a last attempt on her part to wreak vengeance and inflict on him the same amount of pain she suffered. But when he engages in an intense conjuration of her memory, not only does his anger mitigate, but also a proliferation of "voice" and "hand" pops out into prosopopoeic existence: "She seemed to be near him in the darkness. At moments he seemed to feel her voice touch his ear, her hand touch his. He stood still to listen."[38]

In a pioneering study of melancholy and mourning in *Dubliners,* Earl Ingersoll claims that at the end of "A Painful Case," Duffy—when finishing his evening meal—caught sight of "A Painful Case" in the paper beside his plate, and is thus "offered the opportunity to have Emily Sinico for dessert."[39] In other words, Duffy reacts to the prosopopoeic restitution of Emily by incorporating her within, thus violating her otherwise inassimilable otherness. The end of the story, however, seems to me to stress rather an empiphanic moment in which the empathy with Emily's loneliness brings Duffy's gaze to center on his own loneliness. This empiphanic structure begins when he "understood how lonely her life must have been," and comes full circle at the very end of the story when he "felt that he was alone."[40] This last sentence, which certainly conveys the onset of mourning, was prepared for by another sentence: "His life would be lonely until, he, too, died, ceased to exist, became a memory—if anyone remembered him."[41] Far from cannibalistically incorporating Emily within him, Duffy is again gliding chiastically between an empathic approximation of her experience of loneliness, and an empiphanic cognizance of his own ineluctable death, his present loneliness, and her infinite alterity. At one point, "he seemed to feel her voice touch his ear." At another, he "could not feel her near him in the darkness nor her voice touch his ear."[42] Only through the chiastics of proximity and distance can we understand the full surge of the dead Emily Sinico in the expanding and simultaneously withering world of Duffy. Indeed, at the very end of the story, Emily remains near and yet far, *there beyond,* at the crossroads between the transcendence he preaches and the birth of desire he was wont to abhor.

Empiphany, being a transactive interchange between an exterior and interior gaze, does not violate the experience of the other in the process of approximating it, no more than the other's experience itself can be said to violate one's own. Like Duffy's, Gabriel's empiphanic awakening not only lays bare the emergence of Gretta as utterly other (after she has been hitherto caught within the fabric of specular identification with him), but also evokes the emergence of empathy not so much as an overappropriative as a transactive force. While Duffy's story foregrounds his reckoning with the otherness (of Mrs. Sinico, of eros, of mourning, and so forth) that he had always dreaded and kept at bay, Gabriel's brings to the limelight his recognition of the otherness he had always suppressed. By virtue of being married, Gabriel's relation to Gretta is normally—as James Duffy, the author of "[e]very bond is a bond to sorrow," would have pointed out—animated by the foundational conjugal contract of mourning. Yet, Gabriel is presented as absorbed in clearing away the mist of mortality hanging in the horizon of his mortal bond to Gretta, and to his relatives. Immersed in the waters of philosophy, associated with a Roman-Stoic and Nietzschean practice of productive forgetting, Gabriel is spurred by a powerful illusion, masquerading as intellectual triumphalism, and thus eschews everything that smacks of grief: "Our path through life is strewn with many . . . memories: and were we to brood upon them always we could not find the heart to go on bravely with our work among the living." And he adds: "I will not linger on the past. I will not let any gloomy moralising intrude upon us here to-night."[43]

Gabriel deploys a seductive and palliative rhetoric of persuasion in order not only to defuse, but ultimately to transcend, if not occlude, "thoughts of the past, of youth, of changes, of absent faces."[44] His strategy of managing mortality and transience is deeply rooted in the Greek and Roman stoic traditions of philosophy, especially Epicurus and Lucretius. Stoicism has emphatically cautioned against unreserved attachments to objects, persons, or anything mortal, as a preventive armament against any assault of unbridled mourning in the wake of their loss. Thus, death is presented as the cessation of being, which, if rationally compromised at the outset, should foster no unexpected bouts of mourning, nor any unseasonable lugubrious wails. Indeed, in his famous letter to Menoeceus, Epicurus goes on, in a combination of both rhetoric and logic, hammering this very idea home: "Become accustomed to the belief that death is nothing to us. . . . It does not . . . concern either the living or the dead, since for the former it is not, and the latter are no more."[45] The Lucretian argument, following from the Epicurean one, also holds that death is posthumous nonexistence akin to prenatal nonexistence (this is the core of the famous Lucretian "symmetry thesis"). Summing up his cogitation about the radical wedge that death enters between the living and the dead, Lucretius writes, "Death therefore must be thought to concern us much less, if less there can be than what we see to be nothing; for a greater dispersion of the mass of matter follows after death, and no one wakes up, upon whom the chill cessation of life has once come."[46]

In the second of his *Unzeitgemässe Betrachtungen,* recently rendered by Richard Gray as *Unfashionable Observations* (formerly known as *Untimely Meditations*), Nietzsche goes even further than the Stoics and strikes an organic cord between the necessity of forgetting the dead and the past at large, and the possibility of action: "All action requires forgetting" since "historical sensibility makes its servants passive and retrospective."[47] Ultimately, Nietzsche reasons that (historical) memory and the past are sickening, that his age suffers from "*historical sickness*" and from "the memory of its chains," and that the only antidote to this fatal disease lies in "the art and power to be able to *forget.*"[48] This Stoic tradition of philosophy, whose effects have rippled through the ages, is appropriated and ultimately deconstructed, in "The Dead" through Gabriel's character. Actually, the empiphanic moment that Gabriel experiences is but the moment of dispelling the hold such a philosophy has had on his thinking—a thinking that, far from being tempered and particularized by (an) experience (à la Gretta), is simply indulgent in Stoicism, in the pursuance and maintenance of a rational protective buffer—a sort of cordon sanitaire—between the dead and the living.

One could safely posit that Gabriel is just not aware that a pseudotheory of memory (or what in the words of Barbie Zelizer amounts to a "remembering to forget")[49] would not secure an unencumbered present. Although his strategy of transcendence would brook no *return to* the past, it remains perched on the abyss of a possible free-floating *return of* the past in the form of a harrowing and disembodied memory. Unlike the return *to* memory, which is a deliberate, transformational, and generative practice of remembering, the return *of* memory is but the eruption of hitherto latent, but unsubdued force. While the return *to* memory might be described as *mournfulfilling* (i.e., a remembering that works toward the gradual fulfillment of the task of mourning), the return *of* memory is rather *mournfilling* (i.e., it fills the hitherto intellectually triumphant disclaimer of the past with a sudden outbreak of mourning that might eventually slide into a form of prolonged mourning or melancholia).

Laboring under the auspices of the Roman-Stoic tradition of libidinal management, Gabriel's practice of pseudoremembering reaches its limits, where its vocabulary, concerned with prophylaxis, would fall short, as Gretta's case attests to, of precluding the occurrence of a *return-of* type of memory, followed by a focalized conjuration, culminating in a prosopopoeic jolt. Before that occurs to Gretta, however, Gabriel had enjoyed the psychic seamlessness of a specular relationship with her (as his "object-cathexis"). No sooner does he learn that there was "a person long ago" in her life than he is beset by fury: "A dull anger began to gather again at the back of his mind and the dull fires of his lust began to glow angrily in his veins."[50] Such anger, not yet ignited by shame, feeds on the fear of belatedness, on the erotic phobia of having been preceded to the heart of Gretta by someone else. Surely, there is a certain preemptive power that precedence holds over, and exercises upon, belatedness, yet it is not so much the loss of this initiatory power—the power to cast long shadows—that has provoked Gabriel's anger as it is the loss of the powerful illusion that has hitherto spurred and nurtured it. Such an illusion is, moreover, predicated upon holding the other in abeyance, if not suppressing her altogether. As Eric L. Santner points out, "the narcissist loves an object only insofar and as long as he or she can repress the otherness of the object."[51]

While the other for Duffy is a threat to his strategic loneliness, the other for Gabriel is but an extension of the self, invisible as such, and thus harboring no threat to his prolonged egoic monologism. At least initially, then, Gabriel exemplifies Sándor Ferenczi's dictum that, "[i]n principle, man can only love himself; if he loves an object he takes it into his ego."[52] It follows from this that the narcissist's egoic monologism and specular reciprocity with the love-object is shaken at the seams as soon as the object's otherness is asserted. Gretta's otherness is inscribed in her tale of love and loss, and has gradually come into prominence as that very tale unfolded. It is as if the mark of loss, which is really the stamp of grief, were the grantor of that hitherto veiled and denied otherness.

The Inability to Mourn

Gretta's insurgent otherness, along with Gabriel's loss of the illusion of priority, while furnishing the objective prerequisites for a logical outbreak of melancholy (i.e., a process whereby the ego attempts to contain its loss of self-regard), will nonetheless foment no turbulence at all in Gabriel's psyche. The point is that the thrust of melancholia toward the exterior is immediately countered by an interior strategy of *psychoaffective foreclosure.* Although Gabriel is now deeply aware of the fracture of his identificatory mirror with Gretta, he attempts firmly to elide the heightened hues of shame that come to color his face. The active engagement of containing the emotional currents that have swept his ego-narcissism adds to his conviction—or illusion—of mastery over a situation to which he was forced to submit. Gabriel is still dreaming of saving face, of suturing his fissures, and of consoling his ego by sparing it the shame of admitting and displaying its festering wounds. Joyce is careful enough to use the word "instinctively," which suggests that Gabriel is unconsciously defending against the onset of melancholia.

Gabriel manifests the symptoms of what Alexander and Margarette Mitscherlich call the "inability to mourn," which is, in fact, a foreclosure of mourning, an obstinate refusal to submit to what one is literally exposed and submitted to.[53] Precisely, the inability to mourn bespeaks the disavowal of something (here grief) that is nonetheless felt in every iota of one's being. The ego can thus be, as is the case with Gabriel, at a stage of emotional turmoil, overwhelmed with grief, anger, and incipient melancholia, but will still be categorically unwilling to live through its egoic injuries, and thus folds back into a state of primitive narcissism, believed to be the only remaining repository of hope, shelter and protection of (the otherwise constitutive vulnerability of) the ego. This strategy of occlusion of shame, an occlusion of what is there, of what insists on being there, on the face, there for the public eye—coupled with his self-deceptive irony and the insurgent vindictive consolatory gestures he waves to his shattered ego—enables Gabriel momentarily to contain the opening of an abysmal interval in his claustral and specular relationship with Gretta.

Gabriel's persistent refusal to evacuate his egoic stronghold is, however, as Gretta's harrowing tale unfolds, met with an immense challenge: to ward off the massive injury brought down upon his ego by the dawning discovery that not only was Gretta "great with" Michael, but especially that the latter "died for [her]."[54] It is precisely this inimitable legacy that forces on Gabriel a kind of unconditional surrender. It pushes him to give up militating, in a spate of egoic consolation, against an unknown enemy who is neither within range, nor of the same caliber. Indeed, it is an enemy who lives in "a grey impalpable world," and, more important by far, an enemy who had braved death for love: "a man died for her."[55] This immense legacy, which Gabriel would not even toy with the idea of measuring himself against, has hastened the collapse of his militant campaign to recapture Gretta within a structure of specular identification: "It hardly pained him now to think how poor a part he, her husband, had played in her life."[56] Whatever way he would turn to win Gretta back again into his ego, it would hardly prove of any consolation, especially if compared to the monumental heritage of Michael Furey.

Gabriel's whole being now becomes redefined in relation to this predecessor, Michael Furey. Such a relation, which is born on the wreck of his ego-syntonic self—a self formerly wont, in its constant movement to broaden the boundaries of its domain, to introject its love-objects within—relocates him on the plane of mortal desire, that is, on the plane of desire as correlative with mourning. As Derrida explains in *Specters of Marx,* being itself shadows forth "a predestined hospitality" that should never shirk the task of extending a welcome to the enduring, spectral presence-absence of the predecessor, or the dead.[57] To put this somewhat differently, being cannot be conceived separately from inheriting, and since inheriting veils the trace of another being in relation to whom we are, then being is necessarily being in mourning for the being from whom we received our inheritance, and eventually this mourning extends to the very being who is now defined/marked by or identified with the duty/task of inheritance—the inheritor. Thus, as Derrida succinctly puts it: "like all inheritors, we are in mourning."[58]

Gabriel's newly formed alignment with his dispossessor/liberator of the illusion of priority, as well as his relocation on the plane of mortal desire and mourning, become more and more evident in his empathic entanglement with the harrowing memories of Gretta. When Gretta is fast asleep, Gabriel is proffered with the opportunity to empathically slice into her experience, and it is not long before he realizes she is infinitely other: "He watched her while she slept as though he and she had never lived together as man and wife."[59] This alienating sentiment, which is now borne into his mind for the first time, does not so much bespeak, as most critical works on the story attest to, the end result of a hitherto failed marriage, as it so manifestly outlines the premises of marriage itself: the affirmation of otherness and the commitment to mourning. This is also a threshold moment of an ethical response to mourning (to be discussed at length in chapter 5), in which we witness, in the words of Marian Eide, "the experience and expression of sympathy within the preservation of difference."[60]

Gabriel's heightened empathy, however, while actuated by a newly formed alignment with Gretta (and an a posteriori one with Michael), knows no sense of proportion: it dilates and spills over into an a priori process of hetero-mourning:

> Poor Aunt Julia! She . . . would soon be a shade with the shade of Patrick Morkan and his horse . . .
> Yes, yes: that would happen very soon . . .
> One by one they were all becoming shades.[61]

Gabriel is so empathically stricken by Gretta's public expression of mourning that he projects himself into a position in which he will have to mourn the anticipated deaths of his aunts, and potentially of everyone he knows. Gabriel has now attained that stage of awareness in which he would very likely repeat, after James Duffy, that "every bond is a bond to sorrow."[62] In the wake of the empathic involvement with Gretta's inconsolable mourning of the loss of her childhood boyfriend, which is itself a premonitory glimpse of the inevitable death of Gabriel's relatives and of the task of heteromourning awaiting him, there emerges, more important by far, the empiphanic prefiguration of a drastic personal narrative of *automourning* whereby Gabriel lives *a priori* the devastating loss of his "own identity"—an identity felt to be irresistibly "fading out into a grey impalpable world."[63]

Gabriel posits his death before it occurs; he lives in the aftermath of what is yet to come, that is, in the wake of the event that is not yet one. He lives, more precisely, in the anticipation of a loss (death) whose very occurrence would inevitably coincide with his collapse as a subject capable of experiencing or bearing witness to it—let alone surviving it. Death presents itself as that which has not yet been experienced, and paradoxically as that which must have always been (a fact). Thus, the anticipation of death is already inhabited by its very aftermath. In a compelling article, "Fear of Breakdown," A.W. Winnicott associates (the wish for/fear of) death with a persisting infantile "primitive agony" that has not yet been amenable to experience. Winnicott wants to draw attention to the possibility that death must have always happened near the beginning of every individual's life, but was not experienced, "because the patient was not there for it to happen to."[64] According to Winnicott, "it is the death that happened but was not experienced that is sought."[65] While this is not the space for infantilizing the (adult) compulsive pursuit/dread of death, nor for determining for sure whether or not Gabriel "died in early infancy," I find Winnicott's emphasis on the death that "has already been" albeit "not yet experienced,"[66] very pertinent to the present discussion, for that which "has already been" while "not yet experienced" is precisely that which is *constitutive* of being as such.

Death is what structures being and cannot, therefore, be experienced by the very person who undergoes it. To experience one's death, one has, as it were, to live through/past the end, without the end. Such an experience is quite simply impossible. What is within the realms of the possible is a *relational* experience of death. This occurs following the loss of others as objects of love, friendship, kinship, or any other kind of bonds. One's death, insofar as it is a constitutive loss of one's being, can only be experienced as a relational loss. Thus, the experience of one's death commences in mourning; more precisely, in mourning (for) the other's death—that is, in heteromourning. What instigates Gabriel's expression of heteromourning is, moreover, not a relational loss that has befallen him but a relational loss that he anticipates. Such anticipation, it bears repeating, emanates from an empiphanic involvement with his wife's harrowing heteromourning.

Automourning

What is easier to recognize than analyze is the baffling slippage of Gabriel from a process of anticipatory heteromourning into a process of automourning, that is, from a process in which he sees all his relatives being transformed one by one into shades to a process in which he sees his soul fast approaching "that region where dwell the vast hosts of the dead."[67] To be able to see one's own identity "fading out into a grey impalpable world" is the impossible par excellence. It is much like Hamlet's impossible pronouncement: "Horatio, I am dead."[68] Here we are obviously faring at the margins of the philosophical logic of noncontradiction, yet there is still method in such rhetoric. The point is that one's own death—the impossible to experience—is presupposed by the structure that engulfs being, so much so that a heightened awareness of its inevitability suspends the demarcating lines between its anticipation and its aftermath. Under one instigator or another, one realizes that one is born to die and acts as if one were already dead, as if the end were at hand. Hence, the "not yet experienced," in Winnicott's words, falls under the shadow of what "has already been," such that one is left in limbo—suspended between an end that has *already* come and an end that has not *yet* come, mistaking the one for the other. One ends up living in an impossible realm—past the end, yet without the end. One, in other words, submits passively to a state that Jean-Luc Nancy transcribes as—"life/death"—"a suspension of the continuum of being, a scansion wherein 'I' has/have little to do."[69] Only under such a condition can one approximate an experience of one's own death, an experience of one's end.

To be able to pronounce one's death is to move from a position of relative, affective passivity toward a constitutive loss (yet to be experienced) into an active, affective engagement with its aftermath. One's own life becomes the unfolding of a mystifying story of survival and/or waiting for the arrival of death. Mourning the deaths of others—heteromourning—rouses the underpinning structure of automourning. Thus, every relational loss, however anticipatory, translates immediately into a constitutive loss, a flash-forward of the loss of one's own self. *The relational harks back to the constitutive.* The constitutive remains, however, the realm of the impossible to experience.

In this respect, the sadness that seals Gabriel's heart at the end of the story is the offshoot not so much of the *imminent bereavement* hic et ubique of the end as of the *immanent bereftness* hic et nunc of an end. The litany of losses—the ones past (Michael Furey and Patrick Morkan and his horse) and the ones yet to come (Aunt Julia and the rest)—awakens Gabriel to the transitory nature of life, and instills in him what Freud calls "a foretaste of mourning."[70] Yet what makes this story theoretically important is that mourning does not follow, *pace* Freud, from the loss of something (here Gabriel's life) that the survivor (Gabriel as survivor of his own death) cannot seamlessly forsake, but rather from the impossible occurrence *here and now* of that which is destined to occur —in short, from the impossibility of the resolve, in Beckett's words, to "finish dying."[71] As Hans-Jost Frey superbly contends, "What has failed to happen cannot be made up for. Mourning envelops the emptiness from which nothing more can be expected. One mourns less for what was than for what can no longer happen now."[72] What can no longer happen now refers—let us not forget—to the prosopopoeic promise of the end, which is, as already explained, the second moment of prosopopoeia—the moment of an *achieved prosopopoeia,* the fulfillment of the end. Gabriel only allows himself to reckon wearily that "[t]he time had come for him to set out on his journey westward."[73] But, in fact, he is suspended in the aridity of a present bereft of potentiality—a present in which he has, in the words of Nancy, "little to do."[74]

Automourning structures one's relation to a loss (of the unit self, in Winnicott's terms) which, though not yet lived through, pertains to a permanent preoccupation of the mind and is rehearsed endlessly in the imagination. This type of loss withstands no experiencing: it occurs abruptly—it interrupts, and leaves no chance for the subject to experience it posthumously. The subject has, therefore, no alternative but to reconcile itself to it a priori, beforehand. Automourning is the affective apparatus within which such a loss is painted and experienced, as it were, hypothetically, but no less acutely and tensely. This is all the more so when automourning breaks out in response to a relational loss or in empathy with another person (here Gretta) on her painful loss.

That Gabriel should have been lured and immured into such a Pyrrhically mature state of nonbecoming attests to the resonant effects of the two affective experiences with which we have been preoccupied so far: namely, the prosopopoeic and the empiphanic experiences. Indeed, to do justice to the enormity and complexity of Gabriel's suspended-ness (really, suspended-I-ness) in the affect of automourning, one has to speak of a prosopopo-empiphanic imbrication. Actually, a complex signifying dialectical chain is started at the behest of the primal prosopopoeic gesture (extended to the dead but primarily directed in the service of the living): conjuration-empathy-conjuration-epiphany. The reason why "conjuration" is repeated twice in this nodal chaining of an otherwise dispersed and unmasterable affective inter- and intra-relations is because right at the very end of the story Gabriel recreates, and lives vicariously through, the night when Michael Furey ran to Gretta's house and threw gravel against her window. The recreation, however, is so subtle as to escape the inquiring eye. What is important to emphasize here is not so much the imaginative recreation of the scene as its lived and transformative effect on Gabriel. The recreation of this scene in Gabriel's imagination goes as follows: "The tears gathered more thickly in his eyes and in the partial darkness he imagined he saw the form of a young man standing under a dripping tree." Clearly, this recreation blurs spontaneously into a prosopopoeic conjuration whose power and force are such that a "few light taps upon the pane made him turn to the window."[75] The fact is that Gabriel is so absorbed and enthralled by the fictional conjuration of Michael Furey that the lines of demarcation between his imaginative engrossment and reality (narrative reality) collapse at the seams, and the "few light taps upon the pane" are immediately confused with Michael's gravel against the window. Thus, it requires no further argument to stress how the imaginative recreation spills over into a prosopopoeic entanglement whose effect is hallucinatory in that it unsettles the distinction between the modality of the visible and the modality of the palpable or feelable.

Hallucination ensues from the empathic entanglement with the prosopopoeic tidal motion. In other words, hallucination is another name for the empathic revelation of the other in his irreducible alterity. Empathy wields the force and effect, without which prosopopoeia becomes an opprobrious and hackneyed tropological ritual. In the context of this story, prosopopoeia does not, *pace* de Man, so much confer a voice and a face upon an absent entity—here, Michael Furey—as confer a feelable presence upon an otherwise irredeemably absent entity. This presence is not, moreover, exteriorized and staged, that is, made literally available in the world of the text, but is anchored in an insurgent structure of empathy. And empathy, insofar as it is a transferential process aimed at approximating the experience of the other, secures the passage to the merged experience of *empiphany:* the *recognition* of the other at the very moment of his *revelation.*

The dialectic of prosopopoeia acts as the motor force that produces empiphany. In other words, through conjuration and peripeteia, the prosopopoeic generates both the revelation and recognition of the otherness of Gretta, and ultimately the *inclusive,* rather than *alienating,* otherness of the dead. Through prosopopoeia, the topography of the dead becomes the "milieu" in which both the living and the dead tread. Prosopopoeia, briefly put, enacts a poetics of suddenness whose transformative and generative effect cannot be overstressed, but suffice it to mention for now that it has the merit of empiphanic reckoning and of retrospective enlightenment. As the structure of the story attests to, prosopopoeia is not only the vessel, the barge, or the isthmus that "gathers together" the river of the living and the river of the dead, but also the trope of maturity, of surviving dialectic, not unscathed but uncompromising.

On the other hand, the latent threat that inhabits prosopopoeia is not so much the alleged congealment of the living in their own death, as denying them sine die such a constitutive ending. Prosopopoeia awakens one to the ineluctability of death, to the promise of the end, all the while it censures the fulfillment of the end. This is precisely the theoretical reservation that the story registers about the performative reach of the trope. While it magnificently plots the logic of the tropological within its structure such that death boils down, in the words of de Man, to "a linguistic predicament,"[76] "The Dead" reminds us in the final analysis that the tropological—however illuminating and enriching—is far from offering a shelter, a cure, or even the very end (of death) that it so preciously treasures.

The strength of prosopopoeia as a trope, its performative aftereffect on the consciousness of the mourner (who becomes simultaneously the mournee), is paradoxically the locus of its frailty, of its impossibility: it gathers us to the end and paradoxically sets us apart from it. Perhaps prosopopoeia is ultimately, and quite oxymoronically, the force that *gathers us apart* with the end. Indeed, the end of the story in which everything, including "the living and the dead," is leveled out by the snow, such that every place looks like the next is expressive of an unfathomable sadness, not so much over the approach of the end as over its intractable recessiveness. The narrative insistence *on* the end is not so much a signal *of* the end as it is a mark of its baffling absence. At the end of the story, Gabriel, along with the reader, finds himself held in the aftermath of death, past the end, yet without the end. Such a prosopopoeic scenario is enveloped by automourning, the affective fragmentary state in which one feels, in the words of Hans-Jost Frey, "that everything is over except the feeling that it is over." In other words, while everything seems to glide chiastically and irresistibly toward the end—"falling faintly through the universe and faintly falling, like the descent of their last end"—there can be "no end in sight anymore."[77] The end is far from being fulfilled: it is only emblematically communicated in the veneer of the white snow. Automourning is precisely the inability to find the end, or as Nancy would have it, the "suspension in the continuum of being."[78] The danger of automourning is that it, in the words of Hans-Jost Frey, "exposes one to the harsh light of an ineluctable present without potentiality."[79] It is against the backdrop of such eventuality/fatality that the strategies of transcendence and idealization of mortal eros have been after all conceived, implemented, and perpetuated. The importance of Joyce's story, however, is that it forces on the reader the acknowledgment of automourning, preparatory to, in the words of Judith Butler, "agreeing to undergo a transformation," particularly if it is, as in the case of Gabriel and Duffy, of empiphanic proportions.[80]

OTOMOURNING

Henry Staten argues that "what motivates the classical project of transcendence of mourning is the fear not of loss of object but of loss of self."[81] This is to say that the death of the other is, if anything, a memento mori. What the classical project of transcendence wants to transcend is this fear of self-loss—this very automourning that Gabriel arrives at so laboriously. I contend, however, that it is precisely this fear of self-loss that in turn complicates the very idea of transcendence itself, since this fear is expressive of an emergent desire that, in the words of Staten, "would cut the knot of revulsion from organic being that fuels the drive to transcendence."[82] This desire is precisely the desire to be mourned. This is the desire that has, curiously enough, converted James Duffy from an inhabitor of a *transcendentalizing* into an inhabitor of a *desiring* form of loneliness. Loneliness is first presented in "A Painful Case" as a deliberate abstinence from libidinal attachments, in concert with his alibi for breaking up with Emily Sinico (i.e., every bond is a bond to sorrow): "he heard the strange impersonal voice which he recognized as his own, insisting on the soul's incurable loneliness. We cannot give ourselves, it said: we are our own."[83] By the end of the story, however, we are confronted, much to the neglect of generations of Joycean scholars, by loneliness as a symptom of crisis, and particularly as a desire for libidinal investment.

As I have argued, Duffy has gone through a prosopopoeic experience that has eventually slid into an empiphanic apprehension of his own anomalous loneliness. Such a transformationally generative experience has, in addition, left Duffy truncated, defenseless in front of the anticipatory self-loss to be parried: "His life would be lonely too until he, too, died, ceased to exist, became a memory—*if anyone remembered him.*"[84] Beneath this elegiac anticipation of his "ownmost" death—this structure of aut-omourning we earlier associated with Gabriel—we can clearly discern a latent concern over what comes after death, which might indeed be worse than death. Following Adorno, Lyotard, and Derrida, "the worse than death" is an allegory for "the extinction of the very name that forbids mourning."[85] While Mrs. Sinico had ceased to exist, she "had," nonetheless, as Duffy himself admits, "become a memory" for better or worse.[86] It remains, however, to be proven whether he, when dead, would ascend to such a stage, where he would be remembered as a name reverberating in the ear of the other, and inciting her to the contract/task of mourning attendant upon her. James Duffy is horrified by the prospect that his own death might coincide with the absolute finitude (i.e., death) of the infinite (i.e., memory), that is, with the very extinction of his name, of his memory, as a carrier of grief, and as a marker of both death and survival.

Mourning is the emotional response to the gap the loss of the other leaves in the ego of the survivor. At the end of "A Painful Case," mourning had broken on Duffy like an unbridled tidal wave, stymieing the prosopopoeic channels that had heretofore reunited him with Mrs. Sinico: "He began to doubt the reality of what memory told him. . . . He could not feel her near him in the darkness nor her voice touch his ear."[87] The final feeling of loneliness welling up inside him must be understood in tandem with the aperture the loss of Mrs. Sinico had suddenly created in his ego. That Duffy feels bereft and lonely attests not only to his entry into a process of automourning, but also to the success of eros in having sustained the cathectic ties to Mrs. Sinico despite Duffy's will to transcendence. The fissure in the ego that is occasioned by the sudden loss of Mrs. Sinico, and that foments automourning can be sutured, according to Freud, only by means of severing the libidinal ties once and for all with Mrs. Sinico and initiating a new alliance with a new love-object. Such is what is psychoanalytically known as a successful mourning—a mourning that always takes place at the expense of the other whose gap come to be filled by, as it were, another other. Although the ethical issues involved here (which I will discuss at length in chapter 5) bulk large, what is important for us to realize is that the affective gap opened by the loss of a love-object will never be fully filled by the compensation that a new love object might be able to offer. After all, while married to Gabriel, Gretta has not fully worked through the void left in her ego by Michael Furey's sudden disappearance. The same applies to Duffy in relation to Mrs. Sinico, whose very name, encrypted in the droning of the train engine, forbids the affective closure of mourning, as defined by Freud. While Mrs. Sinico's memory then would live on as long as someone like him heard and remembered her name, Duffy is abhorred by the prospect that, once he is dead, nobody would be there to remember him/his name. Such a scenario would be for sure "the worse than death" par excellence.

Rather than as an expression of an inability to find the end à la Gabriel, Duffy's narrative of automourning unfolds as a heart-wrenching pilgrimage on the outskirts of memory, on the possibility of surviving death, of being transformed—as humbly as Mrs. Sinico—into a memory. This is precisely the point at which "loneliness" as a strategy of transcending libidinal attachments is displaced by Duffy's desire to transcend death itself—to "bond" with an other, to exteriorize his automourning, and ultimately to implicate that other in it. The consuming loneliness he feels at the end of the story is not to be seen as "the most obvious way for him to go back to his old habits," but as a cognizance of an "inner maw," of a "void" inside, and of the rebirth, rather than the demise, of the desire for otherness.[88]

Pouring out from an unfathomable anxiety generated by the looming threat of extinction, automourning is at heart a plea for *otomourning,* a silent call destined to fall on the keen ear of the other who would thenceforth have the duty/responsibility to honor it. Mourning, as in Freud, "is a kind of betrayal, the second killing of the (lost) object"[89]—the first being the natural death, and the second would coincide with the passing over of such a death, such a silence, into a more lethal silence, a silence in which no memory would be housed, nor any signs of grieving heard. It is from within the process of mourning the loss of Mrs. Sinico that Duffy plunges into automourning before he emerges on the plane of desire, consumed by the passion for otherness, and by the search for a form of life after death. This desire, however, does not dare to speak its name, and takes up refuge in silence: silently it wants to extract a promise, to contract the other and commission him to remember his name, to hear-say his name, and to mourn sine die.

Since the veracity of autobiography, according to Derrida's reading of Nietzsche in *The Ear of the Other,* is archly dependent on the support and assistance, and ultimately the compliance of the other to whom the signature of what is written is entrusted, it is not hard to see almost the same procedure taking place in relation to one's death, and especially in relation to one's own mourning, the automourning that must have always been in place. And given that according to Derrida, the "proper name" is "the name of someone dead, or of a living someone whom it can do without,"[90] everything seems to hinge on the *survival* of the proper name. One survives as a name entrusted to the (ear of the) other. This is precisely the way Mrs. Sinico's survival is inscribed at the end of "A Painful Case": through the keen ear of James Duffy who was able to hear the "laborious droning of the train engine reiterating the syllables" of E-mi-ly Si-ni-co's name. It comes as no surprise, then, that Eveline and Gretta were both hurled into the abyss of sorrow when *hearing* in two different chance musical performances the encryptions of the names of their lost love-objects.

That his life might drift toward the end without the assurance that he would be remembered afterward ("if anyone remembered him"[91])—and that his death might neither open a gap (in the ego of a love-object) nor his name forbid the closure of that gap—must have confronted Duffy not only with the empiphanic recognition of his own loneliness, but potentially the desire to transcend death itself by embracing, not loathing, mortal eros—that is, by seeking to silently and secretly ensconce his name in the landscape of an other's memory. By virtue of being both the harbinger of absence (death/transcendence) and presence (life/eros), the proper name might be indeed the only thinkable *time-space* in which transcendent eros and mortal eros are "locked," in the words of Henry Staten, "in an unbreakable embrace."[92]

By their uncanny grafting of life and death/desire and mourning within their narrative structures, Joyce's stories not only force on the reader the acknowledgment of mourning, but also implicate him or her as a witness to the making and unmaking of the available strategies of mourning in turn-of-the-century Dublin. The transformations that characters such as Duffy and Gabriel undergo make it clear that mourning is not simply a strategy of adjustment to loss but a force of change in the sphere of subjectivity. It is mourning as a transformational, generative experience that the prosopopoeic narrative figuration of loss in Joyce's stories signifies. And it is by figuring mourning in excess of its potential transcendence that the stories ultimately undo the persistence of the transcendentalizing impulse. In this manner, Joyce's early modernist texts activate and articulate a conception of mourning that is politically urgent today in an age of spectacular ahistoricity, affective indifference, and senseless consumerism.

3

The Vicissitudes of Melancholia in Freud and Joyce

> But what breaks the hold of grief except the cultivation of the aggression that grief holds at bay against the means by which it is held at bay?
>
> —Judith Butler, *The Psychic Life of Power*

WHILE THE SHORT STORIES THAT CONSTITUTE *DUBLINERS* PRESENT US, AS we have seen in the previous chapter, with a wide variety of characters who have variably experienced the pangs of loss, "The Sisters" and "A Painful Case" are nonetheless unique in their exposition of a sequential trajectory that ranges from attachment, loss, and melancholia to mania or suicide. If Joyce intuitively inscribed an interactive relationship between loss, melancholia, and mania through the character of Fr. Flynn in "The Sisters" and a similar interactive relationship between loss, melancholia, and suicide through the character of Emily Sinico in "A Painful Case," Sigmund Freud, writing more than a decade later, would attempt to psychoanalytically articulate the psychic rationale behind the regression of some melancholics into mania and the adoption by some others of a more lethal line of flight—suicide.

This chapter seeks to expose the striking parallels between the literary inscriptions of the turn from melancholia to mania and from melancholia to suicide in Joyce's stories, and the Freudian psychoanalytic exposition of the vicissitudes of melancholia: its ultimate deviation into mania or involution into suicide. Not only will the reconstruction of Freud's struggle with the concept of melancholia enable us to better grasp the psychodynamics of melancholia in relation to other psychoaffective formations, it will also throw some light on the yet to be unravelled mystery of both Fr. Flynn's mania and Emily Sinico's sudden suicide. As such, my concern here could be seen as the reverse of my attempt in the previous chapter to construct the transformational and generative aspects of the narrative work of mourning via the tropologics of prosopopoeia. As I have shown, the trouble with James Duffy and Gabriel Conroy is not so much their inconsolability as their foreclosure of the experience of mourning in the first place. But once they open up to such an experience, they emerge no less unscathed than, for better or worse, transformed. In the case of Gabriel, whose exilic attachment to Ireland and to Gaelic culture has found utterance in a politics of itinerant and unrepentant cosmopolitanism (very much like Joyce's),[1] his experience of mourning culminates in an empiphanic moment of reckoning with otherness, finitude, and, above all, the very cultural heritage from which he detached himself in favor of affiliation with European languages and cultures. At the very end of "The Dead," Gabriel sets out on "his journey westward," toward the Aran Isles, and thus discovers and reclaims his historical and cultural identity.[2]

Having demonstrated how the very access to the experience of mourning is an empiphanic moment that coincides subtly with a critique of the ideologies of policing desire and mourning, and might in turn lead to the rediscovery of one's cultural heritage, I move on to examine the ends of this experience of mourning, its sociocultural conditioning, and its pathological vicissitudes in a city that Joyce dubbed "the centre of paralysis."[3] By closely reading Joyce's "The Sisters" and "A Painful Case" against a number of Freud's metapsychological essays, my aim in what follows is not to apply Freud's metapsychological papers to Joyce's stories but rather to underscore the spontaneous overlap between psychoanalysis and literature as well as between theoretical and literary representations of the complex of mourning. Both Joyce and Freud were closely examining and interrogating the same enigmatic phenomenon of mourning; they were closely reading at a distance, though, since there is no evidence that Joyce at the time he was writing *Dubliners* was reading Freud. At any rate, Freud would officially write about mourning almost a decade after Joyce did, and there is no evidence that either was reading the other at the time. Yet the parallels between Freud's theoretical insights and Joyce's dramatizations of the vicissitudes of mourning and melancholia are striking.

My focus here is not the access to but the excess of mourning. Mourning becomes politically consequential at the moment it exceeds the very conditions from which it proceeds. This is the case with Fr. Flynn, the priest, whose mourning turns into melancholia and then into suicide because it remains utterly unfulfilled by the operative socioreligious structures. Mourning becomes political also when it is called for by the experience of loss but is denied by the existing social codes. This is the case with Emily Sinico (in Joyce's "A Painful Case"), whose mourning of the loss of a proscribed and extramarital desire is condemned to turn in the void, unreconciled to the public means of its channeling. Like Fr. Flynn, Emily Sinico finds an outlet finally through suicide.

When in tension with the prescribed strategies of its fulfillment, mourning becomes a political force that forces the reconfiguration of those strategies. Far from being just a mode of adapting to a changed reality (after the loss of the other), mourning here is a threshold force of sociocultural change. In their detailing of the tragedies of Fr. Flynn and Emily Sinico, Joyce's stories are unequivocal about the imperative to seize the moment of loss and mourning to press forth sociocultural reform. In addition to elaborating a new interpretation of the enduring mystery (both in recent and early studies of *Dubliners*) of

Fr. Flynn's and Emily Sinico's suicides and their subtle political implications, this chapter contributes a theoretically and analytically rigorous formulation of the crucial but overlooked linkages in the triptych: mourning, melancholia, suicide. In addition, by untangling the ties between each of these psychoaffective and psychiatric concepts, this chapter will prepare the ground for the following chapter which will advance catachresis as the master trope of melancholia. Here, we are still caught in a poetics of narrative mourning characterized by prosopopoeic reversals, except that prosopopoeia in these two stories delivers the end—the petrification of the living—which it could only promise as we have seen in the previous chapter. While the lethal prosopopoeic plots will become clear in due course, I will focus throughout the chapter on a constellation of concepts that are metonymically contiguous to prosopopoeia, and that I believe better articulate the prosopopoeic reversal. I will speak about swerves, conversions, and, particularly, vicissitudes. The protagonists of Joyce's stories are no longer on the threshold of mourning, as in the previous chapter; rather, they are in the wake of mourning, in transit and on the threshold of something other than mourning; they swerve from mourning to melancholia and from melancholia to suicide. Can we still speak, though, about a politics of mourning as is implicit in the epigraph by Butler?

Melancholia and Its Vicissitudes

Before we can square the literary inscription of melancholia in Joyce's two stories with the psychoanalytical arguments, analyses, and proposals offered by Freud, we have to return once more to some aspects of Freud's essay "Mourning and Melancholia." By now, it should be clear that, for Freud, while mourning is a normal affect that is accomplished once all object-cathexes are withdrawn from the lost object and displaced onto a new object, melancholia originates in an unfaltering fixation on the lost object and culminates in a regressive process of incorporating, if not devouring, the lost other—a process that might eventually enact a primary narcissism, and that Freud suspects of a pathological disposition. In other words, whereas in mourning the lost object is *integrated,* in accordance with the commands of the reality principle, into the texture of the psyche, in melancholia the object is *engraved* within the psyche, and the cathectic ties with it are intensified rather than relaxed.

Clearly, then, melancholia enacts nothing less than a vicissitude of normal mourning. Yet, while Freud had never fully accounted for the waning of the affect of melancholia after the passage of a certain period of time, he seems to contend that the resolution of mourning cannot take place without the passage through melancholia. "Setting up the object inside the ego," Freud suggests in *The Ego and the Id* (1923), "makes it easier for the object to be given up or renders that process possible."[4] It bears repeating, thus, that melancholia becomes here the condition of the possibility of mourning. This is one of the most puzzling conclusions that could be drawn from a reading of "Mourning and Melancholia" in tandem with *The Ego and the Id*—a conclusion on which Freud does not, much to our bewilderment, reflect further or offer any conclusive remarks. As I explained in the first chapter, the melancholic disposition cannot be clearly accounted for since it originates in a more ambiguous and unlocatable event—the dissolution of the Oedipus complex. What is important for us to bear in mind, however, is that melancholia—when it does not transform into other psychoaffective formations—is at the horizon of all possible mourning. This is to say, by implication, that whenever mourning fails, it is either that the melancholic incorporation of the object has been suspended sine die or denied altogether by the forces, namely, the superego, that override the ego. In either case, the lost object is, as I said above, engraved rather than integrated within the psyche. Such is, loosely speaking, the melancholic state whose mutation, rather than resolution, into other neighboring pathological forms like mania and suicide has relentlessly garnered and frustrated Freud's analytical acumen. Being, at least provisionally, a vicissitude of normal mourning, melancholia generates, as it were, its own vicissitudes.

Already in "Mourning and Melancholia," Freud alludes to the outbreak within melancholia of what he would later baptize the "death drive," the drive that results in the "overcoming of the instinct which compels every living thing to cling to life."[5] While during the phase of libidinal approach and attachment, the ego picks up an object, it proceeds, once the loss of that object occurs, to set it up within (the ego) such that it provokes the anger of the critical agency operative in the ego (and which Freud later calls the superego). The act of relocating the lost object within the ego—which Freud loosely calls "identification," "incorporation," or "introjection"—seems, no matter how conducive it might potentially be for the accomplishment of the work of mourning, at the origin of whatever misfortune that would later befall the whole psychic apparatus. It is, after all, suspected of being at the origin of the "cleavage between the critical activity of the ego and the ego as altered by identification."[6]

In *The Ego and the Id,* Freud elucidates how this act of incorporation of the lost object within the ego occurs: the ego fraudulently "assumes the features of [the lost] object"[7] and forces itself upon the id as its (lost/regained) love-object in such a manner as to hijack and introvert the outward emittance of the id's entire libido. Such an illicit undertaking by the ego, while being "the sole condition under which the id can give up its objects," is of grave consequences: it tosses the whole organism on the verge of a lethal conflict between the ego and the critical agency (or, the superego)—a conflict in which the superego might resort to drive the ego into its own death "if the latter does not fend off its tyrant in time by the change round into mania."[8]

While the loss of a given object-libido is inevitable, survival in the aftermath undoubtedly hinges on the psychic wherewithal of the individual organism of each mourner. In *Beyond the Pleasure Principle* (1920), Freud makes it patently clear that the more a living organism is stimulated into affective attachments, the more it becomes capable of both dealing with (libidinal) stimuli and shielding itself against their loss once they are hypercathected. An individual system that is *highly* cathected implies, by the same token, that it is highly effective not only in moderating and managing the inflowing stimuli, but also in subduing the intrusive (libidinal) stimuli by converting them into what Freud calls, after Breuer, "quiescent cathexis": "a system which is itself highly cathected is capable of taking up an additional stream of fresh inflowing energy and of converting it into quiescent cathexis, that is, of binding it psychically."[9] Following these insightful remarks, one might conclude that melancholia strikes harder in individuals whose affective systems are *lowly* cathected. "The higher the system's own quiescent cathexis," Freud points out, "the greater seems to be its 'binding' force; conversely, therefore, the lower its cathexis, the less capacity will it have for taking up inflowing energy and the more violent must be the consequences of such a breach in the protective shield against stimuli."[10]

Shielding against inflowing libidinal stimuli proceeds by hosting any libidinal cathexes before, as it were, lulling them to sleep. This is, however, neither the affective strategy of Fr. Flynn, whose attachment to the priesthood prompts him to transcend any stimulus that smacks of eros, nor is it, for that matter, the pragmatic strategy of Emily Sinico, who was doomed "to sing to empty benches" after having been cold-heartedly excluded from her husband's "gallery of pleasures."[11] Actually, by virtue of multiplying and diversifying his love-objects, her husband managed to reduce her to the level of a "quiescent cathexis," an ineffectual element in the gallery of his inflowing stimuli and outflowing libidinal attachments. Consequently, while her husband accumulated the psychic resources whereby he would keep afloat within the potential storms that her death might provoke, she was not exposed to as much cathectic stimuli and libidinal exchange as would enable her to fend off the effects on her mind of the inimical stimuli that would stem from the untimely break of her illicit romance with James Duffy.

Both Fr. Flynn and Emily Sinico are, by virtue of their low systems of cathexes, incapable of hosting new inflowing stimuli, much less of managing the strong and unpleasurable stimuli that might break easily through their frail protective shields, thus producing, as Freud goes on to surmise, grave impacts on their mental organs. While some stimuli, such as the blandishments of eros, provoke pleasure, some others, such as the loss of an object-libido, provoke pain, mourning, or melancholia whose vicissitudinal thrust toward death—unless twisted along the round path of mania—culminates in suicide. While the former scenario pertains, I will argue, to Fr. Flynn, whose melancholy sadness and self-incriminating guilt following the loss of his holy vase have pressed him toward death until he took the circuitous route of mania, the latter pertains to Emily Sinico, whose affective system is so lowly cathected that it lethally falls apart following the break of her amorous affair with James Duffy. In sum, "Owing to their low cathexis those systems are not," to use Freud's own words, "in a good position for binding the inflowing amounts of excitation and the consequences of the breach in the protective shield follow all the more easily."[12]

Fr. Flynn's Melancholia and the Change Round into Mania

Bearing the above theoretical concerns in mind, let us probe more closely the affective conditions of Fr. Flynn and Emily Sinico after the crises of loss that have beset both of them. Seeking to offer primarily a reading that traces the narrative inscriptions of melancholia in the two *Dubliners'* stories, I will try to carve out my argument in the hinge between object-cathecting, loss, and the onset of melancholia and its vicissitudes. Precisely, by invoking the work of Freud, I will try to place the emphasis on what emerges, especially in the case of Fr. Flynn and Emily Sinico, as a structural incompetence, a constitutive inability to bind the mobile cathexes that threaten to dislodge their defensive systems altogether.

In *Beyond the Pleasure Principle,* Freud insists that the "*Protection against* stimuli is an almost more important function than *reception of* stimuli."[13] By virtue of being a priest, Fr. Flynn is himself already entrenched in a strategy of protection and forearmament against inflowing libidinal stimuli. As Henry Staten has shown in *Eros in Mourning,* Christianity, much like Platonism and Stoicism, among others, is predicated on an ideology of sublimation and transcendence of mortal eros. Transcendence is a mode of coming to terms with the temporal presence of a loved object flawed by mortality, that is, by the solid absence building in the horizon of its immediate presence. Transcendence is, in Staten's words, "a matter of learning how to extract one's libidinal substance from the mortal or losable objects in which it could be trapped."[14] In this respect, Fr. Flynn, is, as is potentially the case with any priest, involved in the ascesis or praxis of foreclosure or desexualization of every *inflowing* or *outflowing* libidinal stimulus.

Invested in the Platonic-Stoic-Christian strategies of idealization and transcendence, which exhort him to nip eros at the very moment of its inception, Fr. Flynn has neither been able to host any inflowing stimulus nor to foster a system of high cathexis, that is, a system that would enable him to convert efficiently, and by virtue of constant exposure, any mobile cathexis into a quiescent one. Yet, while he denies himself, following the commandments of the priesthood, any libidinal attachment, Fr. Flynn lavishes his desexualized libido on the ladder of transcendence, or the imago of priesthood—the chalice. And while he is armored against libidinal attachments by the chalice (which condenses metonymically his life task: the commitment to the priesthood), he is not armored against the possible break of that very chalice. Fr. Flynn had never painted the loss of his chalice such that he was hurled into the abyss of infinite sorrow at the moment of its loss.

When long before his death Fr. Flynn had reiterated to the boy-narrator that he was "*not long for this world,*"[15] he was certainly spurred by the consoling idea of a better life in the hereafter. In the wake of the loss of his chalice, however, such an aspiration was undercut by a sweeping sense of disappointment, frustration, and hopelessness, as if such a loss had brought in its trail the closure of the horizon the chalice first stretched open. In other words, the conciliatory narrative of automourning that Fr. Flynn was wont to share with the boy gave way, following the breaking of the chalice, to a lethal narrative of melancholy sadness whose "deadly work" had a bearing on the well-being of his whole mental organism.[16] Here, while I agree with Donald T. Torchiana that Fr. Flynn died a natural death, that neither paresis nor syphilis—but the breaking of the chalice—was at the origin of his crisis, I nonetheless disagree, as will become clear in due course, with his conclusion that there was actually nothing wrong with Fr. Flynn.[17] The inability to accomplish the ritualistic task of mourning is precisely, I will argue, what is wrong with Fr. Flynn. Such inability, compounded with his total surrender to self-manufactured guilt, has eventually factored out the role of the life instincts. Of course, I am not suggesting that the task of mourning qua mourning ought to or can be fulfilled; rather, I am exploring the degrees of its fulfillment, and, more precisely, the extent to which one can acquire the psychic wherewithal required for its fulfillment or for the defense against its excesses (since I have already examined in the previous chapter how mourning is oftentimes foreclosed rather than experienced).

While Fr. Flynn must have compromised his mortality by his devotion to the priesthood and, by implication, by his aspiration to a life to come, the breaking of the chalice has proven too overwhelming to brook any compromise. As his sister, Eliza, informs us in a very emphatic manner, it is the breaking of the chalice that instantiated a turning point in Fr. Flynn's erstwhile effective strategy of idealization and transcendence: "*It was that chalice he broke.* . . . That was the beginning of it. Of course, they say it was all right, that it contained nothing, I mean. But still. . . . They say it was the boy's fault. But, poor James was nervous."[18] "The Sisters" thus presents us with a controversial breaking of a chalice (and implicitly of its consecration), which, though reparable, is perceived by Fr. Flynn as a grave blunder, for which he has to suffer interminable grief.

As a sign of commitment to the priesthood, the chalice belongs normally to a system of symbolic exchange and reparation: unless it has become unserviceable, it can be—as the text of the story itself implies—repaired, regilded, and eventually reconsecrated without complications. But as a singular and ideal object—ideal in satisfying, that is, the needs of sublimated sexual instincts—the chalice cannot probably be placed within an economic system of circulation and exchange of object-cathexes. Since Eliza establishes a firm connection between the breaking of the chalice and the onset of Fr. Flynn's crisis, I am inclined to think that the chalice is an ideal object that condenses the economy of priesthood (i.e., Fr Flynn's life task), and as such its loss pertains to the uncompromisable par excellence. As Freud insists in "Mourning and Melancholia," the loss of an ideal object is hardly amenable to the conciliatory work of mourning. What muddy the waters are the associative and connotative implications such a loss conjures up. Such implications are not dissociable from the sedimentations of the socioreligious networks of inhibitions or from the neighboring fountainheads of guilt that inform the psyche. In this regard, I will show how Fr. Flynn's hermeneutic uncertainty, for instance, over whether he had committed a sin when he broke the chalice has served to intensify his sense of having done so and has thus fomented his guilt. This phenomenon (which, following psychiatry, one might easily call a *guilt complex*) is not at all restricted to Fr. Flynn but extends to many other Dubliners, such as Eveline and Mrs. Sinico, as well as to Gretta, and shows with a remarkable clarity how something untruthful and in excess of reality, something that contains de facto no guilt at all, comes to burden the mind of its creator, and at length to put his/her psychological makeup in total disarray.

This seems to me one of the strong aspects of paralysis in *Dubliners.* Feeding primarily on a persisting sense of guilt, this paralysis translates as a self-ordained punishment, a warranty to self-indictment. In psychoanalytic terms, this paralysis might be understood as the upshot of the inacceptance of loss, and especially of the conversion of loss into absence, for the loss of the chalice is not perceived by Fr. Flynn as a loss that can be adequately addressed by the various techniques of reparation the church (as also exemplified by Fr. O'Rourke) makes available, but as a loss that brooks no reparation, and that comes ultimately to lay bare his, as it were, originary sinfulness. The loss of the chalice translates as a loss of the priesthood, which is subsequently converted into an absence of the good, an absence of hope: "There was no hope for him this time."[19]

Dominick LaCapra has recently cautioned against the rampancy of psychic apparatuses that tend unwittingly to convert suffered losses into constitutive absences. "When loss," LaCapra points out, "is converted into (or encrypted in an indiscriminately generalized rhetoric of) absence, one faces the impasse of endless melancholy, impossible mourning, and interminable aporia in which any process of working through the past and its historical losses is foreclosed or prematurely aborted."[20] Joyce multiplies the adjectives that attest not only to Fr. Flynn's guilt-stricken conscience, but also to his envelopment in an overall discourse of absence: Fr. Flynn is described as "too scrupulous always," "crossed," "disappointed," and "nervous."[21] The fact that Fr. Flynn's description of the "duties of the priest towards the Eucharist and towards the confessional" struck the boy as so grave that he "wondered how anybody had ever the courage to undertake them" bears witness to the presence in Fr. Flynn's mind of aspects of what LaCapra calls an "all-or-nothing" tendency—a tendency that hardly tolerates the role of intermediary or transitional processes such as those afforded by the work of mourning.[22] Evidentially, Fr. Flynn's mind is structured in such a manner as to hardly paint any possible reparation for a given transgression (here, the breaking of the chalice) of his duties toward the Eucharist. The perception of the loss of the chalice as an instance of the absence of hope forecloses prematurely any potential prospect for recovery. It thus coincides with the onset of melancholia—an affective process whereby the ego tries to refurbish its habitat and take control of a runaway psychic apparatus. As demonstrated earlier, the ego has no choice but to counterfeit the lost object so as to rechannel the id's outward emittance of (desexualized) libido—an action that comes to further excite the anger of an already infuriated superego.

According to Freud, the roots of the superego or ego-ideal strike deep in the Oedipus complex and relate to the ego's primal identification with the parents. Moreover, the superego, Freud intimates, stands as well for the social and moral agencies whose influences and effects are infused in the child's mind during the early years of his development. In this regard, what is puzzling about Fr. Flynn's alleged sin of breaking the chalice is that, while belittled by the ecclesiastical authorities (that is, by those who partially stand for Freud's superego), it is stubbornly maintained by Fr. Flynn himself. Even if we see Fr. Flynn from a common Foucaultian perspective, as an extensive agent of the brokered socioreligious structures that have informed his psychic makeup, we cannot fail to note the excesses of his autosurveillance and the ways in which his turn against his ego override the ostentatious expectations of the visible ecclesiastical authorities by which such a turn (against his ego) is enabled in the first place. To put it bluntly, Fr. Flynn has *reacted inversely* to the socioreligious attempts (that the likes of Fr. O'Rouke have undertaken) to detoxify him from the exorbitant sense of guilt with which his consciousness/conscience is suffused. Such attempts served, as a matter of fact, only to produce in him an exacerbation of his illness, as if the need for illness had gained the upper hand. He exhibits what Freud technically refers to in *The Ego and the Id* as a "negative therapeutic reaction."[23] Fr. Flynn is his own "harsh taskmaster."[24]

Through Fr. Flynn, Joyce seems to illustrate a crisis in the Christian strategies of transcendence of mortal eros. By virtue of being a priest, Fr. Flynn is undoubtedly entitled to emit only a desexualized form of eros. His bond to the chalice is a means to an "eternal reward," as the boy's aunt put it.[25] Yet transcendent as it is, this strategy is vulnerable to the disturbances instantiated by the break and loss of the symbolic ladder of transcendence: the chalice. Once disturbed, the bond between the priest and his chalice—a bond that makes possible the economy of erotic transcendence—brings the priest into an impasse, and hurls him back into the abyss of grief that he first attempted to bypass through distanciation and sublimation. "It was that chalice he broke," Eliza remarks, and she adds, "That was the beginning of it. . . . *That affected his mind.*"[26] Bereft of the enabling transcending power of his chalice, Fr. Flynn is relocated into a structure in which he is vulnerable to rather than unencumbered by the outbreaks of grief. Such an insurgent structure asks of him to renegotiate his relation with the lost chalice in terms of the affective closure afforded by the work of mourning. However, the last image of the priest "lying still in his coffin . . . solemn and truculent in death, *an idle chalice on his breast*,"[27] albeit sealed in mystery, implies that the priest had not really been able to work through the emotional wreck in which he was driven soon after the break of his holy vase.

How can we interpret the presence of an idle chalice on the breast of a coffined priest? Although this might simply be a mnemonic reference to the time when priests used to be buried with their emblematic objects, there is ample evidence to read it otherwise—really, as a symptom of Fr. Flynn's melancholia, whose vicissitudinal drive toward death ("*I am not long for this world*") was subsequently countered by a change round into mania. To start with, I suggest that the presence of an idle chalice on the priest's breast attests to his utter failure to accomplish the work of mourning, since he has perseveringly maintained the affective ties with the broken chalice rather than detached and reattached his desexualized cathexes. This interpretation doesn't of course obtain unless we assume that the chalice that is now on his breast is not a new vessel, but the very same chalice he broke. The qualification of the chalice as "idle" (i.e., unserviceable) lends credence to such an assumption. Moreover, the fact that Joyce had himself settled on putting "chalice"—after he had formerly, in the Irish *Homestead* journal version of the story, opted for "cross"[28]—on the priest's breast implies that he had reviewed the tragic story of Fr. Flynn in such a manner as to center its origin around a single object: the chalice.

In melancholia, the lost object is incorporated within the psyche rather than abandoned. Indeed, it is the ego itself that dissembles the lost object, so as to exhort the id to direct its libido toward it, thus initiating a process that Freud conceptualized as a regression to infantile narcissism. Freud goes on to argue that such a process provokes the wrath of the superego, the agency which had hosted the id's first libidinal expedition and had ever since stood apart from, and quite at loggerheads with, the ego. Feeling usurped, the super-ego exacts its revenge on the ego by inflicting it with guilt, if not thrusting it into death altogether. It requires no lengthy argument to stress Fr. Flynn's devastation by guilt after he broke the chalice: his nervosity, along with his withdrawal from society into his confession-box, is both a symptom and an effect of his overwhelming sense of guilt. In other words, the symptom of Fr. Flynn's guilt is inseparable from its manic re-turn as self-contented laughter.[29] This manic re-turn, moreover, while attesting to the operative transposition of undue guilt, is symptomatic of aborted suicidal intents. The melancholic, guilt-pressured drive toward death defuses into the horizon of mania. After all, the Hamletian death wish expressed at the very beginning of the story ("*I am not long for this world*") tallies perfectly with Freud's psychoanalytic reconstruction of the turn in some psychic apparatuses from melancholia, in which the super-ego becomes potentially "a kind of gathering place for the death-instinct,"[30] into mania, in which the ego seems to unwittingly compromise its mental functioning in order not only to throw off the object, but especially to occlude the destruction of the whole organism.

To better understand Fr. Flynn's slippage into mania as a counterthrust to the superego's drive towards death, let us quote at length from *The Ego and the Id:* "If we turn to melancholia first, we find that the excessively strong super-ego which has obtained a hold upon consciousness rages against the ego with merciless violence . . . *we should say that the destructive component had entrenched itself in the super-ego* and turned against the ego. What is now holding sway in the super-ego is, as it were, a pure culture of the death instinct, and in fact it often enough succeeds in driving the ego into death, *if the latter does not fend off its tyrant in time by the change round into mania.*"[31] While in the *Homestead* version of the story Fr. Flynn is commonly described as mad, it is not hard to glean signs of his mania in the present, drastically revised story: his moping, wanderings, and hysteric or soft laughs (as when in his confession-box) are symptomatic enough of his "change round into mania." Insofar as mania shelters the ego from the otherwise exigent self-annulment, it might be a price willingly paid to steer clear from the deadly embrace of the lost object, embodied in the workings of the conscientious superego. Yet although thrown off, the object remains close by, flung on the chest of the priest while he is "lying still in his coffin . . . solemn and truculent in death."[32] As Judith Butler suggests, "Mania marks a temporary suspension or mastering of the tyrant by the ego, but the tyrant remains structurally ensconced for that psyche—and unknowable."[33] Mania emerges as an aggressive turn not only against the object but potentially against the socioreligious outposts congealed in the psyche, thus emphasizing the scrupulously critical dimensions of Fr. Flynn's paralysis. Such mania, however, remains easier recognized than analyzed. The present attempt to relate it to melancholia and to Freud's metapsychological studies of the interactive relations between melancholia and the death instinct helps to bring to the limelight the mental side of Fr. Flynn's paralysis, especially that most Joyceans have only drawn our attention to the physical or syphilitic side of that paralysis.

In sum, although amounting to no more than a ghostly presence in the whole story, Fr. Flynn's character is quite complex. The turn into mania as a retaliatory and defensive tactic against the thrust of the superego toward death remains one of the clear tasks that Fr. Flynn's ego managed to accomplish in time before it was eventually swept by natural death. Such a task proves especially wanting in the case of Mrs. Sinico, whose melancholically driven suicidal behavior after the shipwreck of her amorous cruise with James Duffy attests to her submission to her harsh taskmaster, the superego, the "gathering place for the death-instinct," as Freud calls it.[34]

EMILY SINICO'S MELANCHOLIA AND THE TURN ROUND UPON THE EGO

Unlike Fr. Flynn, whose commitment to the priesthood had enabled him to transcend carnal desires, Mrs. Sinico is a married woman *expulsed* from her husband's "gallery of pleasures."[35] Although she has an institutionalized right to satisfy her sexual desires, such a right is hardly respected by the conjugation—marriage—that is supposed to grant it. While the story is partly about an aberrant marriage, it is in a more emphatic manner a critique of the premises of the constitution of marriage itself—a critique of the social disciplining of sexual desire. Emily Sinico's case is painful not only because her desire is of a kind that dares not speak its name, but precisely because her grief must remain unresolved in view of the social and familial contestation with which it would have been met were it to be expressed on the cultural and social spheres. Harboring an adulterous desire and failing so utterly to fulfill it, Emily Sinico finds herself in a position where she not only has to mourn the loss of her love-object (James Duffy) and work through the dams of shame and guilt nursed and solidified by her adulterous intent, but she must especially do so under the duress of loneliness, deprived of the potential solidarity of an empathic witness.

Yet since the accomplishment of the task of mourning hinges crucially on the very externalization and exposition of her guilt, that is, on the public avowal of her *loss of a proscribed desire,* Emily Sinico was unable to accomplish mourning and sever the ties with the lost object nor was she capable of circling the downspout of guilt enacted by her fixation on it. This is especially so because Emily Sinico's psychic apparatus is, after all, marked by a lack of skillful maneuverability of inflowing, unpleasurable stimuli. As I suggested earlier, insofar as a psychic apparatus is not adept in binding mobile stimuli, its protective shield remains prone to dissolve with sudden swiftness once an onslaught from the external world falls on its cortical layer. Silent about her love, silent about her grief, and fixated on her lost object while devastated by inflowing inimical stimuli, Emily Sinico's ego becomes a battlefield between the representative of the super moral codes (the superego, the patrolling agency within the ego, precipitated and infused since its inception by societal regulation) and the representative of the desire to love and to be loved (the ego as modified by the identification with the lost love-object). The lower an individual's psyche is cathected, the slower its convertibility rate of unpleasurable stimuli from a state of mobility into one of quiescence, and thus the more susceptible it is to the chidings of the superego, the precipitate and proxy of sociocultural codes. Although its management of stimuli leaves a lot to be desired, a lowly cathected system is not, curiously enough, as economized in its erotic adventures and investitures as a highly cathected one. Emily Sinico is a case in point.

A close look at the tropological structure in which Emily Sinico is represented enables us to better grasp the ways in which her case is truly painful. Mrs. Sinico is described as a receptacle ("oval face") and an earthly figure ("warm soil"), as well as an introjective and transformational force ("she emotionalized [Duffy's] mental life").[36] In his *Final Contributions to the Problems and Methods of Psychoanalysis,* Sándor Ferenczi defines introjection as an "extension to the external world of the original autoerotic interests, by including its objects in the ego."[37] In other words, introjection is the process whereby libidinally charged objects are gradually included within the ego, thus enlarging and enriching it. In their appropriation of Ferenczi's concept of introjection, Abraham and Torok trace it back to the very early stages of childhood and to the child's entry into language, arguing that it parallels normal biological growth, in that it constantly engages the individual into assimilating and accommodating new and emerging desires. More precisely, "introjection operates," Maria Torok suggests, "like a genuine instinct."[38] Insofar as it sets in motion the whole psychic apparatus, introjection is, in the words of Nicolas Rand, "the driving force of psychic life in its entirety."[39]

It requires no lengthy argument to stress the profound schism between the strategies of introjection pertaining to Emily Sinico and those of transcendence of mortal eros, pertaining to Fr. Flynn. No other case in *Dubliners,* however, resembles Mrs. Sinico's, either in terms of the potential for libidinal expansion and introjection, or in terms of the degree of frustration with which these genuine instincts are rebuked. Unshielded against the ravages of desire and unequipped with the introjective psychotactics of binding mobile stimuli, Mrs. Sinico's story unfolds as a relentless thrust into the abyss of sorrow. The bottom fell out of her world when Duffy recoiled in front of her desire for him. Such an end is, as I will demonstrate, hastened by the illicit nature of her affair with Duffy, and as such by the cultural and social as well as psychic impossibility to articulate and grieve it sufficiently or enough to block the downspout of melancholia and hijack the thrust of the destructive forces gathering within her (superego) by a change round into mania, if not by a discharge of aggression from the "psychical sphere" into the "motor sphere" (i.e., the world outside the self).[40]

Judging from her behavior—intemperate habits, addiction to alcohol, crossing the railway lines late at night from platform to platform[41]—one can conjecture that Mrs. Sinico's life has come to be profoundly scarred by her short foray into the doomed adulterous affair with Duffy. Rather than harkening to the reality principle and severing the affective ties with James Duffy, her object-libido, Mrs. Sinico stubbornly proceeds to forcefully "incorporate" the lost object, James Duffy, within her ego and thereby to fantasize about introjecting the desires that that object failed to mediate, not realizing throughout the whole procedure that she was but singing "to empty benches."[42] This is all the more so since, being a married woman, Mrs. Sinico's extramarital desire is proscribed, and cannot therefore be worked- or lived-through by means of a homeopathic or public expression of grief, which is deemed crucial for its relative success. The desire to grieve, which is also a token of love, must therefore be thwarted by means of a magical maneuver—the secret incorporation of the lost object within the contours or deep recesses of the ego. As Maria Torok argues, "The ultimate aim of incorporation is to recover, in *secret* and through magic, an object that, for one reason or another, evaded its own function: mediating the introjection of desires."[43]

Disregarding the various strategies of encryption with which Abraham and Torok burden it, what is important for us to retain from this definition of incorporation is its structural affinity with Freud's concept of melancholia. In other words, while introjection, understood as a process of egoic broadening and expansion, is affined with Freud's version of an achieved mourning, understood as a process of de-attachment from an object and reattachment with an other, incorporation as the fantasy of ingesting the lost love-object resembles Freud's conceptualization of melancholia: the ambivalent but sustained struggle in the ego between the forces that want to abandon the lost object and the other forces that want to force or transplant it, at whatever cost, within the ego.[44] At length, even Torok's description of incorporation as an "illegal" procedure is in tune with Freud's account of the ego's cunning methods of recovering the lost object,[45] of which melancholia is at once an initiatory force and an effect.

The melancholic is governed by the ego-poetics of simulacra, of feigning to possess what it does not, and thus brings a measure of entropy and chaos on the otherwise intact distinction between reality (truthfulness) and fantasy (falsehood). This is all the more so in the case of someone whose system or living organism is not proficient in hosting and then binding mobile cathexes. Indeed, the whole emotional enterprise beckoning at Duffy and Sinico was so novel to their impoverished and lowly cathected systems that neither of them was able to sense or feel any uneasiness about it (prior to the time) when "their thoughts entangled."[46] As the narrator of "A Painful Case" remarks sarcastically, "Neither he nor she had any such adventure before and neither was conscious of any *incongruity*."[47] Yet, while James Duffy seems to have been cognizant with his lowly cathected system and has therefore opted for a strategy of foreclosure of any out-flowing and introjective stimuli, Emily Sinico did not, by virtue of her introjective nature, have the qualifications necessary for the implementation of such an affective policy.

Unimmersed in the waters of philosophic stoicism and unprepared to transcend any beckoning emotional bond, Emily Sinico is not as well placed to compromise an affective knot by recourse to a Platonic or Stoic thought as James Duffy whose initial argument holds that "every bond . . . is a bond to sorrow."[48] Emily Sinico is but a crude introjective force. Since in lowly-cathected systems the management of grief starts, as James Duffy is well aware of, at the moment of inception of eros (which must accordingly be undermined by a symmetrical procedure of attenuation and sublimation), it must therefore be, as Staten rightly surmises, "too late to master mourning once the loved object is lost."[49] In other words, mourning emerges as the condition of possibility of eros, where, as a rule, the one fuses in the horizon of the other. To master mourning, one must therefore give a wide berth to the temptation of eros, but once eros has taken root, it becomes quite impossible to obviate the outbreak of mourning. While James Duffy managed to extract his substance from the entrapments of eros, Emily Sinico was already captive to the lure of eros such that when she heard Duffy's verdict, she was swept by sorrow, and collapsed.[50]

Since the process of libidinal introjection in which she had been absorbed was suspended sine die, Emily Sinico was led—rather than to renounce the object—to maintain the affective bridges with it. In a lowly cathected organism, the ego, devastated by the sudden disappearance of the object, falls prey all too easily to the incorporative and reparative magic of melancholia. Relying on its plasticity and histrionic gifts, the ego thus proceeds to counterfeit and substitute the lost object in order to *introvert* the attention of the id, and hence the outflow of the otherwise runaway cathexes. Being positioned "midway between the id and reality," the ego, Freud propounds, "only too often yields to the temptation to become sycophantic, opportunist and lying, like a politician who sees the truth but wants to keep his place in popular favour."[51] The incorporation of the object, or the identification with it, does not take place prior to the objectal loss of which it is an effect. It is, however, incorporation, not objectal loss, that instantiates a bifurcation within the brokered relations of the ego. In this regard, the supermoral superego unleashes its aggressive potential on the cowering and cunning ego, obliging it either to renounce the object or to face death.

In the wake of this sadistic side of the special agency in the ego (i.e., the superego), Emily Sinico's psyche becomes the battleground of two contending forces, the one (the ego) seeks to host the id's libido after the loss of the object, the other (the superego) seeks to counter boldly and coercively such an illicit readjustment. As Freud has shown, the superego is "not simply a residue of the earliest object-choices of the id; it also represents an *energetic reaction-formation against those choices.*"[52] In other words, while the superego is an extension of such figures as the parents, teachers, heroes, and any other self-chosen figures, it becomes—once the resolution of the Oedipus complex has taken place—quite autonomous in its object-choices, thus constraining the otherwise duplicative adventures of the ego. Moreover, unlike the ego, which when it succumbs to the thrill and magic of incorporation loses sight of reality, the superego is very acute to the laws of reality, including the socio-religious norms, and does not hesitate to use those laws to instil in the ego a pressing sense of guilt. Indeed, Freud describes the superego as the "germ from which all religions have evolved": it can hardly be localized, but it "answers to everything that is expected of the higher nature of man."[53] What does not pertain to the higher nature of man is therefore experienced by the subject as pangs of conscience or as a harrowing sense of guilt.

The sadistic turn of the superego against the ego gains more momentum the more feelings of frustration, disappointment, and erotic vengeance are not given utterance or denied outward expression—especially when "a *cultural suppression of the instincts,*" as Freud suggests in "The Economic Problem of Masochism" (1924), "holds back a large part of the subject's destructive instinctual components from being exercised in life."[54] As I have intimated earlier, the painfulness of Emily Sinico's case stems primarily from the fact that both her love and her grief are proscribed and must therefore remain closeted and socioculturally unacknowledged. Few things are more tragic than the loss of a love in a culture marked by a lack of the adequate conventions that would otherwise acknowledge such a loss and thereby warrant the homeopathic and communitywide performance of grief necessary for its reparation. As Judith Butler expounds, in a not-so-dissimilar context, "Insofar as the grief remains unspeakable, the rage over the loss can redouble by virtue of remaining unavowed. And if that rage is publically proscribed, the melancholic effects of such a proscription can achieve suicidal proportions."[55] The preponderance in Mrs. Sinico of a melancholic disposition, neither buffered by an outward discharge of grief or aggression nor defused by any social form of solidarity and empathy, must therefore effectuate an inward turn against the ego.

Toward a Politics of Melancholia

While Emily Sinico can be said to have finally, and by means of her very suicide, assumed an active part in her destiny and exacted erotic vengeance on James Duffy (who will thenceforth have not only, as we have seen in the previous chapter, to grieve her death, but also to suffer the guilt emanating from the suspicion of having caused such a death), she has not prior to that final act undertaken any similar acts, although the need—disregarding whether it is socio-culturally legitimate or not—for such acts has certainly presented itself. The need, in other words, to inflict on Duffy as much pain as suffered because of his cowering recoil into his world of exquisite loneliness has been denied concretization, and therefore must have coalesced into an alliance with the superego in its assault against the ego. What has been barred from outward vindictive expression must ultimately refract or return as self-indictment. Establishing a zero-sum relation between the outward and inward expressions of aggression, Freud intones that "the more a man controls his aggressiveness, the more intense becomes his ideal's inclination to aggressiveness against his ego. It is like a displacement, *a turning round upon his own ego.*"[56]

Bit by bit, we begin to grasp the psychic un-method behind Emily Sinico's aggressive U-turn against her ego. I have yet to account for her ego's unwitting masochistic turn on itself. When the sadistic raids of the superego are bolstered by the suppressed need of the ego for vindictive violence, the ego is left with no alternative but to fight back against the assault. In its retaliatory frenzy, the ego might, however, take a step whereby it *unwittingly supplements* the sadism of the superego, and thus speeds up the process of its own diminishment. In this regard, Emily Sinico's intemperate habits, such as "crossing the lines late at night from platform to platform" or "going out at night to buy spirits,"[57] can be read not only as effects of the evasion reflex and as defensive measures against the persecution of the superego, but especially as unwitting masochistic contrivances. Thus, the sadism of the superego, which expresses itself through the whips of conscience, is inadvertently supplemented, in the very process of being countered, by the flight reflex of the ego into alcoholism and all other antidepressive methods, including crossing the lines late at night, which would eventually bring about its death. At length, "The sadism of the superego and the masochism of the ego supplement each other and unite to produce the same effects."[58] Deserted by all protective forces, strolling in the deathly stillness of exquisite isolation, and deceived by its own contrapuntal maneuvers, "the ego," in the words of Freud, "gives itself up," that is, "lets itself die."[59]

Because all forces have contrived against her, Emily Sinico dies, even though "[t]he injuries she had were not sufficient to have caused death in a normal person."[60] The need for self-annihilation has, in other words, gained the upper hand. The aggression that should have found utterance against James Duffy and, by implication, against the sociocultural mores that regulate desire and the mourning of desire is rerouted against her own ego. Nothing "breaks," as Butler rhetorically implies, "the hold of grief except the cultivation of the aggression that grief holds at bay against the means by which it is held at bay."[61] In other words, only erotic vengeance against Duffy would have broken the lethal hold that Emily Sinico's impossible grief has laid on her psychic apparatus. Only an unashamed and public expression of her grief—whether manically or hysterically driven—would have enabled her to survive the abysmal and lethal onslaughts of conscience.

The difference between Fr Flynn's case and that of Emily Sinico proves that only mania has the leverage to resolve and mediate the conflict between the ego and the superego, of which melancholia is both an effect and a driving force. Yet, can we not discern underneath Emily Sinico's suicide the contours of a strategy of sociopolitical protest and posthumous vengeance, not only against James Duffy, who is now himself overwhelmed by the guilt stemming from the suspicion of having had a hand in such a tragic end, but also against the devaluation of mourning practices and of communitywide solidarity in turn-of-the-century Dublin?[62]

4

Kincaid's Claim: The Poetics and Politics of Melancholia

No later undoing will undo the first undoing.
—Joyce, *Ulysses*

WHO WOULD MOURN WERE THERE NOTHING TO BE REMEMBERED?[1] WHAT FOLLOWS is an attempt to work through the manifest rhetoricity of this question by illuminating, in variable depths, two of its structural latencies, two possible ways of taking stock of its otherwise mystifying logic. The question, *who would mourn were there nothing to be remembered?* is formulated thus, not to ask after the one who would in a pathetic and unpitiful style of vicarious victimhood or willy-nilly sense of martyrdom wear a disposition to mourning, but, rather, to ask (1) after the one who would engage deliberately in a process of remembrance of things past, as it were, in the name of mourning, only to discover that the work of remembering tightens, rather than relaxes, the hold of grief, and (2) after the one who would lay a claim to loss, to remembering and to mourning there where, historically speaking, there is indeed *a nothing* to be remembered, that is, there where, in the words of Spivak, there is "no historically adequate referent" for the sake of which remembering and mourning are undertaken, except a "catachrestic" stir.[2] Here, I will demonstrate how the economy of mourning originates in an insistent *identification with* an allegedly lost object whose *identification,* identity, or location in narrative historiography, perennially eludes the mourning subject. Yet, since the work of remembering as such seeks precisely to raise the threshold and broaden the scope and repertoire of what can be remembered and reintegrated into the psyche, the claim made by this mourning subject remains a valid source of uncertainty and, consequentially, of anxiety, especially in light of its persistent "what-if-ness" and potential veracity. After all, we gain nothing by passing over in silence those claims to seemingly empty nothings, to unregistered memories, losses, or traumas, since it is precisely in the nature of the victim, as Lyotard contends, "not to be able to prove that one has been done a wrong."[3] In other words, these claims, however unrealistic or excessive they might seem prima facie, must be taken seriously as threshold moments of historical redress until they brighten, or vanish, on the dawn of new finds or studies.

Who would mourn were there nothing to be remembered? is, then, a question whose economy enables me to paint the broad strokes of the argument of this chapter: after establishing the psychoanalytic importance of the work of remembering to any (envisaged) work of mourning, I will show the excesses of the modern cult of remembrance, not only by provisionally pointing out its catachrestic overtones, but especially by laying bare its alarming convergence—or, in the words of Derrida, "overlap without equivalence"[4]—with acting-out and "repetition-compulsion" (*Wiederholungszwang*), rather than with working-through and mourning. Perhaps one of the laudable virtues of the question *Who would mourn were there nothing to be remembered?* is that it mockingly cements, by means of its rhetorical structure of seductive reasoning, the bond between the work of remembering and the work of mourning, thus setting the trap into which many of our modern reflections on mourning and memory fall. Everything hinges, however, on the way(s) in which we understand *nothing to be remembered.* Are we placed in front of an unwitting void in memory or in front of an insistent memory of void? Do we inhabit or are we inhabited by a void? The nature of the theoretical argument has referred me to one of Freud's most pertinent papers on the subject, "Remembering, Repeating and Working-Through," while the need to interrogate and deconstruct Freud's insights has referred me to aspects of Fanon's theory of violence and to Kincaid's whole oeuvre, and, particularly, to *The Autobiography of My Mother.* In the process, I remain reticent—somewhat in the Heideggerian sense of the term[5]—about the empiphanic latencies of playing off the rigor of the theoretical texts against the insightful adhocracies of their literary counterparts.

Remembering and Its Vicissitudes

In "Remembering, Repeating and Working-Through," Freud attempts to move beyond the old hypnotic method of treatment through which the patient would be transported into an earlier situation, "which he seemed *never to confuse with* the present one, and [would give] an account of the mental processes belonging to it."[6] Under the hypnotic model of treatment, the process of remembering, Freud gauges, "took a very simple form"—a "delightfully smooth course of events."[7] In a new science ever drawn to newer challenges, and never contented with the successfulness of its methods, it comes as no surprise that the hypnotic method would quickly be dismissed. In "Mourning and Melancholia," mourning, by virtue of being a "normal affect," receives the same fate as hypnosis.[8] It is as if psychoanalysis has never really been comfortable in the vicinity of its foundational motive—therapy!

The new technique of "analytic treatment," which comes to replace hypnosis, consists in the face-to-face exchange, "in a new sort of division of labour" between analyst and analysand, in the course of which the analyst relies on the "art of interpretation" in order to locate the analysand's resistances and make them conscious while the analysand proceeds, once he or she reckons with the repressive propensities of his or her resistances, to relate the forgotten situations and to fill in the gaps of his or her memory without any difficulty.[9] Since this new technique is motivated by Freud's courage "to create more complicated situations in the analytic treatment and to keep them clear before us,"[10] it is not long before we are confronted with one of these complicated situations. While formerly the potential resistances of the analysand are preempted through hypnosis, they are now put, in accordance with Freud's new technique, on equal footing with the analyst's transferential inducements. Not that the analysand has become master of the analytic situation; rather, the analytic situation itself has become a real battlefield, a duel of powers and wills.

Through an economy of transferential attachment, the analyst has to release the analysand from "the armoury of the past" into whose fortified fortresses he or she tends to fold back when the transference proves hostile, embarrassing or tense. By "wresting" from the analysand his or her defensive weapons "one by one,"[11] the analyst ensures that he or she does not have recourse to any of them anymore, for while with hypnosis the discrimination between the past and the present is sharpened rather than blurred, with analysis, in which the analysand comes equipped with a license to resistance, the remembrance of the past oftentimes doubles onto the present and usurps it from its radical difference from the past. In Freud's memorable idiom, the analysand is said to be unable to "*remember* anything of what he has forgotten and repressed, but *acts* it out. He reproduces it not as memory but as an action; he *repeats* it, without, of course, knowing that he is repeating it."[12]

While this observation—that the analysand's "way of remembering" is frequently caught within the loop of repetition-compulsion—might serve to invalidate the new technique of treatment, Freud points out nonetheless that the role of the analyst lies henceforth in his or her ability "to keep in the psychical sphere all the impulses which the patient would like to direct into the motor sphere."[13] The analyst must, in other words, have the transferential wherewithal to participate in the memories of the analysand in such a way as to preclude their outward enactment. Elsewhere, I have recast this distinction between the "psychical sphere" and the "motor sphere" into a distinction between the "affective sphere" and the "actantial sphere," respectively. Accordingly, what is discharged, sickly, and sickeningly in action (i.e., in the motor sphere) can be contained within or detoxified along a metonymic chain of affects (i.e., in the psychical sphere)—affects ranging from indifference, mourning, and melancholia to "melanxiety."[14] The questions to which I will turn later are the following: Where do we situate *narrative* in the light of this distinction, under whose aegis the work of remembering takes place, since narrative, at least in Kincaid, is inextricably related to the recollection of infantile inhibitions, suffered losses, sociocultural proscriptions, and colonial traumas? Does narrative offer an alternative transferential economy whereby the process of remembrance and inscription of pain, injustice, and victimization is freed from the compulsion to repeat? Can narrative act as an *affective* container of an otherwise runaway *actantial* repetition-compulsion?

For Freud, it is in the playground of transference that the transfer or transition from the actantial sphere to the affective sphere is made possible. At the time he wrote "Remembering, Repeating and Working-Through," Freud had not yet formulated such concepts as "mourning" and "melancholia," and so remembering—certainly not in Hegel's sense of *Gedächtnis* (mechanical memorization), but, possibly, in his sense of *Erinnerung* (internalizing recollection) —amounted to (and encompassed, if we are to stick to Hegel's *Erinnerung*) working-through and mourning. The new technique of analytic treatment, while not foreclosing the analysand's resistance, asks that the analyst pinpoint the workings of such resistance to the analysand. The analyst has to play on the transferential contract to extract from the analysand the promise of compliance to the rules of psychoanalysis—prior to "curbing [his] compulsion to repeat . . . turning it into a motive for remembering."[15] At the heart of Freud's new technique is an unwavering counter-Nietzschean assumption that forgetting, far from being productive, is in fact the handmaiden of repression: "Forgetting impressions, scenes or experiences nearly always reduces itself to shutting them off."[16] Small wonder, then, that Freud deems it a triumph worthy of celebration if the analyst "can bring it about that something that the patient wishes to discharge in action is disposed of through the work of remembering."[17] Remembering becomes thus the sine qua non for the success of the treatment, on which depends not only the cure of the analysand, but also the acknowledgment of the role of the analyst and of psychoanalysis writ large.[18]

A widening circle of post-Freudians have dwelled almost exclusively on the means whereby a *mournfulfilling remembering* can be achieved. Attentive to Freud's caution against repetition-compulsion and acting-out—and combining the teachings of Bergson and those of the *Aufklärung*—Paul Ricoeur, for example, calls for a *souvenir veritable,* for a *mémoire critique,* as well as for a *mémoire-souvenir* in order to overpower the *mémoire-répétition.*[19] Ricoeur might be seen to privilege a practice of remembrance in which only deliberate and critical *returns to* memory are accepted. Any unwitting *return of* memory in the veneer of a compulsion to repeat is, for Ricoeur, an irresponsible act, ensuing from a subject suffering from a *déficit de critique*—a critical bankruptcy.[20] In the same vein, Simon, Rosenberg, and Eppert call for a move beyond classical practices of remembrance ("remembrance as strategic practice" and "remembrance as a difficult return") to a practice of "remembrance as critical learning." Advancing the pair "remembrance/pedagogy," they call for a kind of regulative, institutionalized body of "what is to be remembered, how, by whom, for whom, and with what potential effects."[21] Perhaps the sharply pragmatic tendency of Simon, Rosenberg, and Eppert is at the origin of their tenuous theoretical formulations.

In their enthusiasm for a cult of remembering against the devastating and overwhelming monster of forgetting, Simon, Rosenberg, and Eppert have overlooked the kind of *return of* memory that might be produced by the *return to memory.*[22] If one is to opt for remembering to the detriment of forgetting, one should not forget to articulate the pitfalls of remembering, and to resituate the tension not between memory and an outsider (forgetting) but within the realm of memory itself and between the *return of* and the *return to* memory. One has, therefore, first to look at the possible ways that would prevent the spawning and eventual reversal of the process of *return to* into that of *return of.* Second, one has, on a par with that preventive inclination, to conceive of the ways whereby a *return of* might spill into a *return to* through a kind of disfiguring reconfiguration. In this respect, what should, perhaps, be retained from Ricoeur, Simon, Rosenberg, and Eppert is the critical task they urge us to engage in, a task all the more incumbent on the mourning subject whose hypercathecting return to memory might awaken several other, hitherto, latent memories—*l'oubli de reserve* (literally, forgetting in reserve), of which Ricoeur speaks in relation to the state of dormancy and divestiture in which memories live on and pop up intermittently and at times devastatingly.[23]

While I am adopting an attitude neither of "objective cynicism" nor of praise vis-à-vis the kind of remembering that fills us with rather than fulfill mourning (really, a *mournfilling remembering* of which melancholia is a product),[24] I nonetheless think that it is time we interrogated the as-yet argumentum ad hominem: that one can remember (the past and one's traumatic losses) and can still accomplish the task of mourning. It is not a matter of defending or fetishizing the somewhat uncanny pleasures of melancholy or those of an unremitting mourning to state that one cannot have it both ways. Nor is it a matter of being pessimistic—though "pessoptimistic"[25] might apply better here—but it is certainly one of suggesting that one is, whenever within the moulds of remembering, already within the contours of a runaway mourning. To go out of mourning—to accomplish mourning—one has, perhaps, to start by excoriating one's memory, by laying to rest the clinical myth of curative remembering. One has, in the words of Derek Walcott, to "return through a darkness whose terminus is amnesia."[26] Hamlet knows only too well the palliative magic of forgetting: "Most necessary 'tis to forget / To pay ourselves what to ourselves is debt."[27]

Here is what he promises to the ghost of his father:

> Remember thee!
> Yea, from the table of my memory
> I'll wipe away all trivial fond records,
> All saws of books, all forms, all pressures past
> That youth and observation copied there,
> And thy commandment all alone shall live
> Within the book and volume of my brain,
> Unmix'd with baser matter.[28]

Here the work of remembrance that Hamlet is exhorted to perform by the ghost of his dead father is inextricably bound to the task of revenge. Hamlet's course of action—of setting right what went wrong, of redressing a tort, and of implementing justice—is undergirded by the instrument of remembering. Remembering is remembering in view of what is to be executed, which boils down to nothing but a *repetition*—a killing that is to be enlisted within the abysmal and immuring gyre of revenge. While in Freud the analysand is said to repress and therefore to repeat, Hamlet is asked to remember *to* repeat. The compulsion to repeat and the impulsion to remember converge mediated by self-conscious repression.

Hamlet's willingness to commit a sheer *memoricide*—to "wipe away all trivial fond records / All saws of books, all forms, all pressures past / That youth and observation copied there"—in order to remember the commandments of the ghost alone implicates him doubtlessly within a selective/repressive structure of forgetting. To commit this memoricide, to commit oneself to this wholesale scale of repression, implies, by the same token, that Hamlet's table of memory will indeed suffer from a "déficit de critique," a critical deficiency, and that the commandments of the ghost can no longer be interrogated by any other criterion that is not answerable to them. Located at the very core of the injunction to remember and to wreak vengeance is, therefore, the kernel of repression. In order to live up to the commandments of the ghost, Hamlet has to thrust into oblivion whatever "baser matter" might eventually dilute the acuity and urgency of the commandments or delay their execution. While Freud's analysand is said to repeat because he or she represses rather than remembers, Hamlet can be said to repress in view of an ultimate repetition.

In *Difference and Repetition,* Deleuze succinctly and acutely parodies and subverts Freud by contending that: "We do not repeat because we repress," but "*we repress because we repeat.*"[29] If we bear Deleuze's dictum in mind, it becomes clear that remembrance masks the repression that repetition unmasks. Yet, we realize this only too late, always too late! It is not that the act of remembering does not take place, but that it is repressed, elided and occluded ex post facto, as it were, so much so that the repetition of revenge in the actantial or motor sphere perpetuates itself. While in the psychoanalytic situation the work of remembering serves to stymie the passage from repression to repetition—and the unwitting repetition of the repressed resurfaces in the form of remembering—in *Hamlet* the work of remembering comes to affirm the fearful alliance between repetition and repression. We do not repeat because we repress; quite to the contrary, we repress because we repeat.[30]

Sanctioned Repetition

> As for we who have decided to break the back of colonialism, our historic mission is to sanction all revolts, all desperate actions, all those abortive attempts drowned in rivers of blood.
>
> —Fanon, *The Wretched of the Earth*

> That the great misery and much smaller joy of existence remain unchanged no matter what anything is called never checks the impulse to reach back and reclaim a loss, to try and make what happened look as if it had not happened at all.
>
> —Kincaid, *My Garden (Book)*

During decolonial struggles, all colonized "nations" were—as they, in many respects, still are in places like Palestine, where settler colonialism is alive and well despite decades of postcolonial enlightenment—possessed by tormented spirits; all "nations" promised, if not contracted themselves, to the fulfillment of the commandments of a nameless horde of ghosts scattered across the globe. The voices of the ghosts still speak to us, with an explosive admixture of irascibility and intransigence, through the pages of Frantz Fanon's *The Wretched of the Earth.* It is as if, at least retrospectively, Hamlet were a nation unto himself or a postcolonial visionary avant la lettre. Generations after generations of men and women who happened to be born during colonization—a colonization for which they were hardly responsible yet against which they were contracted by/from birth to fight—gave utterance to Hamlet's passionate outcry: "O cursed spite / that ever I was born to set it right!"[31]

While Freud introduced analytic treatment and the economy of transference as a technique that makes possible the passage from repetition-compulsion in the motor sphere into remembrance and working-through in the psychical sphere, Fanon—a psychoanalyst, philosopher, and psychiatrist by training—seems, in my view, to call for the implementation of the reverse of Freud's technique. Therapy follows, for Fanon, from the *canalization* (Fanon's notion) of repetition-compulsion in the service of decolonial struggles, and not from the containment of that aggressive compulsion in the interiority of the psyche, since such containment would render the colonized/the analysand docile and passive (which would all too neatly dovetail with the colonial setup).[32] "Discipline, training, mastering, and today pacifying are," Fanon notes, "the words most frequently used by the colonialists in occupied territories."[33] Therapy within the colonial context comes, then, only through the willing suspension of relief in its Freudian analytic understanding—really, only through the willing sustenance of grief (which would then in Fanon's view be harnessed by the natives for decolonial ends).

It is theoretically rewarding to trace the delicate moves that Fanon makes en route to the detoxification of repetition (of violence) from the kernel of compulsion. When I have rounded out my argument, it will become patently clear that the *compulsive* in Freud becomes the *compulsory* in Fanon. In *The Wretched of the Earth,* Fanon rams home the idea that violence should be understood not only within the narrow cultural context of myth and ritual, but also within the vaster historical tide of colonization-decolonization that has spectacularly inaugurated it. I will come back to the psychological and historical reasons for this argument later, but it seems important to underscore right away that Fanon's most contentious theoretical stride occurs, in my view, in his attempt to show how *ritualistic* violence, of possession and exorcism, can be rerouted in the service of *political* and decolonial violence. When the compulsive repetition of violence at the level of ritual becomes—once the *moudjahidines* have laid hold of it and changed its direction—instrumental to the project of decolonization, crude repetition-compulsion transforms into sanctioned repetition, as in the above epigraph.[34]

For Fanon, if the colonial subjugation of the native was born in violence, then the native's revolt and liberation can be forged only in the smithy of a greater violence. If "positive law demands," as Walter Benjamin professes, "of all violence a proof of its historical origin, which under certain conditions is declared legal, sanctioned," no wonder, then, that Fanon's first move is to establish the phenomenon of violence as a product of material history, brought "into the home and into the mind of the native" by the colonizer.[35] From a positivist, historicist, and legalistic perspective, violence can be sought only in the realm of means, not of ends. As Benjamin points out, once violence is established as a means, a criterion for establishing its validity might be made immediately available: "It imposes itself in the question whether violence, in a given case, is a means to a just or an unjust end."[36] While it might seem critically unproductive not to interrogate the catachrestic nature of the figure of justice (a task I largely set myself in the following chapter), let us assume nonetheless—and for the sake of a leap of "irresponsible literality"[37]—with Fanon that justice amounts to nothing less than the use of violence against the colonizer, in view, of course, of an eventual independence. Justice, insofar as Fanon's argument is concerned, seems indissociable from a narrative historiography bedeviled by the runaway force of the dialectic of history and barbarism, according to which colonizer and colonized come to entertain a Manichean relation of "reciprocal exclusivity."[38]

Fanon's forays into the "virtues" of violence in the project of decolonization would have been simple had he confined the spiraling circuitry of his thought to history and dialectic. Soon, however, violence becomes the common impetus that incites, in a quasi-Sartrean manner, the native to move from a state of passive existence into one (in search) of essence—"the 'thing' which has been colonized becomes man during the same process by which it frees itself."[39] Equally, violence becomes, from a loosely psychoanalytic perspective, the rallying cry of the primitive, the possessed, the inhibited, the mentally ill—of the colonized in all his or her damaged fragmentary states. While it is true that the mental disorders from which the colonized suffers might be inextricably bound to the structure of colonialism of which they are indeed an effect, it remains theoretically hazardous to assert that those disorders can be dealt with only on the pyre of colonialism.[40]

The trouble with Fanon's concept of violence is that it cuts through the dividing lines between symptom and cure. Fanon's analysis aims to unwind the subtle meanderings of the concept of violence, yet the urgency with which he writes—and the swiftness with which his thought on violence seeps through the whole porous network of origins, symptom, and cure—tinges the tactical exactness of his analysis with a mystifying whiff: "In the colonial world, the emotional sensitivity of the native is kept on the surface of his skin like an open sore which flinches from the caustic agent; and the psyche shrinks back, obliterates itself and finds outlet in muscular demonstrations which have caused certain very wise men to say that the native is a hysterical type."[41] The gaping wound or "sore" of the native—of which the ritualistic muscular outlets are both symptom and cure—must first be seen in terms of its historical origins: it is, after all, the settler that deposits aggressiveness in the bones of the native: "The argument the native chooses has been furnished by the settler."[42] Furthermore, given that the "settler keeps alive in the native an anger which he deprives of outlet," one can understand why the "native's muscular tension finds outlet regularly in bloodthirsty explosions—in tribal warfare, in feuds between septs, and in quarrels between individuals."[43] Fanon calls these detours into neighborly quarrels nothing more than behavioral techniques of psychic avoidance whereby the natives try to "put off till later the choice, nevertheless inevitable, which opens up the question of armed resistance to colonialism."[44] It is not that these feuds never existed prior to colonization, but that they come to serve in the colonial context a new function—a means not only to avoid the colonizer, but also to dissipate the aggressiveness he nevertheless keeps ignited. Thus, even the otherwise identificatory stamp of myth and magic—that is, of belonging to a community entirely under "magical jurisdiction"—plays, in the colonial context, a role dissimilar to the one it normally used to play prior to colonization.[45]

Fanon's pivotal emplacement of violence within the colonial orbit makes any manifestation of violence (whether symptomatic or curative or both) on the part of the native revolve necessarily around colonial violence. Even the sphere of the occult—in which a chain of violent actions "are repeated with crystalline inevitability"[46]—has now, according to Fanon's cautionary advice, to be studied in terms of the ways in which it bears on and bears the impress of colonial violence. On the one hand, Fanon points out that the natives are a people for whom the colonizer is—compared to the zombies of myth, for instance, not to mention the crowd of maleficent spirits such as leopard-men, serpent-men, and six-legged dogs—too insignificant an enemy for them to bother rising up against, all the more so since rising up against the colonizer is subsumable under the phantasmic intelligence that regulates the natives' lives and is thus always already taken care of by their Gods and spirits. In other words, the natives do not really need to fight against the settlers since ultimately "all is settled by a permanent confrontation on the phantasmic plane."[47] On the other hand, while maintaining that ritualistic violence surpasses colonial violence—if not dismisses it altogether by handing it over to the "invisible keepers"[48] of mythic jurisprudence—Fanon harks back nonetheless to the thesis that ritualistic violence speaks directly to colonial violence, even when it does not aim at it: "The native's relaxation takes precisely the form of a muscular orgy in which the most acute aggressivity and the most impelling violence are canalized, transformed, and conjured away. The circle of the dance is a permissive circle: it protects and permits. . . . There are no limits inside the circle. . . . There are no limits—*for in reality your purpose in coming together is to allow the accumulated libido, the hampered aggressivity, to dissolve as in a volcanic eruption.*"[49] The cathartic purchases of mythic and ritualistic violence cannot be overstated: in fact, they very aptly exemplify the promissory impetus from which myth derives its continuing appeal. The "hampered aggressivity"—that is, the vindictive violence that the colonizer keeps alive but deprives of an outlet—is finally discharged through the purificatory apertures of myth and dance. While paying tribute to the edifying dimensions of mythic violence, Fanon intones nonetheless that such violence does not exist in a balmy elsewhere, unencumbered by the unthinking machine of colonialism. The colonial condition demands that this violence—"formerly lost in an imaginary maze," "canalized by the emotional outlets of dance and possession by spirits," and "exhausted in fratricidal combats" or criminal activities[50]—change directions, find a new line of action, and emerge shot through with insurrection and revolt.

While the analyst in the Freudian analytic situation is required to participate in the memories of the analysand in such a way as to ascertain their inward affective containment and thus preclude their outward actantial enactment, the rebel intellectual/analyst (of whom Fanon speaks) has to participate in the native's mythic canalization of violence in such a way as to enable the native (analysand) not only to embody it but also to direct it toward, or hurl it back on, the colonizer.[51] It is incumbent upon the native to negotiate prudently the delicate balance between the available ritualistic patterns of canalizing violence and the new demands for decolonization. The native is asked, in other words, to keep alive the aggressive impulses and, paradoxically, to direct their ultimate eruption in the battle for national self-determination. "When formerly [violence] was appeased by myths and exercised its talents in finding fresh ways of committing mass suicide, now new conditions will make possible a completely new line of action" and "engender new aims for the violence of colonized people."[52] This is, in my view, Fanon's most daring theoretical venture—that the *compulsive* reenactment of aggression must bleed into a *compulsory* act of revolt against colonization. Once the mythic, fratricidal, and criminal canalization of violent impulses finds utterance in the decolonial struggle, not only do feuds and crimes decrease, but even psychic pathologies such as melancholia become sites of, if not occasions for, resistance to colonialism.[53] Curiously enough, the melancholic no longer harbors autodestructive or suicidal intents, as we have seen in the previous chapter, but rather engages in heterodestructive and homicidal acts.[54] This shift in function is certainly a breakthrough in the understanding of the psychic forces of decolonization movements, yet it has not benefited from the theoretical elaboration that it nevertheless seems to prompt.[55] In the shift from the colonial to the postcolonial situation, however, melancholia becomes, as I will show later, less of hetero-destructive act than a psychoaffective economy of retrospective inquiry into the history of colonialism while enduring its aftereffects.

The problem with Fanon's conception of counterviolence—or what I called, *pace* Freud's repetition-compulsion, sanctioned repetition—and with Hamlet's matrix of remembering, at the heart of which stirs the call for revenge, is that each of them sends history back to itself; each of them falls back on mimetic and visceral reflexes and sends revenge back to revenge, threatening thereof to produce a chain of mirroring effects that is extremely hard to undo. Is not revenge, which is pursued in the name of justice, "merely one of the snares that history and its various influences [set] for us"?[56] Are we not, after all, warranted —not to say, *entitled*—in the words of Derrida, to "yearn for a justice that one day, *a day belonging no longer to history,* a quasi-messianic day, would finally be *removed from the fatality of vengeance?*"[57] Justice in a legalistic sense is indissociable from the structures of its enforcement, from the implements of justice, and therefore cannot cease to fold back into the horizon of violence. Moreover, if from a positivistic legal perspective violence is the product of history—and if the socius itself originates, as Freud's *Totem and Taboo* demonstrates, in violence—can a later violence help redress that first (originating) violence? I can but refer here to the young Jesuit sage of Joyce's *Ulysses,* Stephen, who interjects, with a measure of prophetic gloom, that "No later undoing will undo the first undoing."[58]

Stephen's largely aphoristic statement should be taken not as an open invitation to political inaction, but as an incentive to ponder and outwit the nightmarish dialectic of civilization and barbarism and in the process to help Benjamin's angel regain control over its wings. Hence, insofar as it bears on the actantial or motor sphere—in which one has recourse to violence to undo an injustice—one would willingly want to ratify Stephen's counterintuitive conclusion.[59] Yet, insofar as Stephen's dictum bears on the psychoaffective sphere —in which one is urged to remember and to mourn an originary undoing— one might end up with a sense of paralytic helplessness, if not abuse, over the fact that the work of mourning cannot always undo the psychoaffective undoing (of colonial history) it is called upon to undo. The counter-intuitive force of Stephen's axiom, "No later undoing *will* undo the first undoing," lies, I think, not in merely sabotaging both Freud and Fanon, but in laying bare the conditions of impossibility that prefigure (the conditions of possibility of) any practice—literary, theoretical, or political—whose horizon/primary material is shot through with loss, suffering, and colonial trauma.

It is precisely this condition of impossibility—or of irreconcilability "to what happened," as in the above epigraph—that Kincaid contends in *A Small Place:* "nothing can erase my rage—not an apology, not a large sum of money, not the death of the criminal—for *this wrong* can never be made right, and only the impossible can make me still: can a way be found to make *what happened* not have happened?"[60] While Kincaid proceeds systematically to name the different available redemptive patterns (ranging from "an apology" and "a large sum of money" to the actual "death" of the wrongdoer), which she then summarily declines, she remains nonetheless incapable of *specifying* the *crime* that has, after all, incited this irascible rage. Kincaid cannot but lay claim to "what happened," to "this wrong" that remains either too obvious to need any naming or in excess of language altogether. Or is it that language inevitably rationalizes that which surpasses reason?

Almost every postcolonial writer inherits this claim to *what happened,* to *this wrong* that he has, in turn, to pass on to posterity, wittingly or unwittingly— and perhaps in the form of a phantomatic (and unconscious) transgenerational haunting.[61] It is not that the devious psychic and material effects of *what happened* do not echo down to the present—whether in the form of inferiority complexes and bad governance or corruption[62]—but that the *whatness* of *what happened* never quite coincides with the telling. Here we are, of course, trenching on a recurrent theme, if not actually a common denominator of most post-Holocaust, postcolonial, or postmodern critical practices: unrepresentability. Yet I will not insist on the inextricable bond between silence/unspeakability and representation[63]—at the origin of the cul-de-sac of inexpressibility/unrepresentability—or on its ethical merits (Derrida) or legal demerits (Lyotard), but I will instead attempt to sharpen our understanding of this aporia of unrepresentability by understanding the poetic and psychoaffective structure of which it is a product—namely, the confluence of catachresis and melancholia.

Melancholy Acts, Catachrestic Rumblings

> The past, to which we were subjected, which has not yet emerged as history for us, is, however, obsessively present.
>
> —Glissant, *Caribbean Discourse.*

> Once the reflection on the figurality of language is started, there is no telling where it may lead.
>
> —Paul de Man, "The Epistemology of Metaphor"

The reason why *what happened* is called thus—simply, *what happened*—is that it cannot be located in a narrative historiography, in a historical continuum, but is condemned to remain at the outskirts of history, a species of "nonhistory," as in the words of Edouard Glissant: "Our historical consciousness could not be deposited gradually and continuously like sediment . . . but came together in the context of *shock,* contraction, painful negation, and explosive forces. This *dislocation* of the continuum, and the inability of the collective consciousness to absorb it all, characterizes what I call a nonhistory."[64] In Africa a constellation of forces—ranging, as in the case of Fanon's Algeria, from mythic jurisprudence and political commitment to the mobilization of psychic pathologies—has combined to form what Glissant suggestively calls a "cultural hinterland" that has enabled, in turn, the structures of resistance to colonialism and its aftermath; in the Caribbean context, however, no such cultural repository could be found, since the kind of continuity on which rests the cultures of African nations had been, in the case of the Caribbean nations, brutally interrupted by the dislocatory concourse of the slave trade, colonization, and imperialism. What is worse is that this dislocation is not fused into the historical horizon of the Caribbean people but hangs over it, threatening to dislodge it every time it reaches out for it. It is therefore incumbent, according to Glissant, upon the Caribbean writer to explore this dislocation, not in order to relate it to a "schematic chronology" or to a "nostalgic lament," but in order "to show its relevance in a continuous fashion to the immediate present."[65]

I cannot discuss with due justice herein the complexity, density, and constructive potential of Glissant's patient theoretical postulations—much less interrogate them from Kincaid's perspective—but I think it is sufficiently beneficial for my purposes to examine the ways in which Glissant's reflection on *what happened* has been inaugurated by a tropologically regenerative desire for not only naming but also possessing the *whatness* of *what happened.* In the absence of a master narrative of historical continuity, Glissant is explicit about the paradoxical desire to possess—not *re*possess—what has never been his: "For history is not only absence for us, it is vertigo. *This time that was never ours, we must now possess.*"[66] This desire to possess that which has never been earned, possessed, or lost—that which is still an empty vacuum, an "absence"—is a signal mark not only of the melancholic affect underpinning it but also of the inventive and largely poetic enterprise of the postcolonial intellectual. It is not for nothing that this desire to possess announces itself as both a definitional adventure and a recuperative enterprise: words such as "shock," "dislocation," "nonhistory," "absence," "vertigo," or, as in the above epigraph, the "not yet . . . history"—words in which there is literally "no lack of void" (Beckett's phrase)—have become part and parcel of what Glissant calls "the uncertain possibilities of the word made ours."[67] Not only is the desire to possess the void regenerative (and this is, of course, the law/logic of desire in Lacan), it is equally appropriative—it possesses the void in the very process of claiming and therefore multiplying it. To the extent that this possession (or obsession, as in the Glissant epigraph) is a possession *by* that which has never been possessed—and to the extent that it is constituted at the interface between language and desire, between linguistic appropriation and affective incorporation, or between a *possession of* and a *possession by*—it is the effect, I will argue, of an overlap between melancholia and catachresis, between psychoaffective dispositions and poetic reconfigurations.

It is, of course, impossible to reconstitute *what happened* when it first happened, since this poses not only a chronological but also a topographical problem—a chronotopic conundrum of time and space in which one cannot possibly travel back in time to bear witness to *what happened.* This time-space conundrum is perhaps aggravated if we are to bear in mind that *what happened* is of the order of the traumatic, whose presence insists but also resists articulacy—a "solid shadow," as Kincaid would put it in *Annie John.*[68] Yet the conundrum might, by the same token, become insignificant if we place ourselves in a psychoanalytic perspective, in which the traumatic is said to brook no witness, it being the site of an utter "collapse of witnessing" (Freud, Laub, Caruth). It is, however—and still from a psychoanalytic perspective—what is doomed to return after a period of latency (Freud), or what is fated to haunt posterity persistently if it is allowed to travel free-floatingly across generations (Abraham and Torok). It is in this sense that Glissant's evocation of a past that has not yet emerged, but that is obsessively present, should be understood. It is also in this sense that every reflection on the past should be understood, not as making visible the site/sight of invisibility, but rather as producing the visible, that which can be demonstrated to have been invisible, or of the order of the impossible to bear witness to, let alone register.[69]

What happened is nothing but the "nothing" of *Who would mourn were there nothing to be remembered?*—the question I asked at the very beginning of this chapter and to which I have been trying to gain a fresh entry. If *what happened* is of the order of the *traumatic,* the *dislocatory,* and the *nothing,* one is faced with the hopelessness not only of determining but also of proving it. We are yet to acquaint ourselves with the grave psychic sedimentations of the hopelessness of this situation and with the many hurdles it unwittingly interposes in front of any envisaged transcultural or transnational action, yet we cannot fail to note that the gloomiest part of it lies in the resultant fermentation and dissemination of a sense of victimization to whoever inherits the *nothingness* of *what happened* and gazes at it orphically. This is a hopeless situation, more precisely, because whoever inherits it or reclaims it cannot prove that *what happened* did really happen. If we are to abide by the distinction that Lyotard makes between the plaintiff ("someone who has incurred damages and who disposes of the means to prove it") and the victim (one who is not "able to prove that one has been done a wrong"),[70] we might think of the postcolonial writer as, properly speaking, neither a plaintiff nor a victim, but one who is condemned (in Sartre's sense) to border-dwelling, tending ever so pressingly toward the threshold of plaintiffhood but always falling under the shadow of victimhood. Can, therefore, to rephrase Lyotard, new referents, new expressions, or new idioms be found in order for "the plaintiff to cease being a victim"?[71]

Let us return then to Kincaid, whose only response to the above question seems to brook no response at all, only fresh referrals to a chiastically narrowing and widening negative dialectic:

> What to call the thing that happened to me and all who look like me?
>
> Should I call it history?
>
> If so, what should history mean to someone like me? Should it be an idea, should it be an open wound and each breath I take in and expel healing and opening the wound again and again, over and over, or is it a moment that began in 1492 and has come to no end yet? Is it a collection of facts, all true and precise details, and, if so, when I come across these true and precise details, what should I do, how should I feel, where should I place myself? Why should I be obsessed with all these questions?[72]

Before I eventually come back to reflect on the enormity and ambition of the first question, let me first point out that it is a definitional question. Of course, definitional questions are the most common and simple questions, yet they can be particularly difficult to answer: on the one hand, they presuppose the existence of the "name" of that of which they ask and demand its identification; on the other, they undermine that very name of which they ask. The question and the name become identical: there is no name of which the question asks, only a question. The question asks after "the thing that happened," but does not dare to name it, not because it cannot be named and even specified, but because its very name, its very specification would threaten to thrust it into oblivion. Perhaps Kincaid "overemplots" her fear of naming,[73] but the question, as it is formulated, is the site of an interdiction. It is as if the conferral of a name on "the thing that happened" would irrecoverably prevent us from having access to it, to its weight and enormity. But by the same token, one is struck by the reification of the object of the question. Not to be able to produce a name for it—and to call it "the thing that happened"—makes one wonder at the outset whether one is placed in the pull of excess or inadequacy. This is, of course, the perfect "inscriptional space" of catachrestic maneuvers, of improper usages of words, abuses of some sort; a trope of disarticulation and embarrassment,[74] catachresis preys on blanks and on the absence of referents in order to usurp, transfer, and displace words from one context or proper use into another—so much so that the resultant word, which will, of course, bear the stamp of catachresis, becomes not only an evocation of an original lack but also a staging of the lack of homology between meanings and words.

Since "the thing that happened" does not have a proper name yet, it is opened up, by necessity, to catachrestic malleability, to an infinite set of propositions and appropriations, of enumerations and calculations.[75] Right after Kincaid asks her first question, she proposes a name for "the thing that happened": "should I call it *history?*" (my italics). Hence, "history" should be understood as a catachrestic inscription of "the thing that happened," and continues to exert/command enormous identificatory power, even though it is hardly identifiable in itself. I will come back to the melancholic import of this distinction later, but let me briefly indicate the aporia of identification operative in the first question, which is definitional, and the second one, which is propositional. It seems to me that a question such as *What to call the thing that happened to me and all who look like me?* stages a disjunction between hermeneutic grasp and affective investment. While the *identification of* "the thing that happened" has not yet been articulated, the *identification with* it seems nonetheless to be so deeply seated in Kincaid's historical consciousness that she shares it with "all who look like her." This disjunction—or, more precisely, this disjunctive relation, this *rapport sans rapport,* as Derrida would say—between the *identification of* and the *identification with* "the thing that happened" is an effect of what I call the *melancholologics* of catachresis, a trope of transferral and appropriation, much like Freud's melancholia, in which the ego is said to latch on to a lost object it cannot fully articulate. Where there is catachresis, melancholia will be.

In "Mourning and Melancholia," Freud does not purport to give a coherent and comprehensive account of what melancholia is, only a variation on a theme—a set of observations based on heterogeneous cases. Not infrequently, Freud is very explicit about the impossibility of homogenizing all the otherwise irreconcilable aspects of melancholia. Such expressions as "[i]n one set of cases . . ." and "[i]n yet other cases . . ." testify to Freud's caution against any subsequent critical temptation to elaborate a master narrative of melancholia. I will be concerned, therefore, with an aspect of melancholia in which the melancholic is said to be consumed by an "unknown loss": "In yet other cases one feels justified in maintaining the belief that a loss . . . has occurred, but one cannot see clearly what it is that has been lost, and it is all the more reasonable to suppose that the patient cannot consciously perceive what he has lost either. This, indeed, might be so even if the patient is aware of the loss which has given rise to his melancholia, but only in the sense that he knows *whom* he has lost but not *what* he has lost in him."[76] Freud goes on to add that a melancholic of this type is not uninhibited by "the unknown loss," but his inhibition "seems puzzling to us because we cannot see *what* it is that is absorbing him so entirely."[77] Freud insists that the melancholic "knows *whom* he has lost but not *what* he has lost in him," yet to me this distinction seems elusive, precisely because it attempts to sharpen the already blurred lines between the memory of the person lost (the "whom") and his attributes (the "what"); it purports, as it were, to distinguish between "the dancer and the dance."[78] As we move ahead into the Kincaidian text, this distinction might become useful; however, for the moment, what is important to stress is this maddening unknowability of the object of the melancholic's absorption.

Kincaid wants to condense—as in a dream—the sum total of all "that happened to [her] and all who look like [her]," and wants to give it a name. There is no gainsaying the urgency and the precariousness of the project. The explicit rhetoricity of the question, however, suspends its literality in the impossible. In other words, Kincaid explicitly intones that it is impossible to "call the thing that happened." Yet that very impossibility implies that Kincaid is nevertheless trying—caught, as it were, in the attempt. We are cautioned, however, that the name of "the thing that happened" will not come from memory but from the imagination: "*Should* I call it history?" In other words, it is not that Kincaid tried and was not able to remember the name of "the thing," or that a precise name for it existed already, but that its memory is itself missing and must therefore be invented. The "should" in "Should I call it history?" gives us an idea of not only the arbitrariness of the name but also the necessary catachrestic invention of that of which it is the name. Moreover, at the heart of this catachrestic claim to "history"—to naming and misnaming "the thing that happened" as "history"—we can also see the amount of forgetting involved. Speaking no longer to memory but to the imagination, Kincaid, in dubbing "the thing that happened" "history," threatens to thrust it into oblivion at the very moment when she wants to identify it and bring it to cognition.[79] The inscriptional space of identification is cited/sited in oblivion. The suspicion that "Something monstrous lurks in the most innocent of catachreses"[80] is not totally unfounded, inasmuch as the domino effect of a catachrestic inscription is nothing less than the domestication, and therefore supplantation, of "the thing that happened" with a familiar name. At the very same time that it is instigated by the impulsion to comprehension, naming thus becomes a form of denial of "the thing that happened," much as the resistance to naming would boil down to yet another form of denial of the same "thing that happened"—a melancholic appropriation of "the thing" and a narcissistic mortification of its loss. We must therefore rephrase Lyotard: Can, therefore, a new idiom be found whereby what is named ceases to be named?

Now that Kincaid has imaginatively dubbed what happened as "history," she can no longer arrest the spiraling chain of catachresis, or the resultant mise en abyme of catachrestic rumblings. As de Man states, "Once the reflection on the figurality of language is started, there is no telling where it may lead."[81] These are nothing more than effects of any definitional question, since any such question would carry with it the possibility of staging several propositions, which is to say, the possibility of setting in motion an infinite chain of catachrestic generative transformations. As we will see in due course, catachresis itself is not exempt from this chain of mutations and metamorphoses. Returning to Kincaid's catachrestic inscription of "the thing that happened," we might ask the following question: what does the referent "history" imply if "the thing that happened" is now inscribed as "history"? First and foremost, it implies that "the thing that happened," now baptized as "history," is finally amenable to sensemaking rather than removed from it. To call it "history" means that it can, after all, pass through understanding, be conferred a meaning, and be integrated—rather than engraved—in the historical horizon of the postcolonial subject.[82] Second, since understanding is a function of consciousness, it is presumably conducive to the fulfillment of the work of mourning. No wonder then that Kincaid's subsequent question is, "If so, what should history *mean* to someone like me?" It is worth noting here that Kincaid is extremely sensitive to every delicate move she makes along the path of rhetoric. For instance, having dubbed "the thing that happened" as "history," she is now aware that it has introduced it into language and has therefore opened it up to perspectival differences and to hermeneutic appropriations. She hastens therefore to specify that she is here concerned with her perspective alone: "what should history mean to someone *like me?*" Having made that clear—despite the residual undecidability of the simile "like me"—Kincaid cannot, however, but work within the differential nature of the referent against which she has warned us.

Her response is structured by juxtaposition and focalized by subordination: "Should it be an *idea,* should it be an *open wound* and each breath I take in and expel healing and opening the wound again and again, over and over . . . ?" First of all, how do we understand her use of the word *idea?* Why an idea? What can it be? Is this an implicit concession that "the thing that happened to [her] and all who look like [her]"—and that she imperfectly inscribed as "history"—can be understood? Is not the definitional-propositional impulse at the heart of the question traversed by a homogenizing urge that purports to give, at one stroke, a name for an otherwise heterogeneous concourse of events? If we are to adopt a Benjaminian perspective, we might say that Kincaid's question encourages the formulation of an answer from a historicist perspective, in which "a mass of data" is mustered in order "to fill the homogenous, empty time"—one in which, that is, "a chain of events" is collapsed, in Benjamin's famous idiom, under a "single catastrophe which keeps piling wreckage upon wreckage."[83] While Benjamin decries this historicist perspective and calls for a materialist, historiographical practice of history—in which signs of "a Messianic cessation of happening" or of "a revolutionary chance" to blast a specific era out of "the homogenous course of history" are entertained, enabled, and maintained—Kincaid's definitional question seems to invite just such a perspective. It is worth noting here that Kincaid's fiction is not "shot through," as Benjamin would have urged, "with chips of Messianic time."[84] Quite the contrary, Kincaid's evocation of "the thing that happened" is subsumable under a single catastrophe—an unbridgeable gap between, in Glissant's words, "blind belief" in the "thing that happened" and "clear consciousness" of when, how, and why exactly it happened.[85]

If Kincaid's first definitional question conveys the sense that "the thing that happened" verges on a single catastrophe—and, as such, surpasses our ability to make sense of it, to understand it—then her propositional question "Should it be an idea" should be seen as an attempt to make sense of the otherwise threatening senselessness of the catastrophic nature of "the thing that happened." Insofar as this proposition—as is the case with every proposition that will follow—is an attempt to restore to meaning "the thing that happened," it is inherently an attempt at mourning; it belongs to the logic of the work of mourning provided that this logic is understood as a hermeneutic task in the first place. True, mourning can be seen as a process of sensemaking and of leave-taking, yet it is set in motion by the very assumption—of sensemaking and leave-taking—of what it does not have. Marc Nichanian is right to stress that "*a sense* [not sense in general, but a certain sense or an assumption thereof] *is necessary so that mourning can occur.*"[86] If "the thing that happened" verges on the catastrophic, is not the attempt to name it—to define and condense it in one word—also an attempt to mourn the many atrocities it involved, as it were, at one fell swoop?

The hesitations and equivocalness of the question—"Should it be an idea"—should thus be seen as modalities or functions of the hermeneutics of mourning, by which I mean simply the window(s) of meaning through which mourning enters the house of fiction. The "idea," then, is better understood as the muse of narrative, which is, in turn, the muse of mourning. Once this process is adumbrated, narrative plays off the relations between mourning and sensemaking—two activities that work in tandem and codetermine each other. Having said this, I find that the immediate problem that presents itself in the Kincaidian text is that "the thing that happened"—which is now catachrestically inscribed as "history"—doesn't seem to make sense or to invite sensemaking, and the attempt to make sense of it becomes an attempt to make sense of the senseless. "Should it be an idea?" is a question that is not, after all, addressed to the victim but to the victor; the question, more precisely, challenges the victor to make sense of "the thing that happened." In other words, is "the thing that happened" amenable to sense, to an "idea at the back of it," as Conrad would say?[87]

By and large, to the extent that "Should it be an idea?" is an attempt to apprehend the implacable void of "the thing that happened" in its totality—in other words, to the extent that it purports to define, enumerate, calculate, explain, and, perhaps, prove the concourse of the events that happened, as well as the sum of the atrocities, indignities, and sufferings involved—it signals the limits not only of understanding and imagining but also of mourning. For, as Nichanian rightly observes, "the limit of the imagination is also the limit of mourning."[88] Kincaid's propositional question, however, is subordinated to another more strikingly propositional *and* descriptive question—"should it be an open wound . . . ?" To propose to call "history" an "idea" and then to propose to call it an "open wound" can be seen as an attempt to wrest it from the abstractions (and even pretensions to objectivity) of epistemological discourse in order to ram it home to the psychic and affective sphere. Moreover, to trope "history" as an "open wound" is not only to reemplot what would have been a historical narrative in an "extended metaphor," but also to charge us with particular "emotional valences" in the very process.[89]

It is at this stage that the variably definitional and propositional melancho-logic of catachresis is extended and mutated into the rather descriptive metaphorics of melancholia. When "the thing that happened" has been catachrestically inscribed as "history," it symmetrically opens itself up to further tropological extensions and variations. Since the "history" in question is not a lived experience of "the thing that happened," it cannot be retrieved from the repertoire of memory but only from the protean field of the imagination and must revolve, therefore, in the orbit of forgetting. Arsène Darmesteter was perhaps the first to discern the contours of forgetting underneath the structure of catachresis; such forgetting enables catachresis to multiply itself along the chain of tropological mutations and to segue eventually into other tropes.[90] Once "the thing that happened" is catachrestically inscribed as "history," not only is the possibility of reclaiming it enabled but so is the possibility of grounding the claim, such that the claim becomes identical with the means by which it is made. The means of laying the claim to "history" are anchored in "history"—an anchorage without anchor! In other words, not only is the claim sited in an inscriptional space for which there is—to use Spivak's words again—"no historically adequate referent" in the case of Antigua, but it is also correlatively *cited* as a means of *siting* the claim to that inscriptional space. When the claim and the means of making the claim converge, catachresis doubles or generalizes into metaphor: the catachrestically inscribed "history" spills into the metaphor of the "open wound." Although one would not set on a task of mourning if there were *a nothing* to be remembered, one cannot help but register the tendency in Kincaid to lay a catachrestic claim to loss and, in the words of Derrida, to "the properly spectral anteriority of the crime—the crime of the other, a misdeed whose event and reality, whose truth can never *present themselves* in flesh and blood, but can only allow themselves to be presumed, reconstructed, fantasized."[91]

When the catachrestic rumblings intensify and become too taxing on the imagination, catachresis mutates into, while it encrypts itself in, other tropological configurations. In her work on the French surrealist Louis Aragon, Kristeva illustrates how catachresis comes to be "generalized in metaphor in order to create an image"[92]—the image, here, of course, is of the "open wound," of which Kincaid speaks. Sited in an inscriptional space that it cannot fully accommodate, catachresis cannot but transform and multiply itself on the infinite chain of tropological transformations. In the previous chapter of this book, I showed the ways in which melancholia—being a vicissitude of normal mourning—cannot but create its own vicissitudes, such as madness and suicide; I can now say almost the same thing about catachresis, namely, that it is a vicissitude in the proper usage of words, of names and even tropes and cannot therefore but proliferate and perpetuate the vicissitudinal gesture on which it is founded. At the same time, one realizes that this vicissitudinal tendency of the trope is but a function of the indefatigable desire to master the object of inquiry—"the thing that happened"—a desire that is inaugurated by the retrospective force of melancholia and sustained by its indefatigable thrust toward hermeneutic mastery (which would coincide with mourning proper). It is in these senses combined that we should understand the tropological shift from "history" to "open wound"—that is, in the sense of the intensification of the imagination, which is a function of psychodynamics of understanding, as well as in the sense of the aptitude of catachresis, much like affects, for mutation and change.

I concur with J. Hillis Miller's vision—which is also César Dumarsais's—that catachresis "poisons the anthology of tropes," and I also agree with Spivak's more tautological and Derridean conclusion that all names are misfits,[93] but I think one's immediate task is to aspire for a measure of differentiation and acculturation. Catachresis in the postcolonial context—or at least in Kincaid's work—is not so much a laudable, poststructuralist game that comes to confirm our vaunted suspicion of the indeterminacy of the linguistic sign as a signal of crisis or a sign of abuse and improper use as it is a mark of victimhood and pain—indeed, *a stamp of the abused.* The distance between historical loss and narrative inscription is the real measure of Kincaid's melancholic rage.

At the very end of her essay, Kincaid rephrases and re-clusters her series of interrogations as follows: "What to call the thing that happened to me and all who look like me? Should I call it history? And if so, what should history mean to someone who looks like me? Should it be an idea; should it be an open wound, each breath I take in and expel healing and opening the wound again and again, over and over, or is it a long moment that begins anew each day since 1492?"[94] If we compare this closing passage of her essay with the other opening passage cited before, we will not fail to note the excision of the following questions from the flow of her interrogations: "Is it a collection of facts, all true and precise details, and, if so, when I come across these true and precise details, what should I do, how should I feel, where should I place myself? Why should I be obsessed with all these questions?"[95] This excision is very important because it debunks the epistemological pretensions of history books (these same pretensions have also received a considerable amount of criticism in the work of Wilson Harris) and elides the questions of action, affect, and location ("what should I do, how should I feel, where should I place myself?"). Since "someone else's ordinary dreariness is another person's epiphany,"[96] Kincaid dispenses herself with the "interest in an objective standard" of narrative historiography. She provides no response to the questions of action, affect, location, and obsession, intimating thus that a response is operative in the rhetoricity of the questions themselves. While the questions are rhetorically amplified by the anaphoric repetition of the propositional modality "should it be," they are not indiscriminately so: they prod syllogistically toward constructing "history," not so much as an "idea" but as an "open wound" whose *pharmakon*-like (in Derrida's sense) logic of poison and cure keeps the postcolonial subject stranded along a continuum between mourning and melancholia.

There is no gainsaying the melancholic charge of the figure of the "open wound," whether in Freud's "Mourning and Melancholia" or in Abraham and Torok's *The Shell and the Kernel,* but I would like to interrogate, in particular, the manifest experiential veracity it traffics, by exploring the counterproductive latencies that undermine its rhetorical torsion away from the crisis of signification and trauma of colonialism of which it is an effect. In addition, there is no gainsaying the fact that the illocutionary force of the figure is wheeled out as part of the poetic armature Kincaid deploys to rebut the charges of intransigence and irascibility—of rekindling old animosities and railing over long-departed colonialists[97]—charges foisted on her by a number of polemicists after the publication of *A Small Place.* What interests me is that the figure of the "open wound" is staked not only as a claim to "history," but also as an avenue of functioning of that history, documenting ever more its significance (material effects) rather than its signification (identification). This is what I would call the slide of catachresis into metaphor. In this respect, the figure registers, in my view, the shift from sensemaking to sensegiving—that is, from the threat, as it were, of not making sense of the "thing that happened" (which is why it is catachrestically inscribed as "history") to the threat of not giving it a sense (which is why it is captured as an "open wound"). In short, the figure registers the uncertain leap I announced earlier from victimhood to plaintiffhood. Having said that, I do not, however, wish to assess whether Kincaid has the ability to prove this "open wound," since the means of proving are, as it were, identical with the fiction of the proof; I would like rather to intuit the ramifications of this very unwitting *impulse to prove* at work in the figure of proof—the "open wound."

While troping "history" (or "the thing that happened") as an "open wound" is a manifest claim to memory, loss, and to impossible mourning, its subtle underside is nothing less than the *denial* of the very thing to which the claim is staked. It is, perhaps, the logic of the traumatic not to brook any identification and to keep breaking down at the threshold of signification. Yet it is exceedingly the (postcolonial) subject's very denial of that denial—the denial of the opaqueness that "the thing that happened" builds around itself—that threatens to compromise it irremediably in the very act of disposing of it in the order of the nameable. To trope is to deny the inability to name. To name is therefore a form of repression of this inability to name. It is this very denial/repression that locks the plaintiff in the logic of the perpetrator (of "the thing that happened"). To catachretize is to repress the denial of "the thing that happened" and to trope is to repeat the repression along the chain of tropological transformations. The sociological, psychological, and cultural workings of this denial/repression have been the focus of a number of studies in the case of Holocaust denials in Germany.[98] This denial is, of course, a function of the repression-repetition logic of which I spoke earlier in relation to Freud and Deleuze. But in what sense, then, does the leap from being the victim to being the plaintiff lock the Kincaidian subject in the logic of the perpetrator?

The answer to this question is already at work in the Kincaid epigraph of the previous section, but let us refresh our memory of it: "That the great misery and much smaller joy of existence remain unchanged no matter what anything is *called* never checks the *impulse* to reach back and *reclaim a loss, to try and make what happened look as if it had not happened at all*" (italics mine). Kincaid implies, perhaps unwittingly, that the impulse to reclaim and name a loss is already sited in the denial of that loss, in making it look as if it had not happened at all. To name the unnameable is as miserable an act as the misery it wants to name, and is therefore surreptitiously caught up in the repetition compulsion of that misery again and again. In a compelling theoretical exchange with Marc Nichanian, David Kazanjian points out (in reference to "the Armenian Genocide") that naming the unnameable is a "denial of [the] inability to name or imagine or apprehend."[99]

What is at stake here is not merely the "impulse to reach back and reclaim a loss," as Kincaid's passionate outcry conveys, but rather the "compulsion to prove" underpinning it. The compulsion to prove that "history" is an "open wound," which is implicit in the figure, keeps alive in the subject a compulsion to repeat that the trope is at pains to lull asleep. No wonder then that each "breath" heals, even while it opens, the wound again and again. Kazanjian concludes that "[t]he executioner that we bear in the depths of ourselves always exhorts us: Speak, say the truth, *prove if you can!* And we obey him incessantly."[100] Yet if the trope of the "open wound" is determined by the compulsion to repeat not only the denial of "the thing that happened," but also the opening of the wound at the very moment of suturing it, might not that be a price willingly paid to contain at the level of affective poetics the historical violence of colonialism—a violence that would otherwise be reenacted in the actantial or motor sphere of everyday war? Clearly, the unlikely conjunction I have made between melancholia and catachresis urges more inquiries into the ways in which the postcolonial subject can be empowered to claim a history of loss and grief while enduring its tragic resurgences and demarcations. This might seem to align the postcolonial with the imperial tactics of appeasement, but it in fact initiates the difficult process of seeking a transferential (as in Freud's preference of the analytic over the hypnotic model discussed above) consciousness of history rather than a merely dialectical one—verily, a consciousness as unforgetful as removed from vengeance.

Signifying Remains: *The Autobiography of My Mother*

> The violent intrusions of catachresis and the possibility of transfers that, unwilled, subvert the very model of the controlling subject, are the gothic underside of the mastery of metaphor, the uncanny other of its own control.
>
> —Patricia Parker, "Metaphor and Catachresis"

> All this is possible only because the reactions expressed in their behaviour still proceed from a mental constellation of revolt, which has then, by a certain process, passed over into the crushed state of melancholia.
>
> —Freud, "Mourning and Melancholia"

The question *Who would mourn were there nothing to be remembered?* that I asked at the very beginning of this chapter presupposes, at one level of its rhetorical structure, a relation of *complementarity* between remembering and mourning. I have already pointed out the many different ways in which this complementarity is oftentimes offset. Remembering does not so much deliver the consolation of mourning as create the repository for its conservation. There is no articulable frontier between remembering as an inaugurational or foundational act of mourning and remembering as a conservational or vicissitudinal force of mourning. The injunction to remember and the exhortation to mourn, both feel, therefore, in the same way, abusive, or so is the case, I argue, with Kincaid's *The Autobiography of My Mother.*

At the level of fabula, *The Autobiography of My Mother* can be seen as the narrative mourning of the life of its protagonist, seventy-year-old Xuela Claudette Richardson, whose "mother died at the moment [she] was born."[101] Set in colonial Dominica, and not in Kincaid's native Antigua, the novel takes us through stages of Xuela's life, culminating in a more or less complete portrait. Meanwhile, the narrator draws portraits of her dead mother, her aloof father, her wicked stepmother, her jealous half sister, and her deluded sexual partners. There is no gainsaying the persistent presence of the mother figure in all of

Kincaid's fiction, whether in such early pieces as *At the Bottom of the River, Annie John,* and *Lucy* or in her coming-of-age novels, such as *The Autobiography of My Mother, My Brother,* and, more recently, *Mr. Potter.*[102] It is precisely by tracing the continuity and mutation of the mother-daughter theme that Leigh Gilmore has been able to discern in Kincaid's fiction a "practice of serial autobiography." Since the twists and turns of this mother-daughter relationship drift with no instant of stasis throughout Kincaid's fiction, autobiography—"a one-shot deal" genre—becomes a prolific theme. "That there will always be (another) autobiography means," Gilmore concludes, "there will be no last words and autobiography is a genre of last words."[103] All Kincaid's novels are, in other words, caught up within the loop of autobiography, yet none of them is strictly autobiographical or consistent enough with the rest as to encompass the sum total of an autobiographical master narrative. Autobiography, however, has less to do here with narrative thematics than with narrative poetics. More precisely, autobiography in *The Autobiography of My Mother* is not an episode in the serial practice of autobiography, to which Kincaid is addicted, but rather a figure of narrative construction. In fact, autobiography in this novel is a fiction that begins by appealing to the facticity of autobiography; by virtue of displaying the autobiographical intent in its very title, in other words, the novel wants to hide the simulation of fiction.

Lizabeth Paravisini-Gebert suggests that "of all the characters Kincaid has created, Xuela is the least autobiographical, the most nakedly literary."[104] That the death of the mother is the axis around which revolves the whole narrative lends credence to this remark, since Kincaid's mother did not die at the moment Kincaid was born. Yet while I partly agree with Paravisini-Gebert that Xuela "is meant to be read not as a faithful representation of a flesh-and-blood woman, but as an artefact of the text,"[105] I would like to entertain the idea, at least for now, that Xuela is meant to be read, in a subtly disguised and twisted manner, as autobiographical. More precisely, Xuela is a *hypothetically* autobiographical character. She is the other of autobiography; she belongs, in other words, to *what could have happened* and not to what has actually happened. Let me explain by means of an example: in *Annie John,* Kincaid's first bildungsroman, Annie, the young protagonist, relates how one day, while she was on the shore watching her mother swim and dive, her view was blocked by three ships going by, and, for a moment, she thought she lost her mother: "After they passed out of view, I turned back to look at my mother, but I could not see her. My eyes searched the small area of water where she should have been, but I could not find her. I stood up and started to call out her name, but no sound would come out of my throat. *A huge black space then opened up in front of me and I fell inside it.*"[106] When she finally managed to see her mother out of the area in which she usually swam, "just sitting and tracing patterns on a large rock," Annie was relieved; nevertheless, she "could not wipe out of her mind the feeling [she] had had when [she] could not find her" and she "kept having a dream about [her] mother sitting on the rock. Over and over [she] would have the dream—only in it [her] mother never came back."[107]

If we are to adhere to the overdeterminedly, autobiographical nature of *Annie John*—a view shared by critics and confirmed by Kincaid herself—we might be warranted to argue that *The Autobiography of My Mother* recasts the complex psychopoetic dynamics of inscribing, confronting, and working through the loss of the mother, this most frightening infantile "nightmare."[108] *The Autobiography of My Mother* is then autobiographical, not in terms of factual reality, but in terms of its psychic remapping of infantile traumas. Let me illustrate this twisted, autobiographical nature with yet another example: it seems to me that the antiheroic negativity of Xuela, whether in her embittered motherlessness or in her loveless sexual relations, is an instance of an "intimate revolt" (Kristeva's notion) against the cultural prescriptions of motherhood and proscriptions of what Gary E. Holcomb calls the "slut identity."[109] In "Girl," the one-sentence story in *At the Bottom of the River,* the speaker (i.e., the mother) enumerates a list of dos and don'ts to her daughter, repeating thrice the prescription against sluthood: "[O]n Sundays try to walk like a lady and not like the slut you are so bent on becoming . . . this is how to hem a dress when you see the hem coming down and so to prevent yourself from looking like the slut I know you are so bent on becoming . . . this is how to behave in the presence of men who don't know you very well, and this way they won't recognize immediately the slut I have warned you against becoming."[110] Xuela walks the uncharted road of social and cultural interdictions. She is proud of having more than one sexual relationship, including an affair with a married man, Roland. Roland's wife calls her "a whore, a slut, a pig, a snake, a viper, a rat, a lowlife, a parasite, and an evil woman," but Xuela remains totally indifferent, constantly in pursuit of pitiless pleasure, regardless of inflicting or suffering pain: "when I [open] my mouth I [can] take in volumes, pleasure and pain, awake or asleep."[111] Gary and Kimberly S. Holcomb have traced the "sadomasochistic" excesses of Xuela's character in terms of the master-slave narrative dialectic, in which Xuela is said to "[alter] the meaning of pain itself from its association with colonial punishment and lust to a means of pleasuring the slave's desiring body."[112] While "pleasuring the slave's desiring body" might ultimately be an instance of the symmetrical return of the dialectic, it is also a form of staging and working through sociocultural proscriptions of sexuality, inculcated in the slave's mind since childhood. Xuela might be the girl in "Girl" who, being so warned against becoming a slut, is tempted and strives to become one: "whatever I was told to hate I loved and loved the most."[113] In the process, an intratextual infantile prohibition is staged and worked through. To conclude this foray into the (intertextually) autobiographical subtleties of *The Autobiography of My Mother,* one can say that, by being a strong and manipulative character, Xuela is perhaps the Lady Macbeth of postcolonial fiction. Not only is the fragility of Annie John and "Girl" completely compensated for, but so is the frailty of most female protagonists of postcolonial literature. Kincaid shows little patience with characters who knuckle under or capitulate without a fight: "[Duras's] women are weak, they are abused, they are crumbling, and, of course, Jean Rhys—her women always crumble—even in the *Wide Sargasso Sea.*"[114]

The vaporous border between autobiography and invention, as well as between memory and imagination, cannot be overstressed: it is, in fact, fiction's (acknowledged or unacknowledged) foundational gesture. My interest in the autobiographical in Kincaid is not limited to tracing its serial manifestations or hidden mutations; it strives to articulate instead the poetic and psychoaffective appropriations that the autobiographical intent actuates and simultaneously dissimulates. The autobiographical intent in *The Autobiography of My Mother* marks the attempt to insert oneself into a personal narrative that exceeds the autobiographical framework and that must thereby appeal to the autobiographical only to unsettle it by the stir (into cognizance) of the otherness located at its very core. Autobiography is a haunted genre of discourse. How can someone *other* than the mother write the autobiography of his or her mother? More precisely, how can the autobiography of the mother be written without the mother? Unless the daughter is also the mother, the one and the other, both and at the same time, can there be such a thing as "the autobiography of my mother"?

This question has perplexed most Kincaidians, such that attempts to demystify it have added to its whiff of mystification. Paravisini-Gebert writes, for instance, that the mother "presides over the text of Xuela's life, of the motherless and childless Xuela whose autobiography is purportedly written (if we are to trust the "My Mother" of the title) by the daughter she so adamantly refused to have."[115] While expressing a vaunted mistrust of the title, Paravisini-Gebert implies that the autobiography of the mother is actually the autobiography of Xuela ("written by the daughter she so adamantly refused to have"), but she does not discuss any further *who* that daughter might be, nor the fact that Xuela did not have any children.

Alison Donnell makes it clear that the title of the novel displays "a playful but incisive disturbance in the accustomed use of language."[116] Attending to this dislocatory force of the title, Donnell goes on to argue, quite rightly, that "this work is not seeking to define itself unproblematically as a piece of life-writing which takes either herself or her mother as its subject, but as a piece which addresses the multiple imbrications of self, m/other and writing."[117] In other words, not only does the novel court speculation about its positioning on the continuum between autobiography and biography, but it also alludes to the inevitability of a collusion and conflation between autobiography and biography. While attentive to the topographical aporetics of the title of the novel, Donnell opts finally to rewrite the "autobiography" of the title as "auto/biography," implying thus that Xuela writes concurrently the biography of her mother and her own autobiography. Donnell devotes much of her argument to rebutting Sinister Wisdom's contention that "[n]o-one should 'speak for' or assume another's voice," such that the writerly slippages—"between mothers and daughters, mothers and mothers, fact and fiction, history and literature, autobiography and biography" that are said to characterize *The Autobiography of My Mother*[118]—are reduced to the possibility of speaking for and representing an other, the possibility of speaking "as" other. The force of Donnell's argument wanes away into an attack on the wardens of the politics of silence: "Happier within the protocols of silence than those of risk, it would appear that most feminist and post-colonial critics have been persuaded away from speaking for others."[119]

While energetically demystifying most feminist and postcolonial dogma, Donnell's argument ends up creating its own dogma: the possibility of "restor(y)ing agency through representing an other."[120] Of course, any such "restor(y)ing" must proceed from the assumption or presupposition that agency exists *prior* to its restor(y)ing and not as an *effect* of such restor(y)ing. This restor(y)ing is in tune with the bifurcation that Donnell entered on the "autobiography" of the title of the novel in order for her to argue for the possibility of autobiography and biography to merge. In other words, Donnell's argument boils down to breaking down the compositeness of the title of the novel—*The Autobiography of My Mother*—in the name of restor(y)ing it back to its former compositeness. While the novel foregrounds its compositeness, Donnell unmakes and remakes it in order to arrive at what she calls a "collaborative subjectivity": "In this autobiography, the 'I' looks backwards and forwards, *identifies subject* and *object, writer* and *teller* in an act of collaborative subjectivity which rewrites the violent individuation of the child."[121] While this description elucidates the mechanics of the act of writing, it glosses over the affective and poetic charge with which such an act is packed. Donnell's argument, however appealing, misses the foundational catachrestic violence and affective abuse with which the very title of the novel is shot through.

The catachrestic force of a title such as *The Autobiography of My Mother* does not reside in the backward and forward identification of subject and object, writer and teller—in the way Donnell understands it—but in the very collapse of the act of identification itself. The crisis of inarticulacy that the title of the novel paradoxically articulates does not brook the Manichean logic or polar system of subject and object in which Donnell attempts to reframe it. The "I" that, in Donnell's words, "looks backwards and forwards, identifies subject and object, writer and teller" is not prior to its catachrestic inauguration. The pairing together, if we are to abide by Donnell's argument, of "I" and "she"—or, more precisely, the violent blending of the mixed modes of autobiography and biography—does not presuppose the separability, much less the later collaboration, of the alleged subject and object; it rather attests to the violence, tension, and abuse in which "subjectivity" is birthed and continues thereby to be perpetually unsettled. Neither "I" nor "she," neither "autobiography" nor "biography," can fully account for the intransigence of the birthing of the child into her mother's death: "My mother died at the moment I was born."[122]

The shock and dislocation of being born at the moment of one's mother's death shatter subjectivity at the very moment of its institution. In other words, Xuela is born, embraced as a subject, at the very moment the unity with her mother, on which subjectivity is predicated, is irrecoverably lost to her. As subject, she is born at the very moment the project of her subjectivity is curtailed, if not utterly abandoned: "How to explain this abandonment, what child can understand it? That attachment, physical and spiritual, *that confusion of who is who,* flesh and flesh, which was absent between my mother and her mother was also absent between my mother and myself, for she died at the moment I was born."[123] The foundational embrace of the mother on whose ruins subjectivity is inaugurated (Freud, *The Ego and the Id*) does not take place, since the mother has now to be embraced, not in her otherwise "good-enough" (Winnicott's notion) presence, but in her very absence. The famous Lacanian troping of subjectivity as lack is doubly weighted here, given that the imaginary phase in which needs are immediately satisfied by a good-enough mother has been denied to Xuela.

The primary (Freud), imaginary (Lacan), or semiotic (Kristeva) unity with the mother does not occur either. Xuela, as subject, is born at the very moment her subjectivity will be irremediably shattered, at the very moment the unity with the mother can no longer be entertained, gradually and steadily, but is suddenly *forced* on her in such a manner as to become identical with "who" she is/was: "Who was I? My mother died at the moment I was born. You are not yet anything at the moment you are born. This fact of my mother dying at the moment I was born became a central motif of my life. *I cannot remember when I first knew this fact of my life, I cannot remember when I did not know this fact of my life;* perhaps it was at the moment I could recognize my own hand, and then again there was never a moment that I can remember when I did not know myself completely."[124] Subjectivity is not *prior* to the mother's death—this "central motif" of Xuela's life—but is, rather, an *effect* of it. In other words, subjectivity is paradoxically enabled by the very event that should have threatened to preempt it. While the loss of the mother occurs at the moment of Xuela's birth, the moment of reckoning with that loss does not take effect right away, but stirs into consciousness at the threshold of subjectivity, in the subject's reflection of/on her infantile nothingness: "You are not anything the moment you are born." The subject is not prior to this loss, but coexists with it in constant renegotiation. I think that there is ample evidence here to warrant the pursuance of a notion of *melancholy subjectivity.* The return of/to the loss of the mother marks the subject-formation of Xuela in that it foments in her, in the words of Freud in the above epigraph, "a mental constellation of revolt, which has then, by a certain process, passed over into the crushed state of melancholia."[125] Xuela, as subject, is not prior to the psychic insurrection of loss and its simultaneous canalization into melancholia. Her memory of who she is is coextensive with her memory of her mother's loss. Xuela is, in Kristeva's well-known idiom, a *sujet en procès*—a subject in process and on trial, both and at the same time. These are the revolting trials of loss and the searing trials of melancholia, both of which inaugurate the process of subject-formation. In other words, Xuela's subjectivity cannot be presupposed separately from her mother's loss—and then arrived at collaboratively, as in Donnell's argument—since it is not prior to that loss. Subjectivity is forged in the smithy of melancholia.

That there is no moment at which Xuela can remember when she did not know this fact of her life—that her mother died at the moment she was born—implies that there is no moment at which she can remember when her life ceased to be her mother's, nor when her autobiography, for that matter, stopped being her mother's. The violence of catachresis, of displacement and transferral, at work in the otherwise unintelligible syntagma that forms the title of the novel *The Autobiography of My Mother*—and of which both Patricia Parker in the above epigraph and Northrop Frye speak[126]—testifies to the violence of the debt wedged in the psyche of the subject at birth. For her very being, Xuela is indebted to her mother; for her, "to be" is nothing but to be in debt.

Xuela is indebted to her mother not only for her own being, but also for her own name: Xuela is also the name of her mother. Her being and her name are one with the inheritance. In *Specters of Marx,* Derrida meditates on the structure of inheritance that constitutes being: "That we *are* heirs does not mean that we *have* or that we *receive* this or that, some inheritance that enriches us one day with this or that, but that *being* of what we are *is* first of all inheritance, whether we like it or not. And that, as Hölderlin said so well, we can only *bear witness* to it. To bear witness would be to bear witness to what we *are* insofar as we *inherit,* and that—here is the circle, here is the chance, or the finitude—we inherit the very thing that allows us to bear witness to it."[127] Xuela inherits the very name and the very body that will allow her, in turn, to bear witness to her inheritance: the inheritance is identical with the means of bearing witness to it. No wonder then that any account of the inheritor proceeds from an account of the inheritance and that any autobiography of the inheritor is an autobiography of the former owner of the inheritance—hence the title: *The Autobiography of My Mother.*

The paradox of the title attests to the melanchologic of catachresis, particularly, the uncoupling of affective investment with hermeneutic mastery. Put differently, the paradox of the title dubs the paradox of postcolonial subjectivity as a paradox of identification, namely, the dissymmetry between the *identification with* and the *identification of* the object of the autobiographical intent. The inability to identify the object manifests itself in the tasteless recourse to catachrestic travesties, to the abuse or improper use of language of which the title of the novel is an exemplum. The identification with the object is, in turn, inaugurated by the tropological enigma to which the subject is heir. "Who was I?" asks Xuela perplexedly, and adds, as if to offer an alibi for this identificatory failure: "My mother died at the moment I was born." This *identifying collapse* does not at all impede the *identificatory investment;* in fact, it sustains and invigorates it. The more the identification with her mother intensifies, the more the need for the identification of the mother becomes overwhelming. It is in the spacing between the (leap of) identification with the mother and the unavailable (or yet to be produced) identification of the mother that *The Autobiography of My Mother,* as a narrative of mourning, has become possible. "I had never known my mother," repeats Xuela again and again, "and yet my love for her followed her into eternity."[128] The space between identifying the mother and identifying with her that narrative mourning cannot completely fill is partly the inscriptional space that coincides with the enigma of melancholic identification: "Who you are is," for Xuela, "a mystery no one can answer, not even you."[129] This space can be called, for want of a better catachresis, the space of identificance, of simultaneous referral to and deferral of the object whose metaphoric mastery is persistently interpellated by catachresis, "the gothic underside of the mastery of metaphor."[130]

In the sustained search for the unidentifiable lost object, the postcolonial subject, as exemplified by Xuela, is prompted to identify with a legacy of loss and grief that has come to shape her identity significantly. This is perhaps the prophetic irony of the play of identificance whose object demands and exceeds inscription. In short, Xuela's melancholy subjectivity is the trope that Kincaid deploys in order to address the living legacy of colonialism and imperialism to which the postcolonial subject is heir. The severe irony is for this subject to claim and articulate a historical loss that dates back to Columbus 1492 and that can neither be constructed nor represented or recuperated, not because of the many flaws of representation, but because the object itself pertains to an experience of loss whose heir never lived through it firsthand, even though she became crucially determined by its effects. Melancholy subjectivity is a compound strategy of claiming and resisting colonial history while *enduring* its falling shadow.

While the poetics and politics of melancholia are indissociable from colonial history, which continues to produce and reproduce postcolonial subjectivity, they nonetheless point toward a socio-politically just future, even if that entails in Kincaid's case the resurrection and exposition of the injustices of the past. In the following chapter, I will stop at the ethical limits of narrative mourning as practiced by Kincaid. I will make use of Derrida's deconstructive interpellations of the Freudian work of mourning in light of the alterity and singularity of the other, who is now situated chiastically both in us and outside us, the locus of an unyielding aporia. I will, in turn, interrogate Derrida's ethical concerns for the other from the perspective of the mourner against the concerns of the mournee, the one who is (being) mourned. Ben Jelloun's thought-provoking novel, *The Last Friend,* points at the limits of an ethics of mourning that does not take into account the wishes of the mournee, only those of the mourner, or those of the mournee as constructed by the mourner. In *The Last Friend,* the mournee is not an absentee. Quite the contrary, he sets the laws of mourning both in his life and from beyond the grave. What unfolds is a counterintuitive account of the laws of friendship and of what I call the challenges of mournership; an ethics of narrative mourning, I will argue, can no longer afford to be oblivious to the wishes of the mournee—a concept that remains almost completely overlooked and unaccounted for in the ensemble of current theoretical, literary, and cultural studies of mourning.

5

The Ineluctable Modality of "Posthumous Infidelity": The Ethics of Mourning in Kincaid, Derrida, and Ben Jelloun

> I became a writer out of desperation, so when I first heard my brother was dying I was familiar with the act of saving myself: I would write about him. I would write about his dying. When I was young, younger than I am now, I started to write about my own life and I came to see that this act saved my life. When I heard about my brother's illness and his dying, I knew, instinctively, that to understand it, or to make an attempt at understanding his dying, and not to die with him, I would write about it.
>
> —Jamaica Kincaid, *My Brother*

> [W]hat I thought impossible, indecent, and unjustifiable, what long ago and more or less secretly and resolutely I had promised myself never to do (out of a concern for rigor or fidelity, if you will, and because it is in this case *too* serious), was to write *following the death,* not after, not long after the death *by returning* to it, but just following the death, *upon or on the occasion of the death,* at the commemorative gatherings and tributes, in the writings "in memory" of those who while living would have been my friends, still present enough to me that some "declaration," indeed some analysis or "study," would seem at that moment completely unbearable (original italics).
>
> —Jacque Derrida, *The Work of Mourning*

THE MAIN PURPOSE OF THIS CHAPTER IS TO REFLECT ON THE INCOMMENSURABLE ethical and therapeutic stakes involved in narrative mourning by staging a dialectical confrontation between the distinct writerly impulses of Kincaid, Derrida, and Ben Jelloun. In an age in which the number of memoirs, testimonies, and autobiographies published has tripled from the 1940s to the 1990s, James Atlas might, after all, be warranted to declare: "The Age of Literary Memoir is Now."[1] While this might be the case, not every memoir that is (or has been) written interrogates its own foundational assumptions, including the very activity of writing in which it is involved and of which it is an effect. While it might serve my purposes well to conjecture right away that we write (following a lived experience of loss, death, trauma, displacement, exile, etc.) in order to mourn, let me start by submitting that we write in the name of justice.

I have no intention here to use the word "justice" in the legalistic or universalistic tradition from Kant to Rawls (i.e., distributive justice), in which there is always the lingering potentiality that the rights of a group of people or of one single person might readily be compromised in order for the system of justice to operate. Moreover, it is beyond the scope of this chapter to pursue the veracity of certain controversial memoirs, and mull over, for instance, the scandal that Rigoberta Menchú's, *I, Rigoberta Menchú: An Indian Woman in Guatemala,* or Norma Khouri's, *Honor Lost: Love and Death in Modern-Day Jordan,* have both created separately; nor is it my purpose to bring into my discussion memoirs of civil wars, genocides, holocaust survivors, exiles, honor killings, and so on, although the secondary material I draw upon is inflected by just such discussions. This is not to say, of course, that what I propose here cannot be brought to bear on the more historical and collective narratives of witnessing and remembrance. I choose to start, however, at the level of what Freud calls "family romance," even while perfectly aware that the drama of family relations in Kincaid, for instance, is but an allegory for life under the duress of colonial rule and its postcolonial proxies. I believe that a grassroots reflection on narrative mourning within the intimate space of family (and friends) is sufficiently complex to offer theoretical insights into the more inchoate narratives that bear witness to collective and/or translocal scenes of victimization and suffering in a postcolonial and global context (note, though, that I will come back to these issues in the following, last chapter, which focuses on a Lebanese civil war novel).

My speculation on the notion of justice in tandem with the dyad of mourning and writing stems primarily from Derrida's essay "Force of Law," in which he contends that, unlike law, justice is an indeconstructible concept. While the law—or, to be more precise, the text of the law—is always marked by a fringe of open texture that warrants its future rewriting and perfectibility, justice is that for the sake of which the deconstruction of the law is undertaken in the first place.[2] In other words, the urgency to improve the law, to deconstruct it, is always carried out in the service of ensuring justice, of tending more toward justice, of being *more* just.[3] While justice remains the overriding concept—that in the name of which we deconstruct—both law and justice are in point of fact indissociable in the sense that the perpetual transformation of the law is necessarily predicated upon the contingency of justice. It is in this spacing, in this interstitial disjuncture between the law and the demand for its change (a change of which a more just idea of justice is the driving force) that the concept of justice can be seen as inherently aporetic, as urgently insistent yet always inadequate to the case at hand. All the more so when what is at stake are, in H. L. A. Hart's parlance, "hard" or "penumbra" cases, cases for which we have no precedent, as opposed to "core" or "easy" cases, for which a precedent exists.[4] This makes it, in turn, all the more urgent to reiterate that not only must we demand (that) justice (prevail), we should also perennially raise the threshold of justice by intuiting or discerning the latencies of injustice in every presentist manifestation or application of justice. Since the demand for justice is *infinite,* the justness of justice must constitute in the final analysis no less than a *claim* to justice. The thirst for justice necessitates, perhaps, the deliberate endorsement of a cynically objectivist attitude of a sort that holds that every present justice is but a future injustice. These futuristic leanings should constitute neither utopic portals nor dystopic evacuations of justice but open invitations to the theater of infinite rehearsal, as Wilson Harris would put it.[5]

It is from within this theater that I intend to explore the interrogation marks —namely, the ethical pressures for an ever-perfectible concept of justice—that cluster thick and fast around the question of narrative mourning, of writing oneself to mourning following the death of a relative (Kincaid) or a friend (Derrida and Ben Jelloun). In the absence of a constitution, of a body of laws that would regulate the relations between the living and the dead and between the mourner and the mournee, such a relation (such a case, if we are warranted to construct it as a case of law and justice) registers a vacuum in what Freud would call the forward thrust of civilization. It is a universal lacuna that presents itself with an abiding insistence after every single death, pressuring the mourner to invent his own laws of relationality with the dead. In the absence of precedent, and, really, because there will never be one *just* enough to be emulated, every narrative mourning must therefore engage its thematics in the process of exploring and formulating its axiomatics, its laws and poetics of mourning.

The necessity of reflecting on the rules that must govern our relations with the dead originates primarily in the contention that death—far from being an end—is precisely an interruption. In his largely aphoristic and genre-unspecific book, *Interruptions* (*Unterbrechungen*), Hans-Jost Frey argues that death, to the extent that one survives it, does not constitute an end, only a break or an interruption of that which (i.e., a relation) can no longer be completed, and must therefore live on as mourning: "What stops in such a way that one loses it while it comes to an end is not completed. If it had been completed it would *be.* What stops without having been completed can no longer become what it would have liked to, could have or should have become. The hope of completion ends with the end. The end of hope survives as mourning."[6] This interruption (that is death) ushers us into an infinite relationship with the dead. The relationship is infinite because, since it broke off, it can no longer find the end, or the finitude of which death is normally the harbinger. The end becomes that which is infinitely left behind, that which is irreversibly missed, and that in relation to which we are irrecoverably belated. Philosophically, mourning is the modality under which that which stops—in such a way that it can no longer be finished—survives.

Such a modality of mourning bespeaks Freud's by now familiar concept of melancholia, which feeds on the failure to burn the bridges with the lost love-object. For Freud, mourning, it bears repeating, is only a temporal and phenomenological process of reestablishing the mastery of the conscious after the dizzying rupture introduced by the loss of a love-object. In other words, mourning is the reparative work that aims to suture the affective fissure opened up by the loss of the object-cathexis. Psychoanalytically, as well as ritualistically, then, mourning is the modality under which that which stops in such a way that it is lost is buried. Such a ritualistic, literal, and affective burial (in the sense of the withdrawal and redistribution of libidinal energies in accordance with the commandments of reality and with the economy of libidinal management) of the lost object leaves in its wake a lot of interrogation marks, a whole panoply of ethical disquietudes. Preeminent among these worries has to do precisely with the responsibility for the other, which Derrida, following Levinas, locates at the very heart of justice, and at the very heart of any de rigueur philosophical engagement with alterity and altermourning.

Derrida does not hesitate to reject and stigmatize this therapeutically driven mourning in favor of a more ethically nuanced, heteropathically interpellated, and spatially enduring conceptualization of mourning. If mourning is the law that governs psychoanalysis and ensures its validity, it is also the law that undercuts any hope for a more just renegotiation of our relations with the dead. Any ego-syntonic and ego-consolatory investment in mourning is, in terms of the de-ontological ethics of Levinas, nothing but a betrayal of the other, that in the face of whom one stands humbly, now and forever. If Levinas's ethics is a journey beyond being, an ethics of the otherwise than being, it is also, as Derrida's appropriations make clear, an ethics beyond the egology of cure, which Freud's mourning institutes. Psychoanalysis, laboring under the auspices of analytical couch therapy, seems, in the hands of deconstruction, to speed irresistibly toward its limits, where its vocabulary, concerned with the pursuance of recovery, falls short of meeting the exigencies of the ethics of alterity. Ethically, mourning is the modality under which that which stops—in such a way that it leaves us while it lives on in us—is preserved in its infinite transcendence.

As my two epigraphs make clear, in what follows I engage with writing as an *exemplum* of mourning. I have no intention here to establish writing or narrative as the *paradigm* for mourning, for, for those who *write themselves to mourning,* it seems impossible to do otherwise; for those who do not, it seems impossible to do so. That writing is a work *at* mourning means also that writing is a work *in* mourning. The written text, what I call *narrative mourning,* must therefore constitute a symptom of mourning even though it is the process whereby that symptom is staged, confronted, and even overcome. One of the major characteristics of narrative mourning is that it tends incessantly to slip away from the theme of mourning into the affective structure of mourning from within which the attempt to grasp that theme is made in the first place. The narrative reflection on mourning is so entangled in the cobwebs of mourning that it cannot escape becoming hostage to its inflections. In other words, we witness in these texts a surprising confluence between theme and symptom. Narrative mourning is the symptom of that of which it is the theme.

To the extent that mourning is the law, to the extent that writing is the law of that law, justice is what these concentric circles of law, or mise en abyme of laws, are destined for; justice is what they are answerable to. To the extent that justice is that in the name of which we deconstruct the law, I propose to deconstruct the mode of deployment or application of these laws in the narratives of mourning produced by Kincaid, Derrida, and Ben Jelloun insofar as these narratives swirl concentrically and even obsessively around a single problematic—signifying loss. Such operation—deconstruction—will have made clear the limits of narratives of mourning, namely the inadequate or disproportionate nature of those narratives vis-à-vis the infinite responsibility for the other in the name of whose justice they are produced. Narrative mourning is inscribed, in my view, in a space it cannot fully accommodate and has therefore to be done and not done, both and at the same time, for can narrative desire carry within it, intrinsically so, the obliterating desire for silence? Narrative mourning begins, I argue, where its limits will have been reached.

Mourning Becomes Case History

> As a rule intermediate links have died out and are known to us only through reconstruction.
>
> —Freud, *Civilization and its Discontents*

While Kincaid's fiction is strongly autobiographical, her 1997 *My Brother* on the AIDS-related death of her brother is memoir proper, the second nonfiction work after *A Small Place,* her devastating indictment of the Antiguan tourism industry and neocolonial servitude. This memoir comes to bear witness to her brother's contraction of HIV and his subsequent death. Writing it, Kincaid has faced a lot of challenges and risked too much, such that it is hard (for us as much as it is for her now) to adjudicate fully whether this is a literary triumph or ethical failure, a petty settlement of family matters, or a raid on the enduring colonial legacy. Perhaps, to say that this memoir is all of these at once and none of them specifically might be the strongest possible approximation of a just characterization. I will explain what I mean by this as I move on, but I am most interested here in the ethical issues that this memoir raises—or fails to raise for that matter. While I do not purport or intend to lead a legalistic inquiry into the validity and veracity of Kincaid's factual congeries, I nonetheless think that a reflection on the ethical stakes involved in writing after the death of the other is incumbent upon any critical endeavor. Wither the responsibility for the other in the act of mournfulfillingly writing his memoir?

Before I address this question, a number of observations are in order. Let me stress at the outset that *My Brother* can be seen as a testimonial to Kincaid's brother's life, dying, and death only insofar as it is subject to the laws of historiographical and analytical construction. As Hayden White made patently clear, narrating necessarily involves a measure of "emplotment," which I understand in terms of the writer's liberty to select, foreground or background, and refract the events of what might have, objectively speaking, constituted a chronicle.[7] Simply put, Kincaid's memoir must first be understood as a narrative construction whose form and design is inseparable from its substance.[8] Having said that, I do not intend to perform here a formal analysis of its structure—however unavoidable that might be—but I do find its form and content bearing a number of striking resemblances to the form and content of Freud's case histories. While it might, of course, be said to lack the manifestly psychoanalytic outlook of Freud's case histories, the scientific language of *My Brother* and its many detours into the pharmacological discourse of AIDS makes the aforementioned difference with Freud's case histories more of an echo than a difference.

I find it particularly worth exploring that Kincaid, whose *Lucy* protagonist is referred to as "Dr. Freud," dwells on childhood memories in her very attempt to "understand" the death of her brother. As such, this memoir, this otherwise than memoir (i.e., case history), cannot escape the loop of construction and reconstruction of the past in order to exploit its latencies in the service of illuminating the present, or in the service of accomplishing the painful task of mourning. Kincaid's grappling with the childhood history of her brother reminds us, then, of Freud's case histories, and of Freud's attempt to arrive *analytically* at the point—the primal scene (*Urszene*)—at which any given patient's adult illness might have started. Freud's work on the Wolf Man case history, "From the History of an Infantile Neurosis" (1918), relies heavily on the presupposition of a primal scene, a *coitus a tergo* of some sort, and on the technique of reconstruction as an entranceway into that primal scene. While in *Civilization and Its Discontents,* he pointed out the importance of reconstruction, as in the above epigraph,[9] it was not until years later, with the publication of "Constructions in Analysis" (1937), that Freud addressed what might be called the construction principle in psychoanalysis: "The analyst has neither experienced nor repressed any of the material under consideration; his task cannot be to remember anything. What then *is* his task? His task is to make out what has been forgotten from the traces which it has left behind or, more accurately, to *construct* it. . . . His work of construction, or, if it is preferred, of reconstruction, resembles to a great extent an archaeologist's excavation of some dwelling-place that has been destroyed and buried or of some ancient edifice."[10] While the analyst might resemble an archaeologist in his reliance on the traces of the past, his constructions stand, in my view, at two removes from those of the archaeologist, not only in the sense that the analyst posits a primal scene before having it, but also in the sense that his constructions rely, if we are to disregard the open-ended flow of supplementation, on traces that are themselves oftentimes more of constructions than verifiable or factual memories.

In "Screen Memories" (1925), Freud insists that childhood memories cannot be traced back to an accurate past, but are formed at the moment they are remembered: "It may indeed be questioned whether we have any memories at all *from* our childhood: memories *relating to* our childhood may be all that we possess. Our childhood memories show us our earliest years not as they were but as they appeared at the later periods when the memories were aroused. In these periods of arousal, the childhood memories did not, as people are accustomed to say, *emerge;* they were *formed* at that time. And a number of motives, with no concern for historical accuracy, had a part in forming them, as well as in the selection of the memories themselves."[11] Of course, we are accustomed to Freud's impulsive hesitations, painstaking perfectionism, and nuanced revisionism, which combine to create a whiff of mystery that Freud would thereof feel the urge and urgency of demystifying, whether by means of supplementing his earlier theories or by venturing into new directions altogether. Freud's disquietudes about the interpretive conclusions of his analyses—and about the necessity of ever perfecting and rectifying those conclusions—derive from the unbridgeable gap between the conditions of seriality and supplementarity of his theories and his aspirations to brand the stamp of scientificity on psychoanalysis. In writing his case histories, for instance, Freud was constantly overwhelmed and distressed by the literary outlook of his otherwise scientific treatises.[12] Of course, while such a worry would not normally be expected to weigh too much on the activity of an imaginative writer like Kincaid, it nonetheless, and quite surprisingly, ripples throughout the whole narrative, as if to register stealthily yet steadily a claim to scientificity—a claim to loss, vindication, and redemption.[13]

While Kincaid does not exactly deploy the scientific logic á la Freudienne as an absolute conceptual framework, she nonetheless elaborates a proximate modality that will enable her to *understand analytically* her brother's AIDS-related death as a case history in which the hypothesis of the primal scene plays a central role. As Ashraf Rushdy persuasively argues—and, indeed, *pace* Freud—"the primal scene need not be sexual; it need only be of such significance that an individual would recollect that episode, and not another, at the crucial moment when driven to re-evaluate her or his life."[14] In this sense, the primal scene is a transformational, generative event whose effect cannot be fathomed separately from its retrospective, interpretive reconstruction. Given the temporal disjuncture between the empirical experience and its deferred narrative inscription, it should be safe to add right away that the primal scene emerges at the crossroads of verifiable history and scribal contingency. Instituted by and within this temporal differential, the primal scene is not fully immune to the pitfalls of Mnemosyne, to misprisions and misconstructions, as well as to the intrusions of fantasy and the encroachments of the present of narrative with its compelling dynamics of expediency and exigency. All of these elements of the primal scene play a significant role in Kincaid's memoir.

Kincaid's complex, interwoven narrative threads constantly re-turn to a reflection on two defining events in her brother's infantile history: the first refers to the episode with the "army of red ants" and the second to the episode of her "brother's hardened stool." The first episode will refer us to her mother, who planted the okra trees, the safe haven of the red ants; the second will refer us to Kincaid herself who—when left by her mother in charge of her brother Devon, then two years old—immerses herself in reading and neglects to change his soiled and hardened diaper. As Ned Lukacher suggests, "the earlier event is still to some extent the cause of the later event, the earlier event is nevertheless also the effect of the later event."[15] Lukacher adds, "What the primal scene establishes is that at the origin one discovers not a single event that transpires in one temporal sequence but a constellation of events that transpire in several discrete temporal sequences."[16] Devon's AIDS-related death should then be understood as the (allegorical) product of a constellation of events that, while grounded in family history, nonetheless conjures up colonial and neocolonial history. The red ants are harbingers of a bad omen; they attacked her brother when he was less than a day old: "They crawled up some okra trees that she [her mother] had planted too near the house and . . . went from the okra trees through a window onto the bed in which he [Devon] and my mother lay."[17] In drawing our attention to this foundational episode, Kincaid wants to understand whether it somewhat presaged his present attack by HIV, "whether it had any meaning that some small red things had almost killed him from the outside shortly after he was born and that now some small things were killing him from the inside," and whether, by implication, her mother might be found guilty for her brother's AIDS-related death. Kincaid then adds, "I don't believe it has any meaning, this is something a mind like mine would think about."[18]

This episode might not, of course, have any immediate bearing on her brother's attack by HIV, yet the fact that it is the kind of memory that her mother would have wanted to thrust into oblivion elevates it to the stature of the primal scene. After all, it was her mother who planted the okra trees, which then served as a military base from which the red ants mounted their surprise guerrilla attack on the less-than-a-day-old Devon Drew, Kincaid's youngest brother. Guilt-stricken, Kincaid's mother "tore up the okra trees, roots and all, and threw them away."[19] Her mother becomes all the more responsible for her brother's fate if we remember that in "Girl," the shortest story from *At the Bot-*

tom of the River, she is the one who warns her daughter not to grow okra trees near the house: "this is how you grow okra—far from the house, because okra tree harbors red ants."[20] While this episode might not justifiably be constructed as a retrospective prolepsis of sorts for her brother's attack by HIV, it is nonetheless thinkable since testimony qua testimony speaks, as Derrida goes on to argue in *Monolingualism of the Other,* precisely to the unbelievable: "For one can *testify* only to the unbelievable . . . to what must be believed all the same, whether believable or not."[21]

Whether or not Kincaid's dramatization here of a "hermeneutics of suspicion" and of a poetics of "free association"—in the service of weaving a master narrative, a relation of causality that must have determined her brother's life from the beginning—is illuminating or mystifying is no more important than the calculation of whether or not Kincaid herself had had a hand in the tragic unfolding of such a narrative, of whether or not she could be found guilty for the negligence of her two-year-old brother when her mother left him in her charge. This is the second central event in her brother's infantile history, which Kincaid discusses toward the end of her memoir, as if to imply in a sigh of resignation that all her repressive energies have by then been depleted. This episode relates how Jamaica—then called Elaine—was left in charge of her younger brother, and how she soon became too absorbed in reading stolen books to be able to notice and then change her brother's soiled diaper. As a result of this utter neglect, the deposit of stool that soiled her brother's diaper, "had hardened and taken the shape of a measure of weight [signifying a pound]."[22] Reflecting on the significance of this episode and trying to retrospectively connect it, in a Forsterian ("only connect") gesture, to the unfolding of her family's future, Kincaid writes: "And in it, this picture of my brother's hardened stool, a memory, a moment of my own life is frozen; for his diaper sagged with a weight that was not gold but its opposite, a weight whose value would not bring us good fortune, a weight that only emphasized our family's despair: our fortunes, our prospects were not more than the contents of my brother's diaper, and the contents were only shit."[23] Perhaps it is not surprising in the least that the handmaiden of Mnemosyne can recollect and inscribe this "rememory," yet the glitteringly masochistic, scandalously lucid, and grotesquely revolting prose of this confession verges on a poetics of self-exposure, of precisely luxuriating in or enjoying the exposure of one's symptoms (as in Freud, Lacan, and Žižek). Perhaps whoever succumbs to the cruelty of memory, to its pounding weight—and to the shattering vocation of sense-making and the hermeneutic task of constructing and reconstructing on the shores of logic a sense of a life that is no more—has to necessarily develop a taste for enjoying his or her symptoms, for only then can the symptom, that which is necessarily humiliating, be "remade," as Kincaid herself suggests, "into art."[24]

The case history logic of Freud is all the more important here for a very specific reason (for which Freud would have, perhaps, worried only in the case of the failure of countertransference, which would open, more confirmedly, the floodgates of interminable analysis, as is the case with his most notorious patient, the Wolf Man):[25] Kincaid wants to establish, directly or indirectly, the extent to which she participated in or contributed to her brother's, and by extension to her family's, later misfortune. I am not suggesting that Kincaid is responsible—through sheer neglect—for sowing the seeds of a structure of bad lot for her brother and for her family, no more than I am suggesting that the nature of the confessional is structured by the avowal of guilt and the demand for expiation, and that guilt must have always insinuated itself into the calculating structure of the confessional. One might contemplate, as Derrida does in *The Work of Mourning,* whether the confession and the parallel expiation of guilt (after the death of the other to whom such confession should be made in the first place) is not an opportunistic calculation that leaves the mourner in an ethically unenviable position.[26] When Kincaid writes that "a memory, a moment of my own life is frozen" in the episode of her brother's hardened stool, one cannot simply slough off the latencies of guilt that run through the very fabric of this heart-wrenching image; nor would one want to free the narrative of *My Brother* completely, as Sarah Brophy seems to suggest, from a "compensatory guilt" in which it is nevertheless bathed.[27] Contrary to what Brophy would have us believe, the fact that Kincaid did not take care of her brother then and for more than twenty years after serves to foment the sense of guilt of which narrative is not only a symptom but also an effect and, potentially, an expiatory force.

Moreover, not only is the hardened stool episode at the origin of her thenceforth troubled relationship with her mother, it is also the episode at the origin of the multiplication and dissemination of guilt: her mother has responded to her neglect of her brother by gathering all her books and setting them on fire, thus traumatizing her in the process: "What I felt when this happened, the exact moment of the burning of my books, what I felt after this happened, the burning of my books, immediately after it happened, shortly after it happened, long after it happened, I do not know, I cannot now remember. In fact, I did not even remember that it happened at all, it had no place in the many horrible events that I could recite to friends, or the many horrible events that shaped and gave life to the thing I was to become, a writer."[28] The fluid and dizzying repetitions bear witness to Kincaid's reliving of this infantile trauma again and again. It is always the law in trauma (Freud, Caruth, Laub) that one does not attend to while living through it: no wonder, then, that Kincaid did not even remember whether it had actually happened. This is not a case in which memories emerge, but one in which, as in Freud's "Screen Memories," they are formed and lived through for the first time at the moment they seem to emerge anew. Perhaps Kincaid's suggestive image of "a frozen moment," like the image of the "open wound" in the previous chapter, is a more or less adequate description of an otherwise unmappable traumatic experience. It is always the law in trauma that repetition is first time—that the traumatic situation does not allow the subject caught in it to step outside of it in order to bear witness or testify to it; what cannot be experienced as it happens has recourse to the vaporous vault of the *Zeitlos,* the timeless, and is therefore destined, in a fleeting moment, to break on the seamlessness of consciousness in such a manner that it is experienced for the first time (given that the *very* first time could not have been remembered and located in the past). I will speak at length in the following chapter about trauma and repetition, suffice it to mention here that the peculiarity of a traumatic experience is, in the words of Caruth, that "it simultaneously defies and demands our witness."[29] The eye of the victim cannot, in other words, be interpellated by the (inscriptional/transcriptional) eye of the witness, unless belatedly and after a period of latency.[30] In the same manner, Kincaid's adolescent traumatic experience—the burning of her books—could not have offered itself immediately, at the time of its occurrence, to the indexical repartition of consciousness, but must have flitted by it or slipped through it into the reservoir of forgetting—or, more accurately, into *l'oubli de reserve.*[31] Writing it now, reliving through it now after a long latency period, is thus the modality under which Kincaid not only bears witness to it, but also experiences and works through it for the first time.[32] "The historical power of the trauma is not just that the experience is repeated after its forgetting, but that it is only in and through its inherent forgetting that it is *first* experienced at all."[33]

As we continue to read her brother's memoir, we cannot fail to feel Kincaid's relentless insertion of her own autobiography into her brother's biography. The victimization of her brother, for which she is partly responsible, is juxtaposed dialectically to her subsequent victimization, for which her mother is responsible. She is a victim, no more than her brother; her mother is responsible, no more than her. The narrative is, however, structured in such a way as to map the victimhood of her brother into her own victimhood. It is as if Kincaid is more worried about her autotopography, about her subject-positioning vis-à-vis her brother, rather than about her responsibility for writing her brother's biography. Thus, while Sarah Brophy contends that *My Brother* is "written out of the interruption of the autobiographical I" and "through self-annihilation,"[34] I suggest the reverse position: that the memoir stages rather than represses the interpellative resurgences of the autobiographical "I." In other words, what starts off as a biographical narrative becomes exceedingly the scene of recurrent slides into autobiography. Given that toward the end of the narrative the slide into autobiography becomes ubiquitous, it is perhaps more accurate to suggest that *My Brother* is an autobiographical narrative written in the veneer of the biographical. Whether liminally located at the threshold of the autobiographical or under the shadow of the biographical, or vice versa, narrative mourning reaches its limits the moment it clears its inscriptional space of possibility.

This is not a matter of praising or blaming Kincaid for what she cannot help doing: writing herself into (her brother's) life. It becomes, however, a matter of ethical concern as soon as we start to get the sense that Kincaid is writing out of an egotropological concern, a concern for troping her recovery, a concern for writing as a trope of *survivance* or survival. *My Brother* is, one might think, about Kincaid's unwitting or willing location in a narrative that is nevertheless explicitly addressed to the other—*My Brother.* It is my intention in what follows to continue to register more ethical reservations on this voluntary or involuntary encroachment of the autobiographical on a scene of writing archly set in motion by the biographical. My aim is not so much to mark the limits at which writing must stop or be abandoned as to show how those limits, which must have always been trespassed as soon as writing began, are dealt with, if at all, throughout narrative.

THE ETHICS OF MOURNING

> If you understand the other you have never encountered him.
> —Hans-Jost Frey, *Interruptions*

If Frey is right, Kincaid should have renounced rather than nurtured the desire to understand her brother.[35] On learning about her brother's terminable illness and dying, however, Kincaid decided right away to write about it in order to "understand" it. Of course, such an undertaking is a privileged one: Kincaid indefatigably reminds us that her brother cannot write, let alone write like Kincaid. In her most recent novel about her father, *Mr. Potter,* her protagonist revels in the knowledge that she alone, of all of Mr. Potter's daughters, can read and write. The seductive rhetoric that permeates Kincaid's fiction is that, in accepting to write about those who cannot write (here, I am not necessarily suggesting that Kincaid can be said to have adopted the role of "the native informant"), it is as if Kincaid had stoically and resignedly accepted to carry a burden, a weighty vocation that she was not particularly happy to carry. In her early fiction (*Annie John* and *Lucy*), we often come across references and allusions to a formless weighty substance she carries within her—a substance she can neither comprehend nor disregard.

Regardless of whether it is a burden, a duty, or an asset, writing, Kincaid insists, is for her a matter of life and death. In an interview with Moira Ferguson, she goes as far as to assert, "I had to write or I would have died."[36] Indeed, were one to cite every published interview conducted by several scholars (such as Moira Ferguson, Selwyn R. Cudjoe, Frank Birbalsingh, and Brad

Goldfarb, to name only a few) with Jamaica Kincaid over the years, chances are one would find variations (sometimes, within the same interview) on a now typically Kincaidian formula: writing = life. Writing is here understood in a very loose sense, but that is not the purpose of my argument: I am only concerned with narrative mourning (of which *My Brother* is, of course, an exemplum). While most writing is more or less undergirded by a structure of mourning, writing after the death of a relative, as is the case with Kincaid here, must be mourning proper. Kincaid does it instinctively, as if it were a matter of doing what comes naturally.

In *My Brother,* writing amounts to nothing less than an Aladdin-like magical lamp that would instantaneously concretize recovery-promises. Arrayed in the armor of writing, Kincaid sees herself as a much more competent person at handling grief than, for instance, her husband: "My husband is someone I love. . . . I would rather bad things or unpleasant things happen to me . . . then I don't have to worry about him. And then again, I believe that I am *better* at handling bad things than he."[37] While in her most recent novel, *Mr. Potter,* writing is presented as a catalytic refrain—"I can read and I can write"—in a song of jubilation and intellectual triumphalism, in *My Brother,* it is mostly understood as a prophylactic recipe for self-preservation, much like the special obeah baths she used to take when young or the "little black sachet filled with things" she used to wear under her shirt.[38]

It comes as no surprise that Kincaid made the following statement when she heard about her brother's illness and dying: "When I heard about my brother's illness and his dying, I knew, *instinctively,* that to *understand* it, or to make an attempt at understanding his dying, and *not to die with him,* I would write about it."[39] The italicized words of this quote indicate the interrelated nodes of the following discussion on the ethical demerits of Kincaid's most endeared practice—writing—in the aftermath of her brother's death. The adverb "instinctively" implies that writing is but a behavioral praxeme in league with other instincts of conduct and self-preservation. Likewise, "to understand" and "not to die with him" are two convergent courses of action subsumable under the modality of self-preservative instincts, except that, while "to understand" conveys a will to hermeneutic mastery, "not to die with him" implies a will to repression, the repression of the death instincts writ large.

That writing following the death of her brother is perceived as an instinctive response to such an event means that mourning presents itself to Kincaid as a demand for writing. To say that mourning presents itself as a demand for writing is not, however, to say that writing satisfies that demand. In other words, the satisfaction of the demand for writing is not necessarily accompanied by the fulfillment of the demand for mourning. In *My Brother,* however, because the demand for mourning and the demand for writing converge on the pages of the book, it is normally hard to speculate on whether writing marks the persistence of an impossible mourning beyond the closure of the book or whether writing testifies to the fulfillment of the work of mourning in the very instance of confronting it on the page. We do not here need to make another detour into trauma studies or into the plethora of psychoanalytic theories that insist on the coterminous relation between writing and mourning, for Kincaid argues with great conviction that writing, following the death of her brother, allows her to accomplish just that. How does writing, which presents itself as a response to the demand for mourning, satisfy mourning?

When Kincaid draws the connection between writing and understanding, between understanding and mourning, and between mourning and survival, she is, perhaps intuitively, alluding to the complex hermeneutic and psychoanalytic machine that knits together these otherwise different demands. Since in Kristeva's axiom "when meaning shatters, life no longer matters,"[40] it is not for nothing that Kincaid insists on establishing meaning, on extracting the meaning of her brother's life by setting herself the "instinctive" task of writing (on) it. The search for meaning, for understanding what happened to her (and to her family) after the death of her brother is indissociable, it bears repeating, from the search for the affective closure of mourning. The closure would not take place unless the relationship with the dead relative is severed. And in order for the work of severance to be effective, it has to be founded on a massive work of remembering and working through. Since writing can bear the burden of the clearly "incompossible" (to use a Derridean neologism—a blending of incompatibility and impossibility)[41] demands of the work of remembrance and the work of severance—the work of hypercathecting and subsequent decathecting—it is understandable why Kincaid instinctively seeks shelter in the soft balm of words.

Writing, we realize bit by bit, is mapped into Kincaid's system of defense mechanisms and thus becomes more of an instinct, as Kincaid herself is wont to say, than a function of competence and high learning. Indeed, in her interview with Ferguson, Kincaid reiterates that she is not from a literary caste or class, that she is not interested in writing as an exercise of class, only in writing as an urgent form of self-rescue and survival.[42] Yet the therapoetic urgency with which the demand for mourning (a demand that immediately translates as a demand for writing) presents itself is comparable only to the ethical urgency with which the demand for alterity (a demand that immediately translates as a demand for sustaining, not severing, relations with the other) demands that the demand for mourning be annulled. There is no getting around the phenomenological fact that death introduces a dreadfully asymmetrical power relation between the mourner and the deceased. Whether one should "let the dead bury the dead" or whether one should bury them by oneself, the accomplishment of the task of mourning is also the burning of the last bridge that can otherwise make possible an infinite relation with the dead.[43] Mourning is the second burial.

Through its expansive presentist and self-preservative concerns, through its inscription of an emergence from the shadow of the object (biography) onto the threshold of the subject (autobiography), and through its hermeneutic search for semantic and affective closure, *My Brother* can be suspected of actuating the second burial of its main protagonist in whose name it is written. The primal gesture of an ethics of mourning would start by letting the dead speak, by conferring a voice and a face on the dead, that is, by a prosopopoeic embrace—a citational immersion. Kincaid is, however, too threatened by the reificatory implications ("not to die with him") of the prosopopoeic conferral of voice that she hardly cites her brother; when she does, she puts his words between quotation marks and also between brackets, as if they were "the okra trees" in relation to the house of fiction, and have to be quarantined lest they should contaminate the salubrious and artistic narrative Kincaid weaves.

It is not that Devon does not, much less cannot, speak, but that his language is unintelligible to Kincaid herself. In *Monolingualism of the Other* and "Force of Law," Derrida insists that the hospitability of justice requires that we speak to the other in his language, and that we open up, in the spirit of deconstruction, to the illiteracy and inarticulacy of the subaltern. Yet Kincaid is too uncannily alienated from the language of the island to be able to reproduce or understand it, let alone address someone in it. In this respect, most critics have expressed their dissatisfaction with the ways in which Kincaid fails to reproduce the language of the people of the island.[44] In the context of our discussion of an ethics of mourning, this failure is consequential and significant: it has a bearing on the question of justice, however persuasively it might be condoned on artistic or historical grounds, namely, that Kincaid associates the uncouth language of the island with the language of humiliation and colonial legacy. This is certainly not a question of whether the subaltern can or cannot speak but one of whether we are able to attend to what he says, whether we are able to reproduce what he says. Having said that, the question is also, I think, riven with incommensurable considerations (artistic, political, or individual), and can neither be reduced to the inscrutability of the subaltern, or to the transparency of the "native informant" but remains archly subject to the exigencies or adhocracies of the act of writing.

Kincaid's whole project of writing the memoir is to understand the death of her brother, to confer a sense of wholeness and establish relations of causality between his death and his (infantile) history, yet what is there to "understand" if Kincaid insists on and on that she cannot understand the language of her brother, the language she used to speak, the language of humiliation? Unless the hermeneutic will to understand is understood as a will to mastery, a will to (semantic and affective) closure—and by implication as a fear of the unmasterable, a fear of the latent petrifying threat of any prosopopoeic ethical embrace, a fear that translates ultimately as a will to repression ("and not to die with him"), a will to mourning—unless thus understood, the will to understand, to which *My Brother* testifies, is only a *demand.* But when the demand for mourning translates, in an almost automated way, as is the case with Kincaid, as a demand for writing, how can we be sure that the demand for mourning is not satisfied in the process of writing? How can we be sure that the demand for writing is not subtended by the work of severance rather than of connectivity? Or can the demand for understanding—that which is a demand for writing—thwart the demand for mourning? Can writing defend against the fulfillment of mourning for the sake of sustaining the relation to the deceased or the queer subaltern, as is the case with Kincaid's brother? Can writing institute silence while breaking it? These are some of the questions that will preoccupy me as I head toward a discussion of Derrida's narratives of mourning.

We can now begin to grasp the manner in which narrative mourning must be inhabited by the guilt of which it is an effect. For what is *to write oneself to mourning* if it is not, in many respects, *to write oneself to forgetting?* To write oneself to mourning means to dispose of the other in the service of the disposition to writing; the other no longer lives in me but is purged out of me into writing; the other is displaced from the interiority of the mourner into the exteriority of the text: not only is Devon's privacy and dignity travestied[45] but so also is his desire to be mourned—that desire to which two (or more) lovers or relatives must have always contracted each other (or themselves). Wither such a contract in the act of writing? Does writing annul the contract to/of mourning (by fulfilling mourning) or reinforce it by maintaining the relationality of mourning? Are not libidinal and cathectic contracts always secret and brooking no public disclosure? This is the aporia, the master trope of the ethics of narrative mourning: to contract oneself to mourning is one thing; to accomplish mourning is quite another thing altogether. Respecting the contract implies devoting oneself to a life task of mourning. Yet, the logic of mourning itself, its phenomeno*logic,* demands the cooperation and empathy of a secondary witness—it demands a homeopathic public expression of grief and solidarity. For Freud, the Mitscherliches, and Santner, among others, mourning is a public performance, a sociocultural ritual. It is, in other words, the exteriorization of mourning that is thought to make possible the interior refurbishing and sustainability of the psyche. Such expression, however, must break at the threshold of the reneging of the secret contract to interminable mourning.

The Anxiety of Mourning

> I believe that the activities of thought have another vocation: that of bearing witness to *differends.*
>
> —Jean-François Lyotard, *Political Writings*

> Speaking frightens me because, by never saying enough, I also say too much.
> —Jacques Derrida, *Writing and Difference*

The question of mourning ripples throughout Derrida's oeuvre to the extent that it would have been redundant for him to write a book about it. Be that as it may, the collection of essays, *The Work of Mourning,* manifests a sustained reflection on the intricacies and the implications of or, indeed, the stakes involved in the work of mourning (*le travail de deuil*). I say "reflection" because it is in the nature of reflection not to know a priori the object of its reflection, because it is in the nature of reflection not to stop at the provisional knowledge it might reach about the object of its reflection, and, finally, because it is in the nature of reflection to renew, again and again, its work whenever the demand for more reflection presents itself, as it surely does following the singular death of a friend. "Reflection," Lyotard intones, "requires that you watch out for occurrences, that you don't already know what's happening. It leaves open the question: *Is it happening?*"[46] Since *The Work of Mourning* consists of a collection of writings that range from letters of condolences and memorial essays to eulogies and funeral orations—which Derrida wrote throughout almost two decades on a pantheon of French and American intellectuals in the event of their death(s)—it is better understood as a serial endeavor that raises the question of mourning at the moment of working through it. Yet this body of writings reflects (on) the question of mourning in the negative (of its occurrence), as if by sidestepping or overstepping and occluding its internal workings, all the while refuting the existence of a metalanguage of mourning.

What is at stake in *The Work of Mourning* is the search for an ever-fresh and singular idiom whereby to bear witness to the singular death of each of the deceased friends, including Roland Barthes, Michel Foucault, Louis Althusser, Gilles Deleuze, and Jean-François Lyotard, to name only a few. Not unlike the logic of signature, which is predicated on the coexistence of singularity and repetition, the logic of mourning requires that a new language, a singular language, be invented for each new occurrence, for each repetition of mourning. Can we therefore invent as many languages of mourning as the people we will have to mourn? Or is there only one language of mourning that is not promiscuous and that cannot be used more than once? In other words, how can we mourn again (repetition), each time afresh (singularity)? This is also the consuming anxiety that lies at the very core of Auden's elegy for Sigmund Freud: "When there are so many we shall have to mourn, / when grief has been made so public, and exposed / to the critique of a whole epoch / the frailty of our conscience and anguish, / of whom shall we speak?"[47] The fact that "there are so many we shall have to mourn" threatens not only to make the act of mourning a monotonous and tedious ritual, but also to render the very language of mourning obsolete and stale because of overuse. That "there are so many we shall have to mourn," and that the plurality of deaths must not be confused with the singularity of each mourning, makes us indeed wonder in a mixture of resignation and anxiety, "of whom shall we speak?" That "there are so many we shall have to mourn" makes speaking of one single person an effort traversed by an autonomous desire to speak of everyone else, and eventually of no one in particular. There is always in the act of speaking (for the purpose of mourning) an unwittingly endless slippage from mourning *one* single death into the mourning, or anticipation, of *other* innumerable deaths such that it becomes utterly embarrassing to speak at all.

What I call the anxiety of mourning has to do then with the nature of the language of mourning—a language that cannot be singular enough to do justice to the singularity of each death. There at the very heart of every singular language of mourning lies an excess of plurality, that is, an underlying structural intent to multiply the gestures and to disseminate the act of mourning, as in the Derrida epigraph above.[48] The anxiety of mourning is, in an overtly Derridean fashion, an anxiety about the *singular plural* nature of language, and about the inevitable sliding of address from the singular to the plural. This anxiety intensifies over the irresistible surge of the work of mourning toward emotional closure and triumphal survival. It is not for nothing that Derrida wants to steer clear of the clinical and psychoanalytic understanding of mourning, and ultimately to dispel the hold such an understanding—promoted in or disguised under the name of cure—has come to cast over the ethics of the work of mourning. Indeed, to the initiator of the discourse of psychoanalysis as well as to his disciples, Derrida raises a fundamental question that seeks ultimately to redefine the notion, or motto, of "successful mourning." For Derrida, if so-called successful mourning means the piecemeal libidinal withdrawal and reinvestment of cathexes from one object to another (Freud) or the total introjection and assimilation of the other within (Abraham and Torok), then mourning has necessarily to fail, for failure alone can be apt enough to embody its success.

Mourning is here carved out and elaborated in such a way as to become a deconstructive lexeme, in a league with such other concepts as *différance* and *supplementarity.* Thus, in mourning Louis Marin, Derrida asserts that "whoever thus works *at* the work of mourning learns the impossible—and that mourning is interminable. Inconsolable. Irreconcilable."[49] And he goes on to hammer home this unsettling ethical contention as follows: "You will also understand, for this is the law, the law of mourning, and the law of the law, always in mourning, that it would have to fail in order to succeed. In order to succeed, it would well have to *fail,* to fail *well.* It would well have to fail, for this is what has to be so, in failing *well.* That is what would have to be. And while it is always promised, it will never be assured" (144, original italics). Derrida tries to find, at the crossroads of philosophy and ethics, answers to the question of mourning—a question that is, in fact, more of a paradox that asks of us, on the one hand, to mourn sine die and cautions us, on the other hand, that no matter how rigorously we persevere in our work of mourning, we will not be able to obviate the ineluctable modality of infidelity. Granted that mourning is indeed interminable—and that the ethics of alterity must resist its seductive affective seal in the service of opening or keeping open the wound of attachment to the deceased, even at the risk of narcissistic mortifications—whence the infidelity?

The championing of a kind of infinite mourning seems to follow from the recognition, the resilient acceptance, of the other's infinite alterity, of the other's irreducible difference, as much as of his or her indigestibility. Clearly, what is at issue here is the degree to which one must melancholically incorporate the other within: although Derrida doesn't address the question of proportionality between mourning and melancholia, one can safely conjecture that the degree of interiorization of the other inside us has to be *in proportion* to the degree to which his difference and alterity are respected. "The one who looks at us in us—and *for whom* we are—is no longer; he is completely other, infinitely other, as he has always been, and death has more than ever entrusted him, given him over, distanced him in this infinite alterity" (161).

Thus, incorporation, or the degree of incorporation to which Derrida concedes, does not encourage a melancholy identification with or wholesale appropriation of the other under the all-engulfing *me,* but strives respectfully to allow the other his infinite alterity and irreducible contrapuntality, both of which are operative in the act of interiorization itself, in the very geometry and dissymmetry of the gaze, and in the very conjuration of the name of the dead. Already in every act of appropriation, assimilation, interiorization, and mastery, there is a kernel, nucleus, grain of resistance, and contrapuntal element that aims at demastering, at resisting the tendency to homogenize and the penchant for devouring the dead. The other remains, therefore, near and yet far, immanent and yet infinitely transcendent, inside and yet outside, within and yet beyond—"Far away in us" (161)—"within us but . . . not ours" (44) such that we remain, Derrida provocatively contends, "Together apart" (224).

To submit to the laws of mourning, as popularized by psychoanalysis, is tantamount to dialectizing a death that Roland Barthes called "undialectical," that is, unsublatable, irresolvable (47). Spotting a thought-provoking phrase—*il n'y aura pas de deuil*—by Lyotard, Derrida goes on exploring and disentangling all its threads and ramifications, only to conclude more emphatically than Lyotard, more laconically but no less tellingly, "No mourning, period" (218). Taking on yet another phrase about the fear of "the worse than death" (222)—a phrase that Lyotard had previously spotted in Adorno—Derrida seems to propound that what is worse than death is precisely the suggestion that death comes to put an unsurpassable end to any kind of communication, dialogue, with the dead: what is worse than death, to be more specific, is the tendency to translate the *finitude* that death instantiates into the *finitude* of the *infinite.* Death ushers us into infinity, and from a finite relationship with the other we move into an infinite relationship with him, a relationship watched over by interiorization and infinite transcendence; what is worse than death, then, is the impossibility of such a readjustment, of such a renegotiation in terms of the in-finite; precisely, what is worse than death is the possibility of successfully accomplishing the task of mourning, the possibility of forgetting, or burying, the name of the dead once and for all. "In the case of 'Auschwitz' [what is] 'worse than death,' . . . is the extinction of the very name that forbids mourning, given that this murder of the name constitutes the very meaning of the order 'die,' or 'that he die,' or even 'that I die'" (237). In order to preclude such a fatality—the end of the infinite—mourning has to continue, and the illusion of a point at which it has to be successfully accomplished has to be banished into the dustbin of the unethical and the unfaithful.

For Derrida, the work of mourning is already at work as soon as friendship begins, if not earlier, and the interruption of death should by no means grind it to a halt: "When friendship begins before friendship, it touches upon death, indeed, *it is born in mourning*" (123, italics mine). Friendship is structured, from the outset, by a degree of a priori mourning, a degree of interiorization, of identification, which must have coincided, before the last death, with every previous nomination, with every instance in which the name of the friend is uttered—the name that not only conjures up the singular death of the friend whose name is called, but also multiplies it infinitely every time it is uttered, making it "singular plural": mourning will have begun as soon as the "interiority (of the other in me, in you, in us) had already begun its work. With the first nomination, it preceded death as another death would have done. The name alone makes possible the plurality of deaths" (46).

Yet, notwithstanding this altruistic attitude and unsparing loyalty to the deceased friend, Derrida is still depressingly uncomfortable with the potentially travestying implications of any attempt (whether in speech or writing) to reckon with the deceased, any attempt to recognize and acknowledge our debt to them since any such attempt will necessarily have been born in an unbearable and tasteless act of infidelity. When it comes to determining our relationship, our bond, to the deceased, the daunting question for Derrida is: "How to leave him alone without abandoning him?" (225). This question bespeaks the intransigent paradox of mourning and the poetics of aporia on which it hinges: whatever way you choose to go in order to remain faithful to the departed friend, you would have to perch on the edge of a vast, seemingly bottomless abyss, where the slippage into infidelity is almost ineluctable. Can one, therefore, mourn enough (for not having mourned enough)?

The anxiety of mourning is, it must have become clear, an anxiety *over* mourning. Not only can one not mourn enough, but one cannot even preclude the political implications of the very work of mourning. Such implications have to do with the notion of heritage, legacy, and, above all, with debt, whose very recognition is too entangled with its annulment to allow for any modus vivendi. For Derrida the recognition of debt threatens to neutralize the debt by purporting or pretending, as it were, to have paid it back in the very act of naming, counting, enumerating, and taking stock of it. Furthermore, to acknowledge the debt in the pursuance of forgiveness is an even more travestying act, for from whom (if not from the "without power" but not "without force") are we asking forgiveness when we ask forgiveness from the dead, and in so doing, aren't we just lured by the thought, which belies an illusion, that expiation will follow, and aren't we in the final analysis more concerned about the *me* that has survived the death of the other rather than the we, the he in me, the he outside of me?

We are thus, in front of all these rhetorical questions, lured into a tangled jungle of difficulties and aporias that weigh heavily on the *conscience* of the faithful (friend). In the face of this ineluctable infidelity that the act of acknowledging one's debt to the deceased has come overwhelmingly to imply, there remain only shimmers of redemption—a redemption that the wistful consciousness cannot completely earn even through sacrifice. These narratives of mourning are, one can begin to recognize gradually, haunted by the anxiety of their birth, by the anxiety of their *writing*—an anxiety they face, measure themselves against, and, to a certain extent, obviate through a constant and indefatigable reassuring promise that they are not written yet, that they cannot be written now, and that they will be written in the future. Throughout these eulogies, time and again, Derrida insists that he does not have "the heart to relate stories or to deliver a eulogy," and that "there would be too much to say and [it] is not the right time" (114). Thus, the act of writing, reckoning, and inconsolable mourning, whose flip side is a potential infidelity, has to be done and not done, and thwarted at the same time it is desired—infinitely rehearsed. To write, or not to write—only in foiling one infidelity against the other, can one redeem, albeit slightly, the ineluctable "posthumous infidelity" (16) to which every mourner is heir. This action of writing and not writing—of fulfilling and renewing the promise of writing—has to be rehearsed, it bears repeating, on the stage of interminable mourning. Writing neither fulfills nor undermines mourning but restores it into eternity.

Reflecting (on) the inevitable infidelities inherent in any work of mourning (here, it is the mourning of Roland Barthes that is at stake), Derrida writes:

> Two infidelities, an impossible choice: on the one hand, not to say anything that comes back to oneself, to one's own voice, to remain silent, or at the very least to let oneself be accompanied or preceded in counterpoint by the friend's voice. Thus, out of zealous devotion or gratitude, out of approbation as well, to be content with just quoting, with just accompanying that which more or less directly comes back or returns to the other, to let him speak, to efface oneself in front of and to follow his speech, and to do so right in front of him. But this excess of fidelity would end up saying and exchanging nothing. It returns to death. It points to death, sending

> death back to death. On the other hand, by avoiding all quotation, all identification, all rapprochements even, so that what is addressed to or spoken of Roland Barthes truly comes from the other, from the living friend, one risks making him disappear again, as if one could add more death to death and thus indecently pluralize it. We are left then with having to do and not do both at once, with having to correct one infidelity by the other. (45)

Following the death of the other, one is inevitably left to court one of these two infidelities: either to write on (i.e., cite, repeat the words of, and confess one's guilt to) the other—and therefore "disfigure," "wound," or "reduce"—or to remain silent and therefore "put to sleep" or "kill" the other for the millionth time (44). One finds him- or herself either on the threshold of the former or under the shadow of the latter and has therefore to play the one against the other, in the hope that one might ultimately correct one through the other. Such hope must be sought in the face of its impossibility; it must be sought in the Lyotardian uncertainty of the *Is it happening?* Ultimately, the imperative to mourn translates as an irreparative performative.

There is no getting around these two infidelities, this "double wound" (44), which the death of the other pressures us into committing. While for Kincaid writing following the death of her brother is more or less a question *of* mourning, in the name of which a plethora of rescue tropes are deployed, for Derrida writing is more of a question *about* mourning and indeed an anxiety over mourning; it is, more accurately, a question addressed *to* mourning, to its economy and discontinuous temporality. One can here build on Lyotard's reflections on the ability to speak and the inability to speak in the service of reaching generic statements about the differences between Kincaid's and Derrida's narratives of mourning. Not to mourn is part of the ability to mourn since ability, according to Lyotard, "is a possibility and a possibility implies something and its opposite."[50] To be unable to mourn is not, however, the same as to be able not to mourn. The former can be seen as a deprivation and the latter as a negation. To be unable to mourn is, by the same token, not the same as to be unable not to mourn. The former is, of course, a deprivation, but the latter can be seen as an instinctive impulse of the order of "I can't help mourning." Given this distinction, we can conjecture that while Kincaid is unable not to mourn, Derrida is able not to mourn.

Derrida wants to slip through the intransigencies of the Scylla of writing and the Charybdis of not writing following the death of a friend; he thus ambivalently tries to take a line of flight that paradoxically enables him to evade the very activity (i.e., duty) he is engaged in. Derrida stops at the threshold of writing and on the verge of articulation; all he manages to pen down is, as it were, nothing more than the promise of a return to writing, or so he wants to have us believe. Since writing amounts to insulting the other as much as the voluntary forbearance from writing threatens to kill him for the second time, writing can only emanate from a space in which the writing subject is too invested in the promise of writing to invest enough stamina in the accomplishment: "To go on speaking of this all alone, after the death of the other, to sketch out the least conjecture or risk the least interpretation, feels to me like an endless insult or wound—and yet also a duty, a duty toward him. Yet I will not be able to carry it out, at least not right here. Always the promise of return."[51] That writing is a promise implies that mourning is also a promise: after all, it is only following the death of the other that a number of interrogations begin to cluster thick around the pertinence of writing as a mode of mourning. Only by asking the question *about* mourning can one decide whether or not to dwell in it, whether or not the narrative mode vehicles the ethical concerns of the mourning subject.

Narrative must question its foundational presuppositions; it must give utterance to its metanarrative; that is, it must question its own practice. As Derrida insists, we deconstruct in order to achieve justice. We deconstruct the law; that is, we improve it in order to guarantee justice. So to improve the law is precisely to deconstruct perpetually, not for the sake of deconstruction but for the sake of justice, of a more inclusive and worldly form of justice. What might that law be in relation to the death of the other? It is nothing but the law of mourning, which since Freud, according to Derrida, has been unjust, thus allowing an unethical privileging of the survivor over the deceased. To ensure justice, it is incumbent upon the living to deconstruct and perfect the law of relationality—the law of mourning—that gathers them together apart with the dead. The law of mourning, as a law of relationality, emerges therefore in the spacing (*espacement*) between the promise (of mourning) that urges us to tend ever so pressingly toward justice and the deconstructable figures of possibility that are meant to continually flesh out the promise. That the law of mourning is a deconstructable figure of relationality implies, by the same token, that narrative—whose subsumption under the law of mourning cannot be overstressed—is also as deconstructable.

Narrative is the law of the law. It is governed by the law of mourning—that which is the law of relationality. To the extent that narrative functions under the jurisdiction of mourning, it cannot escape the affective refractivity that permeates mourning. In this respect, narrative can be deconstructed in terms of the affective inroads it opens up in view of an ever perfectible, ever just relation with the dead. To be able to see, for instance, the ways in which narrative carries the potential of paying back a debt at the very moment of registering or acknowledging it does not so much make us despair as entice us to demand the impossible. To the extent that the demand for the impossible opens up horizons of the possible, it is far from being a mere utopian whistling. To the extent that the deconstruction of narrative generates enthusiasm about new idioms—new ways of expression and new ways of relating to those who remain captives in our idioms—it is a laudable task.

Narrative mourning is the field of force in which the asymmetry between the living and the dead is played out in the idiom of the former. It is, therefore, in Lyotard's idiom, a "case of differend" precisely because "the 'regulation' of the conflict that opposes [or gathers] them [the living and the dead] is done in the idiom of one of the parties [the living] while the wrong suffered by the other [the dead] is not signified in that idiom."[52] In this respect, can Devon Drew lodge a complaint—a cri de coeur that would bear witness to what Douglas Crimp, for instance, calls "the terrible vulnerability" or "frailty" of being human,[53] of which the stark fact that AIDS has claimed the lives of the best and most accomplished intellectuals of our times is testimony? More precisely, can he lodge this very cri de coeur in his sister's narrative (of his life and death), and can that *cri* survive the refractive idiom of his sister? Even if Kincaid's narrative speaks to this *cri,* it cannot justly echo it. This *cri* must finally mark the limits of the narrative's imaginative inventiveness. While it must be phrased, this *cri* cannot find utterance. To inscribe it is to *mis*take its insistence for an appeal-to-framedness, an appeal-to-phrasedness. Not to inscribe it is to run the risk of thrusting it into oblivion. Narrative mourning is born in the spacing or interval between the mourning duties (Derrida) or mourning urgencies (Kincaid) incumbent upon the mourner and the continually deconstructable and perfectible laws of mourning. This narrative does well to recognize and bear witness to the differends that animate it. But that this narrative must be bedeviled by the taint of posthumous infidelity is no more lamentable a fact than the indefatigable search for a better justice. It is in this spirit that I now turn my critical gaze to Tahar Ben Jelloun's *The Last Friend.* In it, the very ethics of narrative mourning reach their limits, and we find ourselves, once more, in front of the poetics of aporia that characterize the business of mourning.

The Challenges of Mournership

> One must outlive the other. . . . One must go first.
> —Joyce, *Ulysses*

In *The Last Friend* (*Le dernier ami*), Taher Ben Jelloun, the Moroccan francophone novelist, poet, and essayist, confronts us with the limits, if not the vicissitudes, of the ethics of mourning, and further compounds our anxiety over mourning. This may prompt some to ask whether a pure ethics of mourning is even desirable when the mournee seeks to spare the mourner the very experience of mourning. It is precisely the challenges of the mournee that I want to examine, though, because they are quite simply the challenges of mournership insofar as friendship in the novel is mediated by mournership. Mournership is the name I give to an ethics of relationality and sociocultural intelligibility inaugurated by a constellation of collective and individual interdependencies in which mourning occupies pride of place. Given that the laws of mourning are perfectible, mournership remains a contingent and negotiable relation between the mournee and the mourner. The importance of *The Last Friend* rests in its dramatization of the voice of the mournee. So far, the voice of the mournee has been, as I have shown, absent in Kincaid's memoir; it is present in Derrida's essays but only as a series of citations. Both Kincaid and Derrida are variably limited by the perspective of the mourner. Ben Jelloun's novel reactivates the voice of the mournee but is not limited by it; the novel also dramatizes the voice of the mourner and of the secondary witness.

Suffering from lung cancer and certain about the approach of his death, Mamed, one of Ben Jelloun's two protagonists, decides to abandon his life and work in Sweden to return to his hometown, Tangier, Morocco, to die quietly during the final stages of his illness. In the meanwhile, Mamed gradually but steadily does something else, something surprising, counterintuitive, and perplexing, something that at first glance amounts to nothing less than the coldest betrayal of friendship imaginable: he breaks his friendship with Ali, his lifelong friend (for more than three decades). What is more, in order to swiftly dissolve their bond, he goes as far as to plot and to accuse Ali of taking advantage of their friendship to embezzle him of his hard-earned money (which Mamed sent to Ali from Sweden so that the latter buys him furniture for his newly bought apartment in Tangier). Ali is not only a childhood friend but someone on whom Mamed had always counted, someone with whom he went to school, engaged in leftist politics, which led to their brutal imprisonment and torture in the disciplinary camps of El Hajeb and later Ahermemoun for eighteen months and fourteen days before they were ultimately released. Ali and Mamed stood by each other throughout their carefree university days, revolutionary activist engagements, their college years in France and Canada, and their marriages to women whose jealousy disturbed their friendship. Throughout their disparate careers, and particularly following Mamed's emigration to Sweden to take up a job at the World Health Organization as a pulmonary specialist, their friendship matured and remained so solid and so steady through regular visits and correspondences that it would seem as unthinkable as needless to break it.

The polyphonic narrative structure of *The Last Friend* is so well interwoven that it easily misleads the reader into believing that Mamed is a monster, an ethically irresponsible friend, even a turncoat of sorts, an egoistic and singular beast whose wretched jealousy (of the exemplary devotion of Ali to the bond of friendship) proves more fatal than lung cancer. And so we are led to believe that Mamed "discovered within [himself] a capacity for perversion, a diabolical imagination and a sick pleasure in toying with the emotions of the people [he] loved."[54] Mamed, we are led to believe, "had to stage a breakup with Ali, pick a fight to ruin everything."[55] Verily, Mamed "was in the process of extending [his] hand to the devil. Was [he] doing it out of an excess of goodness? It was more likely weakness, cruelty, selfishness."[56] It is too early to judge, perhaps impossible to judge tout court. What is startlingly alarming, however, is that even though Mamed is self-conscious of the "cruel charade" he initiated,[57] he can't help being surprised to find out how well he can play the game and even derive some pleasure from it, as if the charade were in fact the materialization of a secret fantasy that came to lift up a flap of the veil on the condition of enmity that structures friendship: "I was playing my role," Mamed tells us, "I felt strong. It was curious, the extent to which provoking this dispute with Ali was boosting my energy. . . . It was as if he had become an enemy."[58] It is as if the mask, "harsh about-face,"[59] or antic disposition, so to speak, that Mamed did put on was, indeed, his true face all along; it is as if the real face were already a mask. For no sooner did Mamed put on the harsh about-face, he became capable of expressing himself freely, of creatively imagining and executing the scenario of their fallout with disaffected mastery, intransigence, and cruelty, as if he were indeed doing what comes naturally.

While the theatrical, but intensely staged breakup seems at first an ethically irresponsible and hardly justifiable act, we begin to realize that it originates in Mamed's hallucinatory and counterintuitive desire to protect his friendship with Ali "from the tragedy of death."[60] While Mamed might have friendship's best interests in mind, Ali is kept in the dark about Mamed's intent; he is led instead to contemplate the precipitating causes of Mamed's abstinence, resurrecting, hypercathecting, and deconstructing every little detail, every little event, memory, or misunderstanding that might have triggered the devastating rift; and so he wonders to himself, "Perhaps he wants me to preserve the image of a lively, happy Mamed, at peace with himself. Or maybe he's angry with me. But why? Because I will outlive him? Could it be that simple? No, Mamed isn't like that. I can't believe it."[61] Strange as it is, this hypothesis—that is, that Mamed might just be engineering a self-protective rift before dying to preempt Ali's triumphant survival after his death—is resonant with what goes on in Mamed's head. Indeed, a reassuring interior voice tells Mamed, "He will survive you, he will continue to live out your friendship in sorrow."[62] Friendship begins to sound like a battlefield governed by power duels between, as in the Joyce epigraph above, the "One [who] must outlive the other" and the "One who must go first."[63] As will become clear, what is remarkable about Ben Jelloun's spellbinding novel is the role that the mournee, Mamed, comes to play in the renegotiation and refashioning of the relations between the mourner and the deceased. Since the "mournee" is largely an undertheorized concept in the theories of mourning from Freud to Derrida, it might be beneficial to ask at the outset, how does the mournee mourn?

In what follows, I will formulate partial answers to this question and examine their political implications and above all their challenges to an ethics of mournership, that is, an ethics of relationality between the mourner and deceased, which has so far, especially in Derrida's work, been theorized exclusively from the perspective of the mourner. The posthumous letter that Mamed wrote to Ali provides a good entranceway into our discussion of the mournee, namely, his ethics of mourning. The letter is worth quoting in its entirety, but I will only cite a series of excerpts:

> Ali . . .
> From the day when I first grasped the seriousness of my illness, I wanted to spare you. . . . You see, I'm your friend, and I did for you what I would have liked you to do for me, had a fatal illness had the temerity to attack you. . . . I had this idea when I was at my lowest, at a time when I had not yet realized that death is part of life, and that when we leave life, we should not punish those who survive us. I knew better than most that death is really the illness, not the actual moment when everything stops. What is death? The long days, the interminable nights of insomnia, when pain bores its mark into your body until you lose consciousness. . . . Death is the test results, the numbers, the speculation about the unknown. Death is the silence, the frightening abyss we watch approaching us.[64]

While Mamed might at first sight seem very naive about his understanding of mourning, not realizing that mourning must have already begun once friendship began, there is more to his observations than sheer naïveté: clearly, Mamed wants to spare Ali, not the ineluctability of his death, which would be impossible, but his dying experience, the evolution of his illness, the degradation of his health, the trials of living on borrowed time, and the anxieties of journeying to the unknown. Yet, granted that Mamed wanted to be cruel only to be kind, almost like Hamlet in relation to Ophelia, doesn't the staged breakup add insult to injury and therefore further aggrieve rather than relieve Ali? Let's read on:

> I could not spare my wife and children this grief. But I could spare you, simply by provoking an argument, by questioning your honesty, which I knew to be your most sensitive point. . . . By detaching you from our friendship, I was pushing you away from my death, hoping you could turn the page. . . . Above all, I wanted to avoid having to share my death with you, because I know what you are like. You would have been there, living through every moment of the progression of this damn disease; you would have been at my side and, waiting with me to the end; and I would have had to read the approach of darkness in your eyes. You were a mirror I could not bear to look into, out of weakness, wounded pride, and, I have to confess, perhaps out of a terrible jealousy unworthy of our friendship.[65]

Mamed's argument here is twofold: he wants to spare Ali the grief of his illness and dying and also spare himself Ali's grief—not that Ali's grief would be excessive or anything, but that it would be dictated by the exemplarity of his friendship. Ali's exemplary grief would have made Mamed's dying unbearable, not only because it would confront him diurnally with his own inevitable death, but also because it would confront him with the demand that he die and mourn himself dying every single time he sees Ali and reads the approach of darkness in his eyes. Above all, Ali's exemplary grief would double Mamed's grief insofar as Mamed would also, and in the spirit of friendship, have to mourn Ali mourning him. In other words, not only would Mamed have to mourn himself as he lays/lies dying (automourning)—and he would have to do that repetitively, every time anew, following every encounter with Ali—but he would also have to mourn Ali himself for mourning him (heteromourning or altermourning). What would complicate things further for Mamed is the exemplarity of Ali's grief, which would make Mamed as envious, as guilty of his inadequacy and unworthiness of Ali's grief and friendship. He already confesses in the beginning of the letter that he would have done exactly the same of what he asked Ali to do had Ali been the one who had cancer. In other words, Mamed would have steered clear from Ali had Ali succumbed to incurable illness.

Mamed's character is perhaps reminiscent of James Duffy and Gabriel Conroy and of their attempted foreclosure of mourning. Like them, and insofar as the twists and turns of love relations are no different from those of friendship, Mamed wants to forgo grief, not because it is uncalled for, but precisely because it is inevitable in his case. Paradoxically, however, his posthumous letter to Ali contains one clear will—friendship—and another implied will, as it were: grief. Here is how the letter ends:

> I have found our rupture hard to endure. Many times, I almost flew back to Tangier to tell you what I had done. I never had the courage, and then it was too late. I believed in my decision, and I couldn't take it back. When I seemed to be angry with you, talking about the bills for the apartment, I worked hard to be believable, using all my talents as an actor to pull it off. I needed the strength of my conviction.
>
> Now, I return to you your due. Our friendship was a great and beautiful adventure. It does not end with my death. It remains a part of the life you will continue to live [*Elle fait partie de toi vivant*].[66]

Under what and whose signature will this friendship continue to reverberate in Ali's life? Obviously, it remains paradoxically livable, sustainable, or signifiable only in mourning and under Mamed's signature. It will have become clear by now that Mamed leaves or wills Ali the very thing he wanted to spare him in the first place, the very thing he wanted to spare himself—that is, grief or, precisely, the scenes of grief, its transformational and generative energies. Indeed, it will have become equally clear that Mamed's legacy for Ali is the legacy of mournership—a friendship, a relationship, a union, a community, a homosociality, and a sociality intelligible only through the psychodynamics of mourning—really, the apostrophic or prosopopoeic dialectic *and* continuum of absence and presence, the absence and presence of the other, the posthumous Mamed speaking from beyond the grave, in the pages of the letter and in the folds of a friendship yet to come. It is as if friendship is only a threshold moment, something that can be lived wholly only posthumously, only through posthumous fidelity (i.e., fidelity to the infidel mournee). The posthumous temporality of mournership is thus the litmus test of friendship, the condition of the well and full functioning of friendship, really its ultimate test, period.

While it occasions fruitful reflections on the notion of mournership, Mamed's logic is liable to the inconsistencies endemic to his positioning as a mournee, that is, as the one who must go first and be outlived by Ali. For one thing, Mamed could be seen as *ethically irresponsible:* he plots against his friend, questions his honesty, and brusquely and unjustifiably breaks up with him. For another, he can be seen as *irresponsibly ethical:* he betrays friendship in order to perfect it; that is, he breaks up with Ali in order to allow him to rediscover, explore, and sustain their friendship in and throughout his absence, an absence that is mediated by the virtual presence of the posthumous letter. As a result, Mamed could be seen to have faulted Ali on two counts: he not only positions him as the *losable* (i.e., disposable and ungrievable) object, which is the performative effect of the staged breakup, but, above all, he places himself in such a way as to assume the position of the unlosable object par excellence, which is the performative effect of the posthumous letter.

This line of inquiry makes it perhaps impossible not to read Mamed's inconsistencies in terms of an allegory of postcolonial nationhood. Given the enduring legacy of their past leftist activism in postcolonial Morocco—in which the pro-Western monarch, King Hassan II, consolidated his rule over an overawed population by repressing freedom of expression and suppressing dissent—Ali and Mamed turned their backs on national politics as soon as they were released from prison, got married, and were too entangled in their disparate daily lives and careers to engage again in politics. It could be argued that they are simply two failed old lefties, and that since they fell out in their politics, it was destined that they would fall out in their friendship, especially that Mamed, who initiated the breakup, has never quite recovered from the inedible marks the experience of jail and torture has left on his psyche. In their two different reemplotments of the events that they lived through together, Mamed lingers more than Ali on their political involvement and their imprisonment, which could mean that by breaking up with Ali, by betraying their friendship, Mamed was in fact reenacting the greater betrayal of the postcolonial state (which he must have in turn internalized).

This line of inquiry would make it impossible not to segue into the semi-autobiographical nature of *The Last Friend.* Like Ali, Ben Jelloun was born in Fez and then moved with his family to Tangier. Like Ali and Mamed, Ben Jelloun studied in a French high school in Tangier, and like them he was arrested in 1966 with ninety-four others following his involvement in the student demonstrations of 1965 in Rabat, and, like them, he was also sent to the disciplinary camps of El Hajeb and Ahermemou for eighteen months. It was in those camps that Ben Jelloun read Joyce's *Ulysses* and started writing. Like Ali, Ben Jelloun is a professor of philosophy and, like him, he was once betrayed by his translator and friend for years, Egi Voletranni, over a pirated Italian edition of one of his books. The novel thus engages with different layers of memory and mourning. A friendship that has become alienated and alienating is Ben Jelloun's verdict on postcolonial Morocco, whose sovereignty, inaugurated and sustained by the jealous dedication of its citizens, has become dysfunctional and punishing.

Like Joyce's, Kincaid's, Freud's, and Derrida's disparate writings, *The Last Friend* is narrative mourning at large. Unlike any of them, it delves into the limits of an ethics of impossible mourning. Particularly, it mobilizes the concept of the mournee in such a way as to register some reservations on an ethics of impossible mourning exclusively constructed from the perspective of the mourner, the survivor of the deceased other. If the mourner must be inconsolable in his mourning for the deceased other, as Derrida argues, would that be of any consolation to the mournee? If the mourner ought to do his best to spare the deceased other the finality of forgetting (i.e., the worse than death), the mournee ought to, by the same token, do his best to spare the survivor the gravities of grief. And if mourning has to fail to succeed, so does friendship.

The narrative structure of *The Last Friend* and the chiastic organization of the viewpoint is an allegory of the work of mourning as advanced in this book and ultimately an allegory of mournership insofar as allegory does not exclusively correspond to an established reality but points insistently to a reality to come (as will become patently clear in the following and final chapter). The story is narrated by both Ali and Mamed, and so we get to have the perspective of each one of them and their different refractions of the same events and their views of each other. This dialectic of narration and perception seems soon to surge toward a synthesis when Ramon, their mutual friend, steps into the penultimate part of the novel to give the reader his disinterested take on the events and on the relationship between Mamed and Ali in general. However, the last part of the novel, the posthumous letter, upsets the dialectic and reinitiates a new one. In other words, the dialectic remains unresolved. Likewise, mourning presents itself as a persistent thrust for emotional closure only to be upset by the inconsolability of the mourning subject.

What Derrida's legacy of an ethics (or aporetics) of impossible mourning tends to produce is generally a philosophical *anxiety* over the question of mourning qua question, not qua experience. The intellectualization of mourning threatens, however, much like the litany of televised spectacles of public mourning, to desensitize us to the suffering of others and to thereby deny us the transformational effects of experiencing mourning, which might reach, as

I demonstrated in my reading of Joyce, empiphanic proportions. Derrida's reluctance to recognize this particular transformational validity of Freud's concept of mourning might ultimately heighten rather than diminish the general ahistoricity of our triumphantly consumerist society. Moreover, while richly empowering, an ethics of impossible mourning à la Derrida and Levinas (under whose influences a plethora of recent studies were produced) does not take into account the challenges of mournership, which are the challenges of the mournee, ethical, political, or personal.

Besides foregrounding the particular relevance of rethinking our mourning practices in terms of the eclectic insights of Joyce, Freud, Kincaid, and Derrida, I have so far emphasized the transformational and generative aspects of mourning in its entangled relation to melancholia as a condition of mourning (Freud), of empiphany, suicide, or mania (Joyce and Freud), of heterodestructive violence (Fanon), of postcolonial subjectivity (Kincaid), or as a condition of ethics and critical dissent (Derrida). The challenges of mournership that the mournee presents us with in *The Last Friend* are in no small measure the challenges of a poetics of mourning whose revolutionizing effects must have always taken the subject by surprise and transformed him in the process. Ali says the following of Mamed's letter: "It was a letter intended to destroy me. The signature was my friend Mamed's. There was no doubt about it. Mamed, my last friend."[67] The letter is pure poetics of suddenness! It prompts Ali to rearrange his mourning practices vis-à-vis Mamed in the spirit of mournership, given that friendship had already been lost. The mournee must have already spoken and the mourner must have already been transformed. The challenges of mournership are the challenges of reckoning with our *mutually* human rather than *dueling* vulnerabilities. It is in this spirit that I now turn to examine further the relevance of a poetics of vulnerability to a rethinking of both subjectivity and community in contexts of extreme violence in our globalized and globalizing contemporaneity. Elias Khoury's abstract and experimental novel, *City Gates,* will help us round out our exploration of a general poetics of narrative mourning by confronting us with the particular poetics of narrative trauma.

6

Formless Form: Elias Khoury's *City Gates* and the Poetics of Trauma

History, said Stephen, is a nightmare from which I am trying to awake.
—James Joyce, *Ulysses*

IN *REFRACTIONS OF VIOLENCE,* MARTIN JAY CONTENDS THAT "WE DO INDEED live in such a finite economy in which utter redemption *from* violence is as utopian as redemption through it."[1] Violence, in Jay's chilling idiom, has become a constitutive function of today's world, structuring and sustaining our ways of existence and all sociopolitical and transnational intelligibility. It is "a closed circuit" in which "there is no complete outside," no penumbra of redemption, nor balmy elsewhere or brief reprieve.[2] Similarly to Jay, Michael Hardt, and Antonio Negri argue that contemporary warfare and violence have become "a permanent condition," "the primary organizing principle of society," and "the general matrix for all relations of power and techniques of domination"—in short, violence and warfare have become a "form of rule aimed not only at controlling the population but producing and reproducing all aspects of social life."[3] Predating Jay, Hardt, and Negri but arguing along similar lines, Michel Foucault had pointed out that subjectivity—all forms of sociopolitical intelligibility, and, indeed, all relations—are but the product and, therefore, the extension of the joined-up apparatuses of power and war, or objective and subjective violence. All relations, in other words, are born in "the blood and mud of battles."[4] Small wonder, then, that "the old joke about outbreaks of peace is now a sobering social fact"[5]—that genocides, exterminations and massacres have in turn become, in Jean-Luc Nancy's bleak aphorism, "if not names properly speaking, at least *semantemes* of modernity."[6]

While I by no means wish here to utterly contradict these loosely pertinent observations, I do nonetheless think that they have—however daring their perspicuity and realistic their rhetorical gloom might seem at first sight—grave political implications and need, therefore, to be brought under critical scrutiny. For one thing, they are largely statements *about* war, not *against* it. For another, they are hardly expressive of the viewpoints of those who have been or continue to be at the receiving end of war and violence—those who have (yet to learn) to survive (let alone to live) in the midst of everyday violence or in the aftermath of atrocity. To argue that warfare and violence *structure* our contemporary world is, therefore, to encourage, however unintentionally, the acceptability of these normally exceptional measures (if not, and by the same token, to rationalize the ineluctability of a generalized or prolonged state of exception in which war is simultaneously "life and living chaos").[7] What is worse, moreover, is the underlying assumption that the current wave of warfare and violence, particularly in the Middle East, is discontinuous with the *decolonial* moment of the early and mid-twentieth century, and as such has to do more with the structure of the contemporary world than with the histories of imperial violence *around* which the contemporary world of global capital continues—strategically so—to structure and perpetuate itself.

While it may be true, then, that warfare and violence are compelling and foundational forces of our contemporaneity, it is incumbent upon us nonetheless to probe and pinpoint the nuances—and to discriminate carefully, and if possible conclusively—between the structural currency of violence, on the one hand, and, on the other, the historical grievances it produces and of which it is oftentimes the product. The rigorous and perceptive task of exposing the entangled (foundational, objective, ideological, or symbolic) domains of violence in contemporary societies ought not at all to override or discredit the still necessary critique of the more contingent and concrete forms of violence, and their particular historical origins or precipitating causes; otherwise, the very experience of human pain and suffering might no longer be recognizable and witnessable, let alone sharable or communicable. All the more so given that the increasing ubiquity of violence—whether in the actual, visual, or virtual worlds—might treacherously end up robbing us of the emotional wherewithal with which to respond critically and politically to the perpetrators (and, therefore, engineers of banality) of global violence and warfare as they continue diurnally to kill more and more innocent lives with impunity. What is at stake in the very structural banalization of everyday violence is not only the foreclosure of human loss—and, therefore, the institutionalization of ungrievability, disposability, and posttraumatic stress disorders as ineluctable conditions of human existence—but also the attenuation and marginalization of the very notions of justice, political redress, and forgiveness, without which no meaningful sense of subjectivity, of community and transnational solidarity, however precarious these might remain, could be instilled and nurtured in the survivors of extreme violence and in the generations-to-come, *their* descendants and *ours,* the inheritors of histories of violence, inflicted and incurred.

Insofar as every war "is also a war for the *meaning* of war," the distinction between the structural determinacy of war and its historical contexts becomes crucial to any viable role of politics whether in preventing war or in settling conflicts and redressing damages.[8] The reverse would result in the interminable displacement of the historical origins of war into the (naturalized) nature of the contemporary world, the universality of evil and many such transcendental and transhistorical grand narratives that hammer home the ineluctability of war. We have by now become quite familiar, for instance, with the ways in which the actual dispossession of Palestinians and the occupation of Palestine have been displaced into mythical and biblical grand narratives of legitimacy, privilege and ancient and, presumably, irresolvable rivalry between the two monotheisms: Islam and Judaism. Similarly, the clashes that took place more recently between Sunni and Shiʿi Muslims in Iraq have been propagandistically traced back to a war within Islam (that dates back to the unresolved debates over the succession to the Prophet Muhammad) rather than, as I would argue, to the colonial divide-and-rule scheme implemented by the United States and its allies after the illegal war they declared against Iraq in 2003.[9] Perhaps the attempt to elide or erase altogether Euro-American and Zionist implications in almost every aspect of so-called ethnic or sectarian violence in the Arab world is nowhere clearer than in the case of the Lebanese civil war (1975–90). The very common characterizations of this war as "ethnic," "religious," or "sectarian" not only exonerate Western imperialism and its unexorcised legacies, but also obscure the incubational historical moments of which the war is a product—namely, the *Nakba* or catastrophe of 1948 and the *Naksa* or setback of 1967, both of which resulted in the Zionist expropriation and occupation of Arab land, particularly the occupation of Palestine and the dispossession of Palestinians, and, above all, the creation and intensification of the Palestinian refugee problem, the phenomenon that is believed to be at the origin of the Lebanese civil war in the first place.

It becomes clear in light of these examples that the particular historical and largely colonial instigators of warfare and violence in Palestine, Iraq and Lebanon are displaced and dispersed onto ancient structural deficiencies, or ethnic and religious exigencies that make the actually unnecessary, asymmetrical and unjust violence look inevitable, even if unfortunate. It seems that when it comes to studying the Arab world and the *status-turmoil* that has characterized and continues to define it, analysts have oftentimes given in too easily to the lures of what might be called *licensed displacements:* a variegated number of subtle and protean rhetorical operations that seek to privatize—and, therefore, dispense with—the political, historical or colonial writ large into intransigent models of genetic and transhistorical ailments or predicaments *tout court.* These kinds of discursive and rhetorical displacements of the political, historical and material realities of war are not, however, inconsequential, much less uncalculated.[10] They serve not only the derealizing aims of actual warfare but also the legitimizing narratives that inaugurate and sustain military violence. Indeed, the increasing normalization and institutionalization of war in today's world is inextricably tied to the development and dissemination of elaborate (oftentimes transcendental, abstract and trans- or ahistorical) narratives that sanction the use of violence. The conduct of war hinges squarely on media coverage and the deployment of propagandistic campaigns as well as on the mobilizing powers of narrative legitimacy and credibility such that concepts of history, truth, memory, and justice have become nothing more than effects of narrative designs, will, and power—really, all the adhocracies of combat positions, alliances, and other related vices.

What interests me in this final chapter are not these largely *legitimizing* narratives that feed the urge to make war and inflict pain, but rather the narratives —really, the counter-narratives—that bear witness to the enduring impulse to make sense of war and to discern and expose in the process its concrete traumatic demarcations, calculated structural denominations and profound derealizing effects. I agree with James Tatum that "the one impulse that has proved as enduring as human beings' urge to make wars is their need to make sense of them,"[11] but I would be remiss not to add that this sense-making impulse ought not to slide inadvertently into an ordering gesture of understanding. Making sense of war involves an engagement with the cruelties of memory and traumatic loss via the consolatory vistas of mourning, memorials, and artistic expression. This sensemaking process ought not, however, to posit understanding before having it. For one thing, sensemaking as a hermeneutic process risks conferring meaning on the meaninglessness of war: it threatens not only to neutralize the discontinuous chaos of the reality of warfare it wants to make sense of, but also to legitimize the very structural dominion of violence it sets out to denounce. For another, the sociopolitical and psychoaffective work of memory and mourning may threaten to persist endlessly since the proliferation of war and violence in today's world is indeed a function of what Naomi Klein calls "disaster capitalism," a global economic system that has institutionalized catastrophe as a permanent market resource for corporate profiteering.[12] This is precisely why our preoccupation with mourning and memorials stems less from the fact that we are either a postwar or a prewar generation, but rather from the fact that we seem always already a generation at war. Profit warfare—because it is instrumental to disaster capitalism—will continue to pile up human tragedy, suffering and pain until the otherwise *ephemeral* work of mourning becomes *interminable.* Worse, we live in a time during which there has been a general decline in mourning practices not only in Europe and the United States, as Peter Homans demonstrates, but also, I would argue, almost across the entire globe, particularly with the advent of globalization, the virtualization of social life, the commodification of grief, the racialization of grievability, the desensitization of emotions and the devaluation of empathy, as well as the breakup and dispersal of community into the carefully (or not so carefully) discriminated spheres of the private and the public, the real and the virtual, or the particular and the spectacular.

Because of the increasing institutionalization of warfare and the decline of communitywide mourning practices, it comes as no surprise that the literary (indeed, the aesthetic writ large) has become the most hospitable public space where the performance of memory and mourning oftentimes takes place. It is hardly surprising either (if depressingly ironic) that entire literary traditions have been facilitated by violence and warfare.[13] This has, obviously, been the case with a good number of modernist and postcolonial national literatures as several new studies go to demonstrate.[14] It has also been the case with the national literatures of the Arab states, particularly in colonial Palestine and postcolonial Algeria and, above all, in contemporary Lebanon, where the civil war has indeed acted as the midwife of modern Lebanese literature.[15] As Elias Khoury points out, "In this city [i.e., Beirut] systematically ravaged by civil war, the only space left for memory is literature."[16] The capacity of literature to preserve what, for instance, architecture would have to destroy cannot be overstressed. "The architect can, and is sometimes forced to, destroy what is anterior to his drawings in order to erect the new. The writer destroys nothing," Khoury goes on to argue.[17] If literature, namely the novel, has then taken upon itself the task of performing memory and mourning—or if, for that matter, memory and mourning have found in the novel the appropriate public means of expression—it is because there is no longer any visible community that could bear the burden of grief, or bear witness to the psychoaffective cuts of which grief is the product and the driving force (particularly in a context such as the Lebanese civil war with civilians fighting each other under the thrall of factionalism, the Manicheanism of friendship, or enmity and several other fanaticisms of the moment).

With no visible community to fall upon, the burden of memory and mourning has fallen either on the individual survivor, or, more increasingly, on the arts (and literature in particular) and has therefore given rise to what Homans suggestively calls, "mourning without mourning practices."[18] To be precise, however, while literature holds open a space for mourning—that is, for the emergence of literary or discursive practices of mourning—it is neither likely nor desirable for it to promise the fulfillment of the work of mourning (much less to act on such a promise even though the promise is arguably inherent in literature's very gesture of hospitality—really, of empathy and solidarity). The fulfillment of mourning would, obviously, mean the successful resolution of all psychoaffective and psychosocial dispositions that might range—depending on the emotional scale and magnitude of the loss incurred—from grief and anxiety to melancholia and posttraumatic stress disorder. Clearly, this is not a task that literature can or should accomplish, particularly if the injustices at the origin of mourning in the first place remain unaddressed in the global or international arenas. Nor is this task of accomplishing mourning plausible at a time when the shadow of warfare and violence in the Arab world has never ceased to fall on the sociopolitical and cultural spheres, disfiguring and reconfiguring all forms of intelligibility, not to say all aspects of literary, artistic and intellectual engagements. By *holding* open a space for discursive mourning practices, literature reckons with the enduring challenges of mourning even while it contends that mourning will not be fully resolved until justice is served. Otherwise, literature would only consolidate and perpetuate the rhetoric of structural violence and preemptive warfare that have converged to produce trauma and mourning in the first place. It would only cement the derealizing aims of warfare and violence by displacing (i.e., objectifying and containing) historical loss into the literary artifact. The venture of the literary in the Arab world and in the Lebanese civil war novel, in particular, lies in the continual interruption of the rationalizing continuum between (the) history (of atrocity) and literary form—hence, the generalized adherence to and dissemination of formless forms of novelistic writings. The domain of literature is that of counter-mourning, of activating and simultaneously occluding the resolution of mourning—really, and *pace* Homans, the domain of literature in the Arab world is the domain of *mourning practices without mourning.*

By focusing on Khoury's *City Gates* (2007; *Gates of the City,* 1993; *Abwāb al-madīna,* 1981), one of the most experimental and abstract novels in modern, or postmodern Arabic literature, written in the midst of the Lebanese civil war and first published in 1981, I will examine the ways in which narrative—by virtue of being the product of the conditions of which it speaks—bears witness to, protests against, and ultimately helps us gain empathic *access* to the devastating effects of war without entirely or necessarily proffering us with consolatory reprieve or clear exit strategies. The more the narrative of *City Gates* clears a space for mourning, the more precarious becomes the search for emotional closure. While the novel comes to a literal full stop at the end of the narrative, it rhetorically resists throughout its formal texture any eventuality of narrative closure. By occluding narrative closure, the novel occludes, at least by implication, any corresponding emotional closure. As such, it exemplifies what might be called a *poetics of occlosure* in which the narrative unfolds within and through a chiastic oscillation between the announcement of the end and the pronouncement of its recessiveness or foreclosure. As will become clear in due course, this poetics fans out through and across various tropes (particularly, allegory, chiasmus and metonymy) and experimental narrative techniques ranging from a stylistic obsession with formlessness, fragmentariness, and anacoluthon to polyphony and, above all, repetition and plotlessness. Repetition is indeed the pivotal conceit or the organizing principle of the narrative in *City Gates.* It is in equal measure the means by which the traumatic experience (or lack of it thereof) of the Lebanese civil war is reconfigured in its crude manifestations. The stark correspondence between the narrative structure of the novel and the psychoaffective structure of trauma attests to the performative élan of *City Gates* and marks an allegorical continuum between the novel and the trauma of the Lebanese civil war. Not only is the novel's investment in technical experimentation inseparable from its desire to interrupt the incessant slide of the brutal reality of diurnal warfare under the derealizing chain of metonymic contiguity and signification, but it is also indissociable from its commitment to a postconsolatory practice of mourning at a time when the taboo placed on the memory of the civil war in Lebanon has de facto taken the form of an ideology of forgetting.[19]

The nameless protagonist of Khoury's *City Gates,* anonymously called "a man and a stranger" (*kāna rajulan wa kāna gharīban*),[20] sets out on a journey home, back to the city from which he was exiled, but the lashing athletic elasticity and haunting lyricism of the prose—its economic admixture of excess and inadequacy, indeterminacy and immanence, literality and undecidability, dream and hallucination, semantic opacity and syntactic play, and reality and fantasy—combine to leave him (and us) practically stranded at the gates (also of meaning, recognition and truth), which, by the end of the novel, are nowhere to be found, and everywhere becomes a closing prison, if not a *mass*ive open-air grave. In their tormenting hunt for meaning, readers and critics alike are bound to fall under the shadow of the stranger's quest for the city, for the city square, for the suitcase and, above all, for the truth (of what happened) to which the stranger wants to bear, or be the bearer of witness. Stefan Meyer rightly suggests that while *City Gates* "is clearly symbolic," "it is not a concrete symbolism that can be interpreted."[21] He has forgotten to add that it is equally, if not primarily, a raid on the symbolic and the mythical altogether. Whether in *Al-dhākira al-mafqūda* (*Lost Memory*), a collection of his critical essays published in 1982, or in *Zaman al-ʾihtilāl* (*Colonial Time*), a collection of his journalisms published in 1985, Khoury has passionately argued against the ideologies of symbolism and myth because they let us off the hook of having to take seriously the responsibility and urgency of engaging and critiquing the present (*al-ḥāḍir* or *ar-rāhin*). For instance, the Phoenix-like aura of Beirut—the fact that it was reduced to rubble by seven earthquakes in ancient history and seven major wars in recent history—is exposed and deconstructed again and again in *City Gates* by the economic and strategic use of the iconographic number seven (seven gates, seven women, seven main chapters of the novel, etc.). For, if anything, this myth subtly instills in the Lebanese collective psyche a sort of emotional insouciance, or utter callousness about the civil war and the calamity of destruction by throwing into sharp relief this timeless and mythical fantasy of resurrection and triumphant reconstruction. It is as if myth here serves merely to fuel the compulsion to repeat the destruction of Beirut again and again rather than to institute the impulse to remember and to work through the legacy of the civil war in such a way as to preclude the ghastly calamity of its potential repetition. Similarly, the symbolism of sacrifice and martyrdom (*al-shahāda*) during the war not only helps cultivate, commodify and transform death into a mode of transaction and dialogue, but also reduces such horrendous practices as assassination, hostage taking, and ransom into mere elements in a wider network that might be called a *system of necrocommunication.* As Khoury suggests, somewhat sarcastically, "Writing is no longer a means of exchange, exchange has moved to bodies, corpses have become the means by which viewpoints are announced: bombing, kidnapping, killing or executing. Writing in its different forms has become a mere naming of this announcement."[22]

City Gates should be seen first and foremost as an attempt to forge a new language, a new type of writing and a new mode of critique that would not only respond to the licensed displacements of historical violence into structural violence, but also expose the material and immaterial aftereffects of warfare, particularly trauma and posttraumatic stress disorder. Above all, the novel charts the enabling contours for the emergence of a new type of subjectivity from within the confines of extreme vulnerability—really, from within the traumas and trials of survival in the aftermath of catastrophe. Khoury's attempt here might also be seen as a postmodernist response to a primitive and déjà-vu reality of factionalist and competing narcissisms, colonial and Zionist set-ups and divide-and-rule schemes. Perhaps what is most striking about *City Gates* is its tirelessly sustained experimental style—a new form of writing in modern Arabic literature that risks, however, as Meyer rightly points out, discouraging the reader to go on with the act of reading: "After a certain point, not knowing where he is and what meaning to associate with the test, the reader's attention simply gives out. The simple problem of sustaining such narrative over distance is perhaps the most fundamental reason why Khoury did not continue to write in this vein."[23] This might as well be the reason why this novel received little critical attention in comparison, for instance, with Khoury's earlier novel, *Little Mountain* (1989; *Al-jabal al-saghīr,* 1977). In light of his essay, "The Unfolding of Modern Fiction and Arab Memory," however, Khoury's strain toward formlessness in *City Gates* seems unavoidable, not to say desirable, given, on the one hand, the "formal" and "majestic heaviness" of the Mahfouzian novel, and, on the other, the specificity of war torn Beirut, its extended state of emergency and unpredictable or uncharted state of emergence: "Writing in times of transition takes the form of a journey towards what we do not know and towards the shock of writing what we know, which will lead us to discover how writing changes things and does not only reflect them."[24] There is, obviously, an inherent disorientation and undecidability in the way that the journey leitmotif or technique functions in fiction insofar as the journey almost always turns into a quest that prompts close reading but defers the consolation of an immediately clear meaning or purpose.

The empowering latencies of deferral here should not be underestimated—they suspend and, simultaneously, expand the norms and forms of intelligibility operative at the moment of reading. As the Russian formalist Victor Shklovsky had memorably put it, "The technique of art is to make objects 'unfamiliar,' to make forms difficult, to increase the difficulty and length of perception because the process of perception is an aesthetic end in itself and must be prolonged."[25] For Shklovsky, the cumulative shock effect of defamiliarizing techniques and difficult forms has the potential to disrupt our habits of seeing and thinking because "Habitualization devours work, clothes, furniture, one's wife, and the fear of war. . . . And art exists that one may recover the sensation of life; it exists to make one feel things, to make the stone *stony*."[26] It is exactly this roundabout way of proceeding—through a defamiliarization that aims at a fresh perception and fresh commitment to life, not desensitization to things, to war and to destruction—that animates *City Gates* and that, therefore, need to be read literally, for to learn to read *City Gates* is to learn, to borrow Gayatri Spivak's expression, "to dis-figure the undecidable figure into responsible literality, again and again."[27] It is in this sense that I want to read *City Gates* by looking at the ways in which it looks awry at the historical reality of civil war. I read it less as a mimetic representation of war torn Beirut than as an allegory of the traumatic demarcations of the war—not to say a foreboding prolepsis of sorts of the Sabra and Shatila massacre that would take place in 1982 (just one year after the publication of the novel). Thus, the novel hardly serves the purpose of knowing the Lebanese civil war as an object of study; instead, its "purpose is to create the vision which results from [a] deautomatized perception," the vision which emerges through "the slowness of the perception" of the otherwise deadening monotony of the war (if it were to be approached simply as a knowable object, an object of knowledge).[28] Insofar as this vision is, for Shklovsky, nothing less than a fresh perception that rearranges the norms of sociocultural intelligibility—a renewed commitment to life that includes a "fear of war"—it is a vision *of* the human that seeks *to* rethink the human *for* the human. I believe the vision that *City Gates* creates can be seen along intensely similar lines. Through the allegorically performative dramatization of trauma, the novel strives, ultimately, to institute vulnerability as a condition of subjectivity and to redistribute human ties along trauma ties—ties that the traumatized (and trauma-tied) subject dreads, yet keeps returning to and rediscovering at a relatively removed experiential distance from the originating traumatic event; it is these centripetal and centrifugal movements—which drive the stranger away from the city and, simultaneously, back into it—that I find of particular relevance to rethinking human agency, if not social intelligibility altogether, particularly in the context of traumatized and trauma-tied subjectivities and collectivities.

From Sigmund Freud to Cathy Caruth, the traumatized subject has been broadly defined as someone who cannot bear witness to the traumatic event at the moment of its actual occurrence. Dori Laub has termed this historical and temporal gap the "collapse of witnessing."[29] Not only is this, as I shall demonstrate, a matter of discursive (and, consequently, experiential) failure, but also, as Laub goes on to argue, a matter of circumstantial (and, particularly, psychological) unfeasibility, "it was also the very circumstance of *being inside the event* that made unthinkable the very notion that a witness could exist, that is, someone who could step outside of the coercively totalitarian and dehumanizing frame of reference in which the event was taking place, and provide an independent frame of reference through which the event could be observed."[30] This frame of reference will only become plausible, if at all, in the aftermath of the traumatic event, once the survivor is situated at a critical (also discursive and temporal) distance from it. The burden of Khoury's writings lies in his attempt to generate a space and an ambiance conducive to experiencing and bearing witness to the traumatic event retrospectively, at the moment of its discursive recall and recreation. For instance, in the beginning of *Little Mountain* (*Al-Jabal al-Saghīr*), the earliest novel about the Lebanese civil war, the narrator relates how a group of right-wing militiamen stormed into his house, looking for him: "Five men come, jumping out of a military-like jeep. . . . They search for me in the house. I wasn't there. They search the books and the papers. I wasn't there. They found a book with a picture of Abdel-Nasser on the back cover. I wasn't there. They scattered the papers and overturned the furniture. They cursed the Palestinians. They ripped my bed up. They insulted my mother and this corrupt generation. I wasn't there. I wasn't there."[31] The ability of the first person narrator to tell us he "wasn't there" becomes possible only belatedly, when he reinserts himself into the narrative gap, and reproduces the absence (the "not being there") to which he was subject, but not yet a retrospective witness. Laying claim to an absence from the scene of the traumatic event at the moment of its unfolding becomes belatedly the inaugurational moment of the discursive reconstruction of what happened. For the first person narrator of *Little Mountain* to go on repeating again and again (in a chiastic vacillation of sameness and difference) the circumstantial sequence of this arch event throughout the narrative is indicative of the ways in which repetition becomes here a narrative device or an organizing principle of narration: not only does it sustain the rhythmic unfolding of the story, but it also frames the very painstaking and gradual transformation of the traumatic event into a belated experience. Here the compelling poignancy of Eva Hoffman's insight—indeed, chiastic double bind—cannot be overstressed, "Those who don't understand the past may be condemned to repeat it, but those who never repeat it are condemned not to understand it."[32]

In *City Gates,* chiasmus, metonymy, and repetition are among the tropological tools that Khoury deploys to register and, simultaneously, loosen up the hold of trauma on the psyche. Consistently occluding narrative closure, the novel unfolds in a dizzyingly recessive circuit, engaging the reader in the act of witnessing and enduring the traumatic experience as it unfolds, thus proffering Khoury with a vantage point from which to signal the political urgency of knowing and acknowledging human dignity and reinstating vulnerability at the core of communal, social and transnational ties. The stranger in the novel roams throughout the city, or what remains of it, looking for his home—"And when the man returned to the square, he felt that his home was here"—yet, no sooner does he fall on or head toward a point of reference (*un point de repère*), the farther away he gets from it, and the further he is led astray: "And suddenly he saw black dots in the distance shimmering amidst the whiteness, and he couldn't make out are they birds in the sand searching for something? He came close to them but after he had traveled for hours and hours he felt as though he was getting farther away from them"[33] Literally deprived of what Caruth calls a "locus of referentiality,"[34] the stranger becomes, and by virtue of his nomadic existence, the proverbial locus of trauma. Stylistically, *City Gates* unfolds like a trauma whose cadence, rhythm and haunting lyricism match only its opacity, recessiveness or intricate evasiveness. It is a performative trauma, literally. The disrupted circular plotline of the story begins with a stranger who returns to an unnamed city, which is, most probably, the scene of the traumatic event (whose deferred action sets the trauma of the stranger and simultaneously the deformed narrative of *City Gates* in motion):

> He was a man and he was a stranger,
>
> He didn't tell his story to anyone, he didn't know he was a story to be told. He thought, he used to think, the way we think, and he was like everyone was, but he didn't tell anyone, because he didn't know that the things that had happened could be told to anyone.
>
> He was a man and he was a stranger,
>
> He doesn't remember how his story began, because he was busy with its ending. And when the ending came he found that he didn't know the ending either, because the ending can't be known, because the ending is an ending.[35]

It is not for nothing that the style here is deliberately self-conscious and somewhat overwrought—it expresses in convoluted form the traumatic venture of the story and of the traumatized state of the anonymous protagonist (whose story reads, at least initially, as an utterly unreadable report). Given that *City Gates* was published in 1981 (and was most probably written after 1977, the year when *Little Mountain* was published to great critical acclaim), this man and this stranger might easily correspond to, or dramatize, the lived experience of a survivor of the 1976 siege and massacre of Palestinians in the refugee camp of Tal al-Zaʿtar in the suburbs of Beirut. He cannot tell his story partly because he does not know whether it can be *framed* as such and partly because he does not remember how it began, much less whether it did actually reach an end. The story (in which the stranger finds himself caught) has not ended yet—indeed, *the* ending has proven nothing more than *an* ending. Because of the unwitting and unremitting repetitive reenactments of the traumatic event (on the threshold of experience), the story might never find the ending, at the end of which it could possibly be framed as a story to be told to others. This is the paradox of *City Gates:* it reenacts the trauma whose story it wants to tell. This performative élan does not seem to allow for the establishment of the kind of formal coherency constitutive of a story to be reconstructed through, or read for its plot (especially since plot normally reorders or distributes and disperses the chronological sequence of events that constitute a story into a coherent narrative rendition of an otherwise chaotic reality).

While a story is an effect of a given plot and while plot is always already a story, *City Gates* is as much a story in need of a plot as a plot in need of a story. Neither a story can be teased out of a narrative without a plot nor can a plot be discerned from a narrative without a story. Little wonder, then, that a solid void starts building steadily as soon as reading starts. Because the novel recreates a traumatic event that, in the words of Caruth, "simultaneously defies and demands our witness," it does so as well in a "language [that] defies, even as it claims, our understanding."[36] That the stranger cannot tell his story means in the final analysis that he cannot frame it into a coherent narrative whose meaning and meaningfulness, while not reflective of the discontinuous chaos of reality, hinges on the development of a horizon of expectations for future potentialities, for the meaning of an event is, in the words of E. van Alphen, "derived from an anticipation of events to follow" (note here, by way of comparison, that death, for instance, is a dreaded event precisely because it lacks a "narrative framework" that would make it possible "to anticipate future events").[37] Clearly, the stranger seems unable from the very outset of the novel to activate a narrative framework that would make it possible to anticipate coming events: he is completely preoccupied with the ending of his story which he nevertheless keeps missing. He is presented to us at the outset very much *past* the end *without* the end. What arises out of the lack of a narrative framework that normally makes possible the anticipation of future events is precisely a narrative (of that) lack. In no small measure, this is the *challenge* to *City Gates* (insofar as it seeks to inscribe that lack) and simultaneously this is the *challenge* of *City Gates* (insofar as it has gone lacking and has reenacted that narrative lack in order to bear witness to it without inadvertently filling it out). Above all, this is *our* challenge—really, the challenge of reading the lack at the structural rib of *City Gates.*

While the beginning of the novel has proven more of an uncanny foreclosure of narrative potentiality, the ending of the novel is no less disconcerting—it sends us back to the very beginning (a beginning that can no longer be thought to have begun at the very beginning of the novel but indeed to have followed from its very circular ending):

> The stranger said he was dying all alone. He said and he looked and he saw the fire devouring everyone, he caught a glimpse of the woman and the man, he caught a glimpse of the women, and they were all being colored by this light blue that spread over the eyes . . .
>
> The stranger moved forward, and the people were forests on fire, approaching one another and collapsing. And the odor was the same, the odor of the square where the king is, the odor of old embers extinguished with water, and the brackish water was on top of him and around him.
>
> The storyteller said.

> Then the sea came. The sea ate up the fire and spread over the city. The sea ate up the walls and spread over the gates, and the gates collapsed, and the remains of corpses floated over a blue rooftop and dark domes. Everything was floating, and nothing remained of the city except weeping voices coming from the entrails of fish and rising to where no one can listen to them. (97)

This blaze and this storm—this baptism by fire and by water, this mixture of atrocity and amnesia, the two poles that have sustained the Lebanese civil war—that strike at the end of the novel would have already taken place when the narrative began with a preamble aptly titled, "Beginning." This preamble is a compressed and composite narrative—simultaneously proleptic and retrospective of the main events to follow or that have taken place in the seven different chapters of which the novel is composed. Since the first chapter is titled "The Stranger" and the seventh (and last chapter) is also titled "The stranger," the structure of the narrative is without a doubt circular (and perhaps in a vicious or absurd way) and subsequently with no determinable beginning or ending (even though the preamble seems to fall, at once, inside and outside the narrative circle, or the structurality of structure). Yet the preamble can be said to escape the circularity of the narrative design of the novel only in the sense that a traumatic event can be said to escape the seriality of repetitions of which it is a product, only in the sense perhaps that the preamble (much like the traumatic event) sets narrative in motion, but does not provide it with a *discernable* experiential anchor or locus of referentiality—only in the sense, really, that the preamble can be seen, in the words of the frame narrator of *City Gates,* "like a point turning into angles, and like an angle turning into circles, and like a circle shrinking into a distant point."[38] That a point (supposedly, a point of departure) should convert into a circle—and that a circle should chiastically revert back into a point, again and again, in cyclical repetition—goes to suggest that *City Gates* performs the unbearable *plotlessness* of trauma (i.e., that experience of being past the end without the end; that is, that lack of narrative framework) even while submitting to the rhythmic and chiastic vacillation between the repetition of trauma and the return to the traumatic event. As Peter Brooks argues in his discussion of the work of repetition in relation to the economics of narrativity, "repetition speaks in the text of a return which ultimately subverts the very notion of beginning and end, suggesting that the idea of beginning presupposes the end, that the end is a time before the beginning, and hence that the interminable never can be finally bound in a plot"—"Any final authority claimed by narrative plots, whether of origin or end, is," Brooks concludes, "illusory."[39]

City Gates reenacts the chiastic recursivity of the traumatic event along the circular chain of repetition where each repetition approximates but never fully coincides with the trauma of which it is a product. There is obviously in the economy of repetition here a heightened sense of uncertainty—an uncertainty about whether what happened *did* actually happen and, simultaneously, an uncertainty about whether it has *ever* ceased to happen. For instance, the cataclysmic events that take place at the very end of the novel have already been announced in the preamble:

> The stranger walked and walked.
> And beside him walked another man.
> And beside the other man walked another.
> And they all walked to the faraway city, and in the faraway city they lit a fire, and in the fire they die, and in the fire they are afraid, and in the fire they write a story that begins where it should have ended, and when it ends it is as though it never began.

City Gates tirelessly invokes its raison d'être—its attempt to represent the lack of a narrative framework—not only because it is an allegorical performative of trauma, but also because it is in a more rudimentary meta-fictional sense intensely aware of what Hans-Jost Frey calls, "the sadness of the novel, whose story can never come to completion because its end is always followed by its narration. In the posthumous present of narration everything has already happened, and only the pale suspicion remains that nothing more can happen than the narration of what happened. That the story turns into narration is sad because it shows that it has not found its end and that it must keep ending in the narration, unfulfilled."[40] Clearly, there is something largely foundational here about the way in which the novel, or narrative, relates to sadness, or mourning. There is what might be called a poetics of narrative mourning, or, more precisely, an inaugurational entanglement between narrative and mourning, not only because the end in narrative does not coincide with the completion of the story, but also because it results in the loss of the story and, above all, in the loss of the hope of its completion (which is what causes mourning in the first place): "The hope of completion ends with the end. The end of hope survives as mourning."[41] What makes narrative even more inextricably bound to mourning is that the narrator or storyteller survives or lives through the end of the novel in order to tell about it to those who have not lived through it: "The narrator is no other than the surviving of the end that, since it has not been one, bathes the narration in sadness about the fact that no end is in sight anymore."[42] While the structural currency of mourning in narrative cannot be overstressed, *City Gates* treads the fine line between the structural and the historical dimensions of mourning, ensuring that the latter does not unwittingly slip into the former. The narrator or storyteller here is not only the survivor of the end of the novel or the mourner for the loss of the story (or, more precisely, of the hope of its completion), but also the survivor of the traumatic event that the novel *presents* performatively—really, the survivor of a history of trauma whose psychic demarcations match only "the very inaccessibility of its occurrence," and, above all, the very lack of a "narrative framework that makes it possible to anticipate future events."[43]

City Gates presents us with more than a structural poetics of narrative mourning. Mourning in the novel is more than a function of the structure of narrative and storytelling. If we abide by what Peter Brooks calls the "textual energetics" of the novel—the ways in which the novel is "inhabited by energies" which "correspond to the arousals, expectations, doubts, suspense, reversals, revaluations, disappointments, embarrassments, fulfillments, and even the incoherences animated by readings"[44]—it becomes possible to *see* how the energies released by the traumatic event (whose very locus of referentiality is precisely the site of a radical collapse of witnessing) in *City Gates* manifest themselves at the level of language, syntax, and narrative form. So far my discussion of the chiasmus between repetition and the search for psychoaffective closure and narrative end should have made it sufficiently clear how trauma comes to weigh on the forms of its expression and experience. The novel presents us with an allegorical continuum—and not a mimesis—between its form and the chaotic reality outside of it. I will say more to this effect further down, when I discuss the fragmentariness of the narrative of *City Gates* and the collapse of the narrative voice, but let me first proceed by untangling the loose relations I have established so far between the traumatic triad: event, experience, and representation. Given that a traumatic event cannot be experienced during its actual occurrence, it bears reiterating here that repetition is precisely the very experience of the traumatic event *for the first time.* This implies that living through a traumatic experience occurs only belatedly and through the work of remembering and/or compulsive repeating. Is it possible, however, one might ask, to experience *belatedly* an event that could not—in the first place—have been experienced when it happened? The impossibility of experiencing a traumatic event while living through it firsthand has more to do with the *discursive* nature of experience than with the extremity of the event itself. As Ernst van Alphen persuasively argues, the problem here "is not the nature of the event, nor an intrinsic limitation of representation; rather, it is the split between the living of an event and the available forms of representation with/in which the event can be experienced," for an "experience does not really exist until it can be named and placed in larger categories."[45]

Experiencing a traumatic event is coextensive with its representation. Representation is not, however, identical with the event. To experience here is precisely to dispose of the traumatic in the realm of the discursive; it is to situate oneself at a safe remove or distance from the event. In short, "experience is the transposition of the event to the realm of the subject. Hence the experience of an event is already a representation of it and not the event itself."[46] *City Gates* attests, however, to the collapse of this continuum between experiencing and representing a traumatic event. In a sense, the traumatic event (that is precipitated by the Lebanese civil war) could not be channeled into experience "because a distance from it in language or representation was not possible."[47] Because experience is a discursive process and because the discursive process in this case has stalled, experience has failed to come about, which is what causes trauma, or, more precisely, what has been recognized since 1980 by the American Psychiatric Association as posttraumatic stress disorder. If experiencing (i.e., representing) trauma means *integrating* it into one's own past (i.e., binding the free-floating stimuli that cut through the protective shields of the psyche), then failing to do so would mean that the trauma would start leading a life of its own and become dissociated with one's own life. As Ruth Leys points out, "The experience of trauma, fixed or frozen in time, refuses to be represented *as* past, but is perpetually reexperienced in a painful, dissociated, traumatic present. All the symptoms characteristic of PTSD—flashbacks, nightmares and other experiences, emotional numbing, depression, guilt, autonomic arousal, explosive violence or tendency to hypervigilance—are thought to be the result of this fundamental dissociation."[48] If experiencing trauma is indissociable from representing it—from discursively locating it in the past and psychically integrating it into one's own past—how can a *failed experience* of trauma still be represented? A failed experience implies here that discourse has failed to bring about a timely experience of trauma or that the inextricable relationship between discourse and experience has been unsettled in such a way that, instead of experience, there follows a *collapse* of experience. *City Gates* should be seen—in light of these remarks—as an intense dramatization of this collapse of experience in an abandon of repetition. "The whole drama," as J. Hillis Miller aptly puts it in a similar context, "is ending and beginning at once, a beginning/ending which must always presuppose something outside of itself, something anterior or ulterior, in order either to begin or to end, in order to begin ending. The moment of reversal, when tying becomes untying, can never be shown as such or identified as such because the two motions are inextricably the same, as in the double antithetical word "articulate," which means simultaneously putting together and taking apart."[49] In both experiencing and representing or writing trauma, repetition marks the impossibility of "ending and beginning at once": (1) the traumatized subject must repeatedly return to the scene of the trauma in order to work through it and extract oneself from it and (2) "Writing, which must always have begun in order to be able to say that it has, must always continue in order to be able to say that it is ending. It always ends too early or too late, and therefore does not end at all, for it misses its own end."[50] The chiastic oscillations that ensue between the beginning and the ending of narrative and between the return to and the return of trauma—in short between the repetition and articulation of the failed experience of trauma—are precisely the meanwhile of narrative lack, the meanwhile of trauma, and, potentially, the meanwhile of redistributing social ties along trauma ties.

The ethico-political wager of *City Gates* consists in delving into the empowering potential of engaging with failure; this wager does not only materialize in its attempt to bear witness to a failed experience of trauma, but also in its failure to bear witness to that very failure (without which it cannot impart an accurate sense of the failure it wants to represent). What better way to represent failure than by failing well! If representing is always already coterminous with experiencing trauma, failing to represent should inversely impart a sense of the correlative failure to/of experience (which is what *City Gates* sets out to represent). While the failure to represent has more to do, as I mentioned earlier, with the intrinsically discursive nature of experience rather than with the extrinsic extremity of the event, it is important to point out (*pace* Alphen) that the extremity of the event itself must have weighed on the symbolic orders or regimes—in this case the novel form—available for experiencing the event. The weight of the traumatic event thwarts the emergence of a meaningful narrative framework, which brings about the collapse of representation. *City Gates* vacillates chiastically between the excess of the traumatic event—its narrative lack or unrepresentability—and the inadequacy of the novel to bring about the experience of the event except in the immanent play of repetition. The failure of the novel as a symbolic form to represent the event (a failure intrinsic to discourse) is inextricably tied to the overwhelming nature of the event (i.e., its unrepresentability and indeterminacy, which is in excess of discourse per se, and pertains rather to the magnitude of the event). There unfolds a chiasmus, then, between inadequacy and excess, the inadequacy of the symbolic order and the excess of the traumatic event. This is a chiasmus that I find to be the master trope of narrative trauma. Far from thrusting forward dialectically, this chiasmus proceeds in reversible and oft-crisscrossing movements, reproducing the transformational generative play of repetition, by which the novel starts in medias res and *by* which rather than *toward* which it is driven. It is in this chiasmus that the highly experimental and postmodern venture of *City Gates* must be situated. Since I have already addressed two aspects of this chiasmus—repetition and the search of narrative/emotional closure—I will now address two final aspects: fragmentariness and the collapse of the narrative voice. My aim here is not to exhaust all the aspects of this chiasmus of inadequacy and excess; rather, it is to be more explicit and specific about how central chiasmus itself is, as a trope, to narrative trauma. In the meanwhile, I will pave the way to my discussion of the specific concept of subjectivity that the novel forges in the smithy of formlessness.

The fragmentariness of *City Gates* is the most daunting hurdle facing any reader or critic of the novel. What is perhaps more consolatory than revelatory is that the reason why the novel is very fragmentary seems simple: it wants to *literalize* the failed experience of trauma (i.e., the failure of representation to bring about an experience of the event at the moment of its occurrence). How does one represent the failure of language to represent a traumatic event that demands yet defies representation, that demands yet defies understanding, and that demands yet defies mourning? How can one adequately represent all the symptoms associated with posttraumatic stress disorder—flashbacks, nightmares, repetition-compulsion, dissociative fugues, or dissociative amnesia, etc.? Here is just one more example, in addition to the preceding citations: "But . . . the truth is I didn't say anything, I wanted to say, but . . . no now I want to say, now after everything has happened I think that I wanted to say, or that I should've said. Now, I want to be there in order to say. But I'm not there, and I don't say anything."[51] The man and the stranger dramatizes here the chiastic oscillation between the survival of trauma and the trauma of survival itself, between having lived through and having missed the traumatic, and between being there and not being there (even though still, but not quite, there). The weight of the disjunctive temporalities of the there-and-then and the here-and-now cannot be overstressed—they are definitional of trauma. What is important to stress is that the desire "to say" is constantly being checked by/against the inability (or, worse, the missed opportunity) to "say anything" in the present of narration. Were it possible to be transported back to the scene of the traumatic event, it would have been possible to say, to represent and to experience the event at the moment of its occurrence. Above all, it would have been possible to distance oneself from it, but the fact that that did not obtain then precludes the possibility to make it happen now. It is precisely because that discursive distance did not take place then that *City Gates* does not attempt to make up for it or undertake it on behalf of its traumatized protagonist now; quite the contrary, the novel produces the lack of that distance (or would-be-discursive distance), the failure of representation, and the collapse of experience/witnessing the traumatic event at the moment it occurred.

"Then no, not possible to, perhaps, or" (*thumma lā, lā yumkin ʾan, rubbamā, ʾaou*)—says the stranger as he sets out searching for his lost suitcase (19). Soon afterwards, he asks: "How do I search for the suitcase?" (20). It is hard to grasp the symbolic meaning of this suitcase which we are told contains, on the one hand, "papers, pencils, and notebooks," and, on the other, "things that no longer had any meaning" (9). What is more puzzling, still, is that the stranger was the one who "threw his suitcase on the ground and it split open" before he left it there and walked (14), only to remember afterwards that in "his ripped suitcase there were papers and pencils" (15), a picture of his father and round pieces (24), and so he went back looking for it. When the first woman leads him in search of the suitcase, however, it becomes clear that the search verges on the absurd: "Seven times she walked and seven times he walked behind her, and the seventh time she said here, he said here, and he dug and didn't find anything" (25). The search for the suitcase becomes here an allegory for the search for the truth of what happened—the traumatic event whose locus of referentiality is inaccessible. Indeed, in Arabic, suitcase (*ḥạqība*) could actually be a pun on truth (*ḥạqīqa*)—both words are after all near-homographs as well as near-homophones.[52] Ultimately, this search for a lost suitcase becomes a journey into what Bessel A. Van der Kolk and Alexander C. McFarlane call in an article of the same title "the black hole of trauma," a vast and empty time-space of muted history, which arises following a traumatic encounter, or event. In the seven chapters that constitute the thoroughly dreamlike narrative of *City Gates,* the man and the stranger splits into multiple voices, becomes at one point in the beginning of the novel almost like a Kafkaesque character before the law, except that he returns to a mythical city with seven gates in front of each is a woman more or less beautiful than the other; in his way to the city square and in his search for the suitcase, he meets with surreal creatures, including a thousand-year old man with no eyes but who still managed to lead him to the city square; a thousand-year old virgin with tiny worms coming out of her insides and who dreamt of making love to a stranger like him;[53] a woman made of yogurt (33); a king in a grave of stone (36); a man eating salt and drinking water until he "transformed into a lump rolling in the middle of the square" (47); a woman who splits in two (55); foul-smelling animals (80); "women weeping over bloated corpses reeking of death" (83); and, finally, the city to which he longed to return fades away in a cataclysmic fire and storm; nothing remains of it "except weeping voices coming from the entrails of the fish and rising to where no one can listen to them" (97). Clearly, there is nothing even remotely mimetic, not to say realistic, about the events that the man and the stranger experiences in his journey back into the city (i.e., Beirut whose resurrection from the ruins of destruction has been replayed over and over again throughout history such that it had become a transhistorical myth, which served to defuse the nefarious material and immaterial repercussions of war and destruction).

While the novel reads and feels like a parable, a fable, a surreal, or fantastic narrative of sorts, it is important to stress again that *City Gates* does not proceed mimetically, but, rather, allegorically. It looks awry at the reality of violence. The events hardly resemble reality or the metonymies associated with reality (here, the reality of the Lebanese civil war obviously); rather, they point *at* and *toward* reality in a more circuitous, urgent and enduring manner for that matter. Like the dizzying seriality of nightmares, from which the man and the stranger keeps trying to awake throughout his journey into the black hole of the traumatic encounter, the reality of the war might not be properly apprehended if it cannot be discerned through the eerie and improbable events, as well as mysterious encounters described in the novel. For one thing, neither can the reality of civil war be walked through firsthand, nor can it be witnessed, or experienced without recourse to free-wheeling fictional qualifiers, or interjections such as "surreal," "preternatural," "senseless," "absurd," etc., all of which could be aptly applied to *City Gates.* For another, the sense of sustained disorientation, formlessness and adventurousness that characterize *City Gates* is not at all unwarranted or uncalled for if the novel is to be understood as a fierce representation of the failure of representation and of the collapse of the experience of trauma in the first place. How can posttraumatic stress disorders produced by the war not bring about correlative disorders at the level of the form of the novel? Edward Said describes Khoury's attraction to "formless works" as an attraction to what "Western theorists have called 'Post-Modern': that amalgam principally of autobiography, story, fable, pastiche, and self-parody, highlighted by an insistent and eerie nostalgia."[54] While Said's remarks were written specifically on *Little Mountain,* his references to the postmodernist formlessness and affective homelessness of Khoury's work (here and in other parts of the article) do, indeed, apply to *City Gates* whose partially postmodernist challenge consists in putting forward "the unpresentable in presentation," to use Jean-François Lyotard's phrase." According to Lyotard, "The postmodern would be that which, in the modern, puts forward the unpresentable in presentation itself; that which denies itself the solace of good forms, the consensus of a taste which would make it possible to share collectively the nostalgia for the unattainable; that which searches for new presentations, not in order to enjoy them but in order to impart a stronger sense of the unpresentable."[55]

City Gates strives to stretch the limits of the *presentable* even while it is highly sensitive to its inadequacy in front of the unpresentable trauma that paradoxically demands and defies representation. In its defamiliarizing and elusive style—simultaneously lyrical and postelegiac, compelling and unyielding at every turn, elliptical, at times, and aphoristic, or apocalyptic at others—*City Gates* clearly takes up the challenge of articulating (by means of a sustained and deliberate, even self-indulgent, inarticulacy) that failed experience and that failed representation, that is, the encounter between its protagonist and the traumatic event (presumably the catastrophe of the Lebanese civil strife). After all, "it is in failed experience that the close interconnectedness of discourse and experience is disrupted. This disruption enables us to see what exactly is discursive about experience."[56] This commitment to formal experimentation does not exist in a sociopolitical vacuum; it is not an aesthetic end in itself, nor is it a function of disinterestedness, or art for art's sake. Quite the contrary, the postmodernist tendencies in modern Arabic literature arise out of profoundly presentist concerns: "In societies in transition," says Khoury, "you cannot separate what is political from what is literary. . . . Literature, in our situation must put together two elements: seeing and inventing; it must tell the truth and lie; it must combine the real and the fantastic at the same level and at the same moment."[57] The late Magda M. Al-Nowaihi reaches a similar conclusion in her reading of Muḥammad Barrāda's *The Game of Forgetting:* "in distinction to western texts where postmodernity and commitment often seem to be mutually exclusive, we have here a narrative that is postmodern in sensibility and structure, but is also fiercely concerned with the here and now and committed to struggling for its improvement."[58] While I do not necessarily think that the entirety of western postmodern literature and theory has surrendered, or compromised its political edge, I agree with Al-Nowaihi's overall argument, whose pertinence has to do more with the actualities of Arabic literature than with the postmodern character of western literature. I cannot overstate the allegorical venture of *City Gates* which proffers us with a way to relate to the discontinuous chaos of war rather than with a documentary and mimetic rendition of its diurnal reality. By defamiliarizing us with the material history of war, the novel points at the invisible and unquantifiable psychic cuts whose history demands yet defies witness. The formlessness of *City Gates* attests, therefore, to the materialization of the immaterial history of these cuts at the level of language and form. From this perspective, the formlessness of the novel puts us on trial before (muted) history.

After having addressed the major formal and stylistic characteristics of the novel, I now want to conclude by addressing one final aspect in which the novel attempts to produce and present the failed experience of trauma; I will address instances of the collapse of the narrative voice in order to stop at the ways in which *City Gates* presents us—in the final analysis—with the drama of depersonalization and vulnerability as a means of rethinking responsible subjectivity. Insofar as it can be read traumatically as a product of the novel's centripetal and centrifugal trauma ties, vulnerability becomes, in turn, a potential psychosocial concept for reenvisioning sociopolitical, communal and human ties (all of which can at any time be invoked or retreated from, particularly in contexts of everyday violence). The narrative voice meanders jerkily between third and first person narration. The "man and the stranger," the anonymous protagonist of the novel, splits—because of the acute dissociative disorders from which he suffers and which are associated with PTSD—into the "man," the "stranger" and the "storyteller," imparting thus a heightened sense of an authorless narrative, shading into anonymously and indistinguishably multiperspectival, protean and confusing narrative voices, including that of the frame narrator. First and third person narrative voices are continually fusing and collapsing into each other: "I said I'll bend down and I'll lean over and I'll go to sleep. The stranger said I'll bend down and I'll lean over and I'll go to sleep."[59] At times, the first person narrative voice splits in two: "The woman calls to me, I say to her, I am not me/I know you are not you, but she calls to me" (38). When the narrative voice finally reasserts its authority, it sounds far less than reassuring: "And I say, I am the one who says, I am the one who" (89). The first example shows how the first person narrative voice identifies with the stranger. The second example shows how the first person narrative voice splits itself in two and disidentifies with one part of its own self. In the third example, the first person narrative voice clears any confusion caused by the chiastic vacillation between identification and disidentification and reclaims its authority over the narrative (even though it is clearly an attenuated form of authority). As a rule, however, whenever the narrative voice is the agent of a given action at the moment of trauma, it tends to identify with otherness (as in the first example); inversely, it tends to disidentify with all forms of otherness whenever it is the object of an action (as in the second example where the woman's call interpellates the first person narrator). It is as if the very subjective ambiguity of the experience of trauma—in which the traumatized subject experiences simultaneities of, or alternations between, deliberate *returns to* and disembodied *returns of* the traumatic event—dictates the economy of identification and disidentification. It is as if the back and forth shifts from the first to the third person narration are expressive of the anonymous narrator's fantasy of mastery over a situation to which he is nevertheless submitted. If such is the case, this fantasy of mastery is nothing more than an agentive fallacy. The traumatized subject is in most cases the object, not the agent, of the traumatic event. The protagonist of *City Gates* is no exception. One need not neglect, however, the role of this fantasy of mastery, not only in the process of experiencing and bearing witness to the devastations of trauma, but also in the formation of a new form of subjectivity out of that very exposure and vulnerability.

The fantasy of mastery is first and foremost a symptom of the unmasterable trauma. It neither fully shelters the traumatized subject from, nor keeps him entirely defenseless in front of the obsessive returns to the shattering traumatic moment (associated with PTSD-related symptoms). Above all, not only does this fantasy hold open the possibility of experiencing and representing trauma, but it also makes possible the endurance of the traumatized subject in the process of (processing) trauma. At the level of the failed experience of trauma that *City Gates* performs, this fantasy of mastery transforms and generates other fantasies, particularly the fantasy of storytelling: "And I, I was speaking, I see and I don't speak. I said I won't tell my story to anyone. I don't know the story, so what's there to tell?" (69). It is ironic that the fantasy of storytelling throughout the novel repetitively announces the very foreclosure of storytelling, only that the narrative voice had to live through that very foreclosure in order to announce it. *City Gates* is, in a nutshell, the name of that announcement (of foreclosure), except that the announcement is reiterated again and again, without end. It is as if the announcement must continue announcing itself in order to say it is being announced. It is ultimately through, and in the meanwhile of, this repetitive announcement of narrative foreclosure that the novel inscribes the catastrophe it failed to represent:

> And the storyteller tells what he saw, and the storyteller bears witness to what he witnessed, and the witness dies as the victims die, and the witness knows no more than walls and doors and eyes in which hands burn, and hands that stretch out to smoldering eyes.
>
> And the one who witnessed writes about his eyes, and walks beside the man who walked and doesn't leave him alone and he will not be except where he found himself. (5)

This is the ending of the preamble, which is, as I mentioned before, a compressed version of the entire narrative, except that it is at once inside and outside its circular structure. The ending of the preamble is a bit different from the ending of the novel, which I cited before and which puts forward a vision of the end in which nothing remains except "weeping voices coming from the entrails of fish and rising to where no one can listen to them" (97). While both endings depict an apocalyptic destiny, the ending of the preamble injects a glimmer of hope for a different future provided that bold steps are taken. These do not even remotely amount to a blueprint for action (especially given the constant disorientation and abstractness of *City Gates*), but they revolve around an eclectic number of keywords that can be extracted from both endings. The first three keywords are explicit: *storytelling, witnessing, listening.* The other three are implicit; they include the notion of *vulnerability* (tacit in the description of victims that die and hands that burn), *solidarity* (latent in the determination not to leave the other man alone), and, finally, *subjectivity* (which is sufficiently encoded in the references to the conditions of being and selfhood). This is by no means a finite list, much less so especially if it is to be taken, as I do here, to apply to the entirety of the novel. What is important here is to articulate the potential relations between these keywords that the novel itself points toward. I propose to do so by reexamining the fantasy of mastery and the fantasy of storytelling that propel the narrative voice in its self professed mission: to listen, to tell and to bear witness.

While the fantasy of mastery over trauma may largely be a product of an agentive fallacy, it is nonetheless crucial to the process of coming to terms with a compromised subjectivity. Similarly, while the fantasy of storytelling is continually overridden by the foreclosure of storytelling, it nonetheless imparts a heightened sense of the urgency of the present (*al-ḥāḍir*) and the pressing need to put forward narrative acts—acts that are never more to be desired than at a time when not even the witness (i.e., the stranger) is (being) spared, as the passage above makes unequivocally evident, the fate of those *to* whom and *for* whom he seeks to bear witness. Both fantasies are in point of fact gestures of inconsolability, symptomatic not only of the experience of lonely suffering that the stranger lives through—"This has not happened before, it hasn't happened that everyone and I have not remained except alone" (90) / "The stranger said he was dying all alone" (97)—but also of the endurance of his subjectivity in the process. Above all, both fantasies are symptomatic of the ways in which the stranger attempts to redistribute solitary suffering into cultural and public memory, which is after all the foundational gesture of *City Gates* as a whole. This process, I argue, cuts across the private and public, the personal and communal, as well as the subjective and collective.

The fantasy of mastery is precisely the fantasy of bearing witness to one's own desolate experience of solitary suffering when no secondary and empathic witness can be found. In "The Most Intimate of Creations: Symptoms as Memorials to One's Lonely Suffering," Peter Shabad deftly reveals the symptomatologic workings of witnessing—the logic whereby the symptom becomes the personal device of witnessing suffering. Accentuating the disjunctive temporalities between the occurrence of a traumatic accident and the psychic and affective response to it by the lonely individual who experienced it, Shabad explains how unwitnessed solitary suffering transforms into trauma and how only "the transformation of experienced suffering into witnessed reality at the moment it occurs that inoculates experience against traumatization."[60] In the absence of another person, who can validate our solitary experience of suffering, however, "we are forced into the awkward, involuted position of bearing witness to our own experience" (200). Individual consciousness becomes, as such, "a powerful homegrown overseer" (198), or, in the words of Paul Russell, whom Sahbad cites, "a camera photographing its own imagery" (202)—really, a camera "bearing the responsibility of remembering and testifying to the actuality of one's suffering" (201). It is as if the mind itself becomes an autowitnessing machine, or a posttraumatic shock recorder, converting the traumatic event into experienceable material.

In a provocative move that is partly reminiscent of Nicolas Abraham and Maria Torok's concept of encryption in *The Shell and the Kernel,* Shabad maintains that the conversion of a trauma precipitated by lonely suffering must pass through the intimate and creative path of symptomatology. Symptoms are self-invented "communicative actions intended to build a lasting monument once and for all for one's experience of suffering" (207)—a "monument that will be remembered and that will testify to the actuality of our own existence" (197). Shabad calls this also "a moment in the sun," blurring thus the materiality of the symptom with its belated temporality (197). The dissolution of the symptoms is dependent upon the engineering of a "credibly empathic witness" and "of bringing the dignity of recognition, sometimes many years later, to a person's experience of lonely suffering" (210). As reiterative acts of lonely suffering generated by, or driven toward the traumatic event, trauma ties not only traumatize the survivor, but also become the animating impetus and optimal fostering ground for the formation of social and communal ties. The protagonist of *City Gates* is estranged from yet tied to the anonymous city; his constant comings and goings between the city gates and city square present us with a poetics of relationality that is profoundly exiled and rooted at one and the same time—this is a chiasmus of exilic ties, which might be, in point of fact, at the very basis of an ethico-politics of relationality. As Kai Erikson argues, "trauma has both centripetal and centrifugal tendencies. It draws one away from the center of group space at the same time drawing one back . . . estrangement becomes the basis for communality."[61] Estrangement allows for what Ricoeur calls, in a book of the same title, "the course of recognition" (*parcours de la reconnaissance*) to unfold from "self-recognition" to "mutual recognition," from "identity" to "otherness," and along a "background" "dialectic between recognition and misrecognition."[62]

City Gates dramatizes throughout its narrative collapse this course of recognition, which is consistently expressed (in Khoury's, by now, routine indirectness) as an unremitting sense of estrangement, rootlessness and exile. For instance, the protagonist of the novel is called "the stranger" (*al-gharīb*) and does, indeed, feel "a stranger in his own city."[63] No wonder, then, that only toward the end of the narrative does he remember that he came to the city carrying a suitcase *and* a mirror which he also lost: "I don't remember, I don't. I'm looking for my mirror that got lost and for my things that I lost."[64] The loss of the mirror (in the Lacanian sense) must have literally retarded the potentiality of misrecognition, but, given that the narrative is refracted through mirrors and through a continually split or splitting narrative voice, the stranger must have already confronted the spectral dimension of his subjectivity. This spectral subjectivity has to do more, though, with the historical magnitude of warfare and violence than with the structural constitution of subjectivity, of which Lacan speaks in his well known essay on the mirror stage.[65] What is important to stress is that the stranger's name (or lack of it thereof) does not only suggest that those around him fail to recognize him—and, therefore, recognize, or misrecognize him as a stranger, perhaps, even, as less than human—but also, and more important by far, that he is himself both alienated from himself and his surroundings. It is in the course of estrangement that a transformational and generative formation of subjectivity and community takes place, since, as Erikson argues, "drifting away is accompanied by revised views of the world that, in their turn, become the basis for communality."[66]

Erikson goes on to argue that traumatized people, by virtue of their estrangement and alienation, "calculate life's chances differently. They look out at the world through a different lens. And in that sense they can be said to have experienced not only a *changed sense of self* and a *changed way of relating to others* but a changed *worldview.*"[67] The type of recognition that is furnished by estrangement and defamiliarization suspends the existing norms of intelligibility that determine the apportioning of recognition and open them up to the dynamics of empathy and epiphany (i.e., what I had termed *empiphany* in chapter 2). It is as if only by becoming totally unrecognizable to oneself and one's surroundings—only by undergoing, that is, a limit experience, such as trauma—does one aspire to be transformed and, more important, to transform the existing norms of intelligibility that grant and withhold recognition. Indeed, the ending of the preamble I cited above points toward a concept of recognition of empiphanic proportions, one that involves both cognitive insight and empathic reckoning, or, as Rita Felski argues, "knowledge" and "acknowledgement": "The former is directed toward the self, the latter toward others, such that the two meanings of the term would seem to be entirely at odds."[68] It is, however, the bidirectional crosscutting of recognition that becomes obvious in the last passage in the preamble: "And the one who witnessed writes about his eyes, and walks beside the man who walked *and doesn't leave him alone and he will not be except where he found himself* (*wa lā yatrukhu waḥīdan wa lā yakūn ʾillā ḥaythu wajada nafsahu*)" (5, italics mine). Recognition here cuts across all of the above keywords, particularly subjectivity, vulnerability, and solidarity. Only in solidarity with the vulnerability of the anonymous other—which is the flipside of our own exposure and vulnerability—can we become subjects.

In league with trauma and mourning, as well as other psychoaffective coordinates, vulnerability here institutes and points toward a counterintuitive mode of subjectivity—a subjectivity that can no longer afford to harbor any illusions about its implication in and exposure to the vulnerability of the other anonymous man who walks beside. In no small measure, this is also the communal and sociopolitical dimension of vulnerability, whose force *City Gates* brings to the fore. Rather than reconcile us to its structural overdetermination in an age of disaster capitalism, Khoury's novel puts us on trial before its historical trials. The novel points at and toward a way of thinking trauma and politics in tandem: form. The vulnerability that the anonymous stranger goes through and endures materializes in the formless form of the novel. It makes itself known more closely through the relentless chiastics of survival. Chiasmus is the figure of traumatic survival and vulnerability. Vulnerability itself is, as I hope I have successfully demonstrated, indissociable from the actual poetics of mourning that govern or fail to govern texts. To continually discriminate between historical (i.e., singular-plural) vulnerabilities *and* structural vulnerability (i.e., the primary vulnerability that inheres in our thrownness into the world, in the Heideggerian sense, of course) is a task that I cannot overstress here—it is one of the most enduring preoccupations—and, ironically, one of the habitually overlooked lessons of the poetics of narrative mourning as charted in this book. It has been the inaugurational and animating gesture of this final chapter. I should like to make it its ending and, hopefully, enduring point.

Coda: The Politics of Mourning

SIGNIFYING LOSS COMES AT THE END OF AN ERA OF CRITICAL THINKING ABOUT mourning and melancholia—really, at the end of the dialectic between mourning and melancholia and, more precisely, between the imperative to mourn and the imperative to refuse consolation, which is the fundamental tonality variably audible throughout most studies on the subject from the Mitscherliches and Abraham and Torok through Eric Santner and Julia Kristeva to Derrida and Butler and beyond. Broadly speaking, I believe these studies have, in one way or another, been constrained and, simultaneously, sustained by Freud's seminal essay, "Mourning and Melancholia" (1917). Not that this is not a good starting point; indisputably, that is precisely the case. However, Freud's later work, especially "The Ego and the Id" (1923), helps us reassess—as the more recent post-Derridean studies demonstrate—the rigidity with which the distinction between mourning and melancholia has been sustained in contemporary discourses on mourning even while Freud himself had already attenuated and diminished its premises. In my examination of "Mourning and Melancholia" within the scope of Freud's work, I reinterpret melancholia as a function of mourning and therefore as existing in a continuum with rather than in opposition to mourning. This view is not an entirely original one since Eric Santner had already formulated it in *Stranded Objects,* but I felt it necessary to revitalize it here in order to stress the continua of convergences rather than divergences between mourning and melancholia.

The point is neither to accentuate nor to attenuate the differences or similarities between mourning and melancholia, but to see the ways in which they both allow us to straddle the study of modernist, postmodernist and postcolonial narratives. Signifying loss is an inaugurational principle of these traditionally and continually separated fields of scholarship. And while I do not necessarily think that modernism is to postcolonialism what mourning is to melancholia, I nonetheless contend that the signifying impulse of mourning is a common denominator of both fields. Much like psychoanalysis and deconstruction, both modernist and postcolonial discourses are marked by their respective heritages of loss from the Two World Wars and the decolonization struggles (not to mention, particularly in the case of postcolonialism, ethnic civil wars and continual neocolonial and proxy wars of various kinds).

This is not to say, of course, that loss is signified in the same way across all the literary and theoretical writings I dealt with, much less across the fields to which these writings normally belong. The point is not to argue that loss is experienced in the same way across modernism, postcolonialism, psychoanalysis and deconstruction, but, rather, to show its distinct yet enduring reverberations, turns and returns. For Joyce, for instance, while the experience of mourning could reach empiphanic proportions, it can also congeal into melancholia and result in either madness or suicide. For Kincaid, however, melancholia is as useful as mourning, depending on the case at hand: while the signifying practices of melancholia enable her to stake a claim to losses that would otherwise be completely assimilated by colonial history, those of mourning allow her to survive the death of a brother without dying with him, and precisely by writing about his death, which renders narrative mourning literally a sanctioned discursive survivalist practice.

It has become quite obvious to me that a remarkable consensus (somewhat on the literary critical Left, I believe) seems to have emerged in recent studies on mourning: that the literary work of mourning does not console; rather, it exercises and incites inconsolability.[1] While I cannot gainsay the pertinence of this argument (since I do actually demonstrate how it works in Kincaid's unclassifiable auto/alter/biography, *The Autobiography of My Mother*), I do nonetheless think that inconsolability has to be deployed carefully in terms of the geopolitical stakes involved. Otherwise, former colonizers and colonized peoples, alike, would equally stake claims to inconsolability, the former for their loss of the old empire status and the gains that come with it, the latter for their loss of their precolonial sovereignty, culture, language, and for the indignity fomented by those losses—an indignity that never ceases to excite projects of redress, financial and moral, the latest of which took place between Libya and Italy.

The political leverage of inconsolability in Kincaid consists in the imperative to claim and signify, however poorly, the disembodied memories of loss and suffering as they flit by in the frailty and contingency of the imagination. This argument is in line with Ranjana Khanna's reactivation of melancholia's critical and political potential—a potential that is latent in Freud, Fanon and Abraham and Torok. However, Khanna's and Kincaid's practice of melancholia is different from that of Paul Gilroy who aligns it with the pathological disposition that has now become prevalent in a former imperial power: England. These differences in the use of the same concept are understandable given that Freud did not elaborate a grand narrative of melancholia, only an allegory of the very crisis melancholia brings about. They are also understandable because Freud's heirs have tended to foreground one aspect of melancholia at the expense of others. This is the case, for instance, with the wide ranging study by the Mitscherliches, *The Inability to Mourn,* in which melancholia becomes important precisely because the conditions for its emergence are in place, only that melancholia itself does not emerge; it is, instead, foreclosed, disavowed or congealed.

Signifying Loss points at *and* toward a tactical and differentiable theory of mourning—*a geopolitics of mourning*—that can attend to the particular historical circumstances in which mourning arises or refuses to arise; persists or ends; transforms or deforms; counts or does not count; in short, materializes or fails to materialize. Ultimately, it is in those vigilant acts of critical distance and close reading—or what I call critical distance at close range—that signifying loss matters, and matters significantly, particularly at a time when the tendency to construct mourning as a sharable experience capable of troping the communal and the social into practical existence has been constantly undermined by the very structures of determinacy that produce and reproduce mourning as a discursive predicament.

When Derrida declares that "all work is also the work of mourning,"[2] the question that comes to mind is not whether this is a true or false statement, for there is a lot of truth in it; rather, the question is the following: what are the political implications of such an assertion? Does it not risk displacing the actual—historically and geopolitically located and locatable—devastating experiences and works of mourning into structural determinacy? It becomes crucial to distinguish, therefore, between the foundational practices of mourning on which all subjectivity is hinged and the painfully historical, deeply disturbing, and oftentimes impossible, mourning tasks that the colonial, diasporic, dispossessed or racialized subject might be called upon to accomplish. I particularly discuss this in chapter 6 in relation to the institutionalization of violence in today's world, but this seems to me in more broad terms one of the continually present and continually disturbing legacies of deconstruction.

Commenting on Paul de Man's wartime writings, Eric Santner has eloquently hammered home this very point I have been trying to locate at the basis for the emergence of a geopolitics of mourning: "The error of Paul de Man in this historical series was, I suggest, that he sought to displace and disperse the particular, historical tasks of mourning which for him, as is now known, were substantial and complex, with what might be called structural mourning, that is, mourning for those 'catastrophes' that are inseparable from being-in-language. And since so much recent critical theory has followed de Man's lead in reducing historical suffering and catastrophe to a series of structural operations depleted of affect—the appeal to human subjectivity is taken as a sign of lack of rigor, nostalgia, sentimentality—the error of Paul de Man, despite the very particular features of his history, becomes exemplary."[3]

I have attempted throughout the different chapters that constitute this book, but particularly in the last one, to point toward a form of subjectivity and community at the crossroads of psychoanalysis and politics. While language remains our predicament par excellence, I believe it has allowed and allows for the formation of forms of agency and collectivity, which in my view emerge and materialize as investments in form—particularly, in the tropologics of signifying or narrative poetics proper—in the texts I have examined.[4]

In the twilight of the first decade of the twenty first century, the political stakes involved in mourning are as high as they have been in the aftermath of 9/11. The question that Butler posed at the time is still an urgent one, "If we are interested in arresting cycles of violence to produce less violent outcomes, it is no doubt important to ask what, politically, might be made of grief besides a cry for war."[5] The fact that individual and national grief in this case was harnessed into a cry for war—which is still going on in two fronts, and as I write: Afghanistan and Iraq—is indicative of the ways in which mourning can be manipulated to serve ideological and political aims.

The prolonged state of exception that followed 9/11 has resulted in the heightened politicization and manipulation of mourning in such a way as to practically normalize the discrimination between "mournable" and "unmournable" —and, subsequently, "disposable"—subjects. The differential conferment of "mournability," which runs in tandem with the production of "disposable subjects," eclipses what Butler calls, in a suggestive phrase, our "primary vulnerability to others."[6] The scramble to action that followed 9/11 is symptomatic, not of the recognition of our primary vulnerability to others, but of a regression to a Freudian state of "primary narcissism,"[7] in which the injured ego (of the nation) attempts to regain mastery over a situation to which it was suddenly forced to submit. The manipulation of mourning in the service of vindictive and global military adventures eclipses, in an equal measure, the opportunity to imagine new modalities of conceiving subjectivity and community and of thinking through mourning as the basis for the emergence of what Butler dubs a "global political community."[8] Given that the devaluation of the concept of mourning is the direct result of the breakup of community, only by reinvigorating the vitalities of mourning—which can reach empiphanic proportions, as I demonstrate in my reading of Joyce—can one aspire to rediscover and rebuild the communal at a transnational and global scale.

What seems to me of critical urgency is the necessity of mapping further, expanding and particularizing, not only the poetics of narrative mourning, but what I have tentatively called a geopolitics of mourning. A couple of questions have animated and still animate my thinking on the necessity of elaborating this geopolitics of mourning; I close with them: Can a rethinking of the human in terms of the contingencies of exposure to (and not solely the exploitation of) the vulnerabilities of others release us from the illusion of our own invulnerability? Can such rethinking lead to the production of viable affective bonds that might in turn foster a sense of transnational solidarity and global community structured by *mutual* rather than *dueling* vulnerabilities?

Notes

Preface

1. Homans, Introduction to *Symbolic Loss,* ed. by Peter Homans, 9.

2. See Cheng, *The Melancholy of Race,* 6.

3. "Of all genres, the elegy especially requires and provides," Peter Sacks argues, "a perspective [from which to reexamine the connections between language and the pathos of human consciousness], for it is characterized by an unusually powerful intertwining of emotion and rhetoric, of loss and figuration" (*The English Elegy,* xii). If elegy is such a sanctioned signifying practice—or the genre par excellence—for signifying loss, it risks being co-opted by the ideological and normative practices of mourning that might be in place in a given community or society at a given point in time. The question, then, becomes how could this genre spearhead or incite dissent from normative practices of mourning if it is already outmaneuvered by those very practices?

4. Ramazani, *Poetry of Mourning,* xi. See also Gana, "War, Poetry, Mourning." A consensus about the antiredemptory significance of the modern elegy seems to have been reached. "What is clear is that those [Ramazani and Shaw] at the cutting edge of elegy studies," William Watkin argues, "reject the consolatory role of elegy within the western paradigm of mourning rituals as emotional therapy and this *must* be the future direction of all studies of the genre" (*On Mourning,* 78, [italics mine.])

5. See Adorno, "Commitment," 189. Adorno's original ban on poetry as such—"To write poetry after Auschwitz is barbaric" (34)—appeared in "Cultural Criticism and Society," an essay written in 1949 and published in 1951.

6. Žižek, *Violence,* 4–5.

7. See Freud, "Mourning and Melancholia," 253; Derrida, *The Work of Mourning,* 142.

8. Ricciardi's *The Ends of Mourning,* 3; Watkin's *On Mourning,* 14.

9. Brooks, *Reading for the Plot,* xiv.

10. Said, "After Mahfouz," 325. Said describes Khoury, along with Darwish, as an artist "who gives voice to rooted exiles and the plight of the trapped refugees, to dissolving boundaries and changing identities, to radical demands and new languages." Not without differences, of course, Joyce, Kincaid and Ben Jelloun are rooted exiles in their own ways.

1. Thresholds of Mourning

1. Joyce, *Ulysses,* 138.

2. Freud, "Mourning and Melancholia," 251.

3. Ibid., 252.

4. Ibid., 253.

5. Geoffrey Galt Harpham, "The Business of Mourning," 539. I am thinking here of Foucault's felicitous remark in his *Remarks on Marx:* "If I had to write a book to communicate what I have already thought, I'd never have the courage to begin it. I write precisely because I don't know yet what to think about a subject that attracts my interest" (27).

6. See J. Hillis Miller, "The Critic as Host."

7. See Joyce, *Ulysses,* 247.

8. For a comprehensive and sharp introduction to "object relations theory," see Jay R. Greenberg and Stephen A. Mitchell, *Object Relations in Psychoanalytic Theory.*

9. Freud, "Mourning and Melancholia," 253.

10. See Ricoeur, "What is a Text?," 344. Of course, such stages of desire are, as will become clear in the next section, structured by death and mourning, but it does not always follow in real life that whoever falls in love contemplates death. In "Thoughts on War and Death," Freud speaks of "the tendency to exclude death from our calculations in life"—a tendency that "brings in its train many other renunciations and exclusions" (79). In *Being and Time,* Martin Heidegger shows how death, the fundamental question of Being, is defused and forgotten by Dasein's withdrawal into the "idle talk" (*Gerede*) of the "they"—the "Self of everydayness" (296). Joyce's attempt in "Hades" to recreate the graveyard scene from *Hamlet* can be seen as an admixture of a harsh reminder of the *reality*—and a severe critique of the *banality*—of death in a world that has become, in the wake of the Great War, no longer cognizant of, let alone beholden to, either aspect.

11. While mourning remains mostly an enigma in all of Freud's writings, it will have become clear nonetheless that Freud was more often than not disinclined to believe in the very possibility of mourning. In fact, mourning seems to be possible only in the realm of literature and theater: "There alone," Freud argues in "Thoughts on War and Death," "the condition can be fulfilled which makes it possible for us to reconcile ourselves with death: namely, that behind all the vicissitudes of life we should still be able to preserve a life intact. For it is really too sad that in life it should be as it is in chess, where one false move may force us to resign the game, but with the difference that we can start no second game, no return-match. In the realm of fiction we find the plurality of lives which we need. We die with the hero with whom we have identified ourselves; yet we survive him, and are ready to die again just as safely with another hero" (79). In chapter 5, I will inquire whether the staging of death and mourning in narrative fiction can help bridge the gap between the cruelty of the experience of reality and the benevolence of the experience of fiction.

12. Freud, "Analysis Terminable and Interminable," 228.

13. Freud, "Mourning and Melancholia," 253.

14. Freud denotes here the process whereby the mourner sets out to reassess thoroughly the relationship to the lost love-object preparatory to ending it. This process entails, among others, an arduous labor of recollection, reattachment, and severance.

15. Joyce, *Ulysses,* 145.

16. In *Ulysses*—and in the "Hades" episode, in particular—mourning can be constructed as a public ritual that is at loggerheads with the more private sensation of grief. Bloom is dressed in mourning for the sake of Paddy Dignam's funeral, yet what he feels—or rather lives through—is grief for the loss of both his father and his son. Paddy Dignam's funeral serves, therefore, as an occasion for Bloom to paradoxically perform the task of mourning for a father who committed suicide and a son who died prematurely, as much as to veil such psychoaffective performance from public display. What is interesting to note here is that Bloom goes *into* mourning for Paddy Dignam—a person he neither knows well nor has any affinities with his religion—only to go *through* the process of mourning for the loss of both his father and his son before he hits the exit door of the cemetery. Bloomsday of mourning becomes here an allegory for the simultaneity of going into, going through and going out of mourning—really, an allegory for the conjunctive and disjunctive contingencies of mourning.

17. Shakespeare, *Hamlet,* ed. Susanne L. Wofford (Boston: Bedford Books, 1994), 1.2, 36.

18. In *The Ends of Mourning,* Ricciardi argues that Freud's notion of the *Trauerarbeit* "takes as its ultimate goal the replacement of the lost object and thereby honors the modernist imperative to 'make it new.' Yet it should be noticed that the tempo he assigns to the mourning process coincides with the pensive meticulousness of analysis rather than the transformative speed of modernity" (25).

19. Freud, "Remembering, Repeating and Working-Through," 152.

20. Henry Staten, *Eros in Mourning,* xi.

21. On attachment theory in relation loss and mourning, see John Bowlby, *Loss,* vol. III of *Attachment and Loss.*

22. While partially inspired by and indebted to Lacan, my reflections on the question of desire are deliberately stripped of Lacan's lexicon, not only because Lacan's conceptual armature is ostensibly opaque, but also because it threatens to hijack the forward thrust of the argument of this book into endless explanatory forays of Lacan's "phallophanies" (or linguistic epiphanies). The reader might be relieved rather than aggrieved to find out that it is still possible to speak about desire, not Desire, after Lacan without necessarily having to use such formulations as "Other/other," "object *in* desire," "object *a*" (*l'objet petit a*), or even Lacan's triadic conception of Desire: the split between demand (*demande*) and need of which the voracious veracity, as I call it, of Desire is an effect. By and large, I draw on Lacan's most common texts in English translations, especially on *Écrit: A Selection, The Four Fundamental Concepts of Psychoanalysis,* as well as on Lacan's essay on *Hamlet,* "Desire and the Interpretation of Desire in *Hamlet.*" A reading of these texts makes it clear to me that Lacan's conception of Desire is indissociable from a constant graveyard whistling, a relentless retrogressive pushing toward a lost or prenatal immortality. In his essay on *Hamlet,* for instance—after having demonstrated, quite cogently, how Hamlet is uninterruptedly suspended in the (time and desire of the) Other—he concludes that an object *in* desire becomes an object *of* desire only when it can no longer be possessed. Referring to the graveyard scene and to the burial of Ophelia—Hamlet's no-longer-possible love-object—Lacan contends that "Only insofar as the object of Hamlet's desire has become an impossible object can it become the object of his desire" (36). Emerging and reemerging in the unbridgeable split between demand and need, desire is a constant slide along the metonymic chain of signifiers. Since the object of desire remains lacking along the chain of signifiers, it can be named and embraced only when it is irrecoverably lost to the signifying system. In this sense, mourning becomes more of a linguistic interruption than a relational and historical predicament: "The Work of mourning is first of all performed to satisfy the disorder that is produced by the inadequacy of signifying elements to cope with the hole that has been created in existence, for it is the system of signifiers in their totality which is impeached by the least instance of mourning" (38). For a critique of Lacan's conception of mourning in relation to lack rather than historical loss, see Dominick LaCapra, "Trauma, Absence, Loss," and Alessia Ricciardi's *The Ends of Mourning;* for a focused conception of desire as a relentless descent into the immortal world of the non-object (that is, the world of Yorick's skull, the world of the "contentless particularity of the self-that-is-nothing"), see Staten's "The Bride Stripped Bare, or Lacan *avec* Plato"; for a more contextual framing of Lacan's reconstruction of Freud's notion of drive (*Trieb*) and instinct (*Instinkt*) in terms of the triad of Desire, demand, and need, see Ellie Ragland-Sullivan, *Jacques Lacan and the Philosophy of Psychoanalysis.*

23. Staten, *Eros in Mourning,* xi.

24. Lacan, "Desire and the Interpretation of Desire in *Hamlet,*" 37

25. Ibid., 38.

26. Staten, *Eros in Mourning,* 5.

27. Quoted in Staten, *Eros in Mourning,* 5.

28. Ibid., 10.

29. Smythe, *Figuring Grief,* 12.

30. Freud, *Civilization and its Discontents,* 264.
31. Ibid.
32. Ibid., 274.
33. Freud, "On Narcissism," 84.
34. Freud, "Inhibitions, Symptoms and Anxiety," 332.
35. Freud, *Group Psychology,* 134.
36. By "gender trouble," I am alluding to Judith Butler, *Gender Trouble: Feminism and the Subversion of Identity.* In *Group Psychology and the Analysis of the Ego,* Freud explains two psychologically distinct emotional ties that a little boy can develop: "a straightforward sexual object-cathexis towards his mother and an identification with his father which takes him as his model" (134). Only when these two types of ties are confounded does the oedipal struggle arise. The sexual rivalry over the mother destabilizes the boy's mimetic identification with the father, since it is crisscrossed with the prohibition of incest. It is noteworthy here that identification is from the outset the playground of a number of ambivalent emotions: love for the mother (which is coupled with the interdiction of *having* her) and mimicry of the father (coupled with the interdiction of impersonating him) that slips into hatred as soon as the father becomes an obstacle in the way of the boy's desire for the mother. This will prove helpful when we move on to a discussion of the melancholic upsurge in which the identification with a lost object is colored by hatred. By and large, Freud's Oedipus complex remains a problem that post-Freudians from Lacan to Judith Butler have not ceased to interrogate. Were my focus here the question of sexual identity, I would discuss the implications of Freud's theory in relation to homosexuality and to what Freud calls, in *The Ego and the Id,* "constitutional bisexuality" (371). For me the question is not, as Butler formulates it, of "melancholy gender," which comes to *structure* identity, but one of melancholy subjectivity, which is a *historical* marker of the devastations of colonialism/imperialism, as I will demonstrate in chapter 4. While Freud distinguishes between the "identification with the father" (in which "one's father is what one would like to *be*") and "the choice of the father as an object" (in which one's father is "what one would like to *have*"), he avows not to be able "to give a clear metapsychological representation of the distinction" (135). Because the dissolution of the Oedipus complex cannot be witnessed, and because normative heterosexuality is not a given, sexual identity remains largely unaccounted for and therefore open to endless heterodox constructions. How is it that an originally blind libidinal identification becomes sexually bound and discriminative? How is it that identification is at the origin and end of the Oedipus complex? While Freud chose in *The Ego and Id* to adopt the heterosexual and "more normal" version of the Oedipus complex (371), Mikkel Borch-Jacobsen is nevertheless right in singling out the two main scandals in which this complex resulted: first, "not that there is infantile sexuality and that the child harbors incestuous and patricidal desires but that access to genital heterosexuality is not a foregone conclusion" and, second, that "the first 'emotional ties' with others," which are not oriented along lines of sexual difference, "are additionally shot through with a hate and violence that are all the more essential in that they are confounded with love" (271).
37. Freud, *The Ego and the Id,* 368.
38. In "Mourning and Melancholia," Freud had already contrasted melancholia—albeit inconclusively—to mourning, arguing that, while the former results in affective closure, the latter acts like an "open wound" in which egoic consolation and flights into infantile forms of narcissism occur simultaneously with the chidings of the super agent in the ego (to be conceptualized later, in *The Ego and the Id,* as the "superego")—an agent that does not condone the ego's identification with and interiorization of the lost object, that is, the setting up of the lost object in the ego for the sake of calming the id's unquenched libidinal desire. Melancholia, however, as constructed in *The Ego and the Id,* is not an interminable process, but is the very condition of the fulfillment of the work of mourning itself. In other words, melancholia has become subsumable under mourning. What is common in most theoretical or critical work that dis-

cusses or applies Freud's theories of mourning and melancholia is that the discussion of mourning oftentimes serves as an excuse to dwell, much as Freud himself does in "Mourning and Melancholia," on melancholia. In melancholia, the shadow of the object is said to fall upon the ego; in most critical discussions of mourning and melancholia, it is rather ironic that the shadow of melancholia falls on mourning. In this respect, the collection of essays, *Loss: The Politics of Mourning,* largely perpetuates this tendency to overlook Freud's later reconceptualization of melancholia in terms of mourning. In this study, I discuss melancholia from within the horizon of mourning.

39. Freud, *The Ego and the Id,* 367, italics mine.

40. Ibid., 368, italics mine.

41. In "The Apocalyptic Imagination and the Inability to Mourn," Martin Jay had conceptualized the "inability to mourn" as the affective instance in which a love-object is not completely lost and cannot therefore be completely mourned: "the continued presence in what we might call the real world of the object whose apparent loss we cannot mourn . . . in the case of the collective 'loss' of mother surrogates such as the earth. . . . There is no reality testing that permits us to let go the libidinal investment we seem to have in an object that has *not fully disappeared* . . . , [that] is *still around* to nurture us" (97, italics mine).

42. Butler, *The Psychic Life of Power,* 134.

43. Ibid., 137–38.

44. Ibid.

45. Joyce exposes his style in a letter to his publisher, Grant Richards, May 5, 1906. See *Dubliners,* 262.

46. As it will become clear later, a concern about the *ends* of desire is of paramount importance to thinking through Freud's and Derrida's legacies on the question of mourning. It is precisely this libidinal factor that most recent studies (e.g., Ricciardi, Durrant, and Spargo) on the intersections between literature and mourning have neglected (as if reenacting Derrida's original neglect) in their formulations of an ethics of mourning and responsibility. Spargo, for instance, elaborates an "ethics of melancholia," which is in turn an ethics of dissent from normative practices of mourning. If normative mourning amounts to abandoning the lost love object for a new one, an ethics of melancholia would require that the mourner's relation with the lost love object be maintained ad infinitum. Yet, Spargo does not take account of the pathological implications of melancholic attachments to lost objects (as is evident in the writings of Freud and Abraham, and Torok) which might lead to either madness or suicide, if not to the cannibalistic incorporation of the other rather than in the prescribed ethical sustenance of the relation with him or her. Not that an ethics of melancholia is, thus, clearly phantasmagorical, but insofar as it does not account for the incorporative libidinal force that constrains and sustains melancholia, it risks dispersing and displacing it, as Spargo ends up doing, into a rhetoric of "wishful intervention" on behalf of the lost (love) object (25). In chapter 3, I argue that an ethics of melancholia has to be constructed not on the pyre but on the brink of the pathological.

47. Freud, *The Ego and the Id,* 368.

48. Ibid., 378.

49. For more on the topic of resistance to psychoanalysis, see Derrida, *Resistances of Psychoanalysis,* and, "Let us not Forget—Psychoanalysis."

50. Freud, *The Ego and Id,* 378.

51. Ibid., 376.

52. Derrida, *Specters of Marx,* 133, italics mine.

53. Kincaid, "In History," 153.

54. Gayatri Spivak, *Outside in the Teaching Machine,* 60.

55. The political leverage of the melancholic affect in Kincaid consists, I argue, in the imperative to claim and signify, however poorly, the disembodied memories of loss and suffering as they flit by in the frailty and contingency of the imagination. I build on the established work

of Freud and Frantz Fanon in order to intervene in the recent debates around melancholia's enigmatic and controversial status vis-à-vis critical and political action. For instance, while in *Postcolonial Melancholia* Paul Gilroy revives the Freudian pathologization of the affect, in *Dark Continents* Ranjana Khanna reactivates melancholia's critical and political potential—a potential already adumbrated by Freud, Fanon and Abraham and Torok, among others. Kincaid's fiction, I point out, brings to prominence these two warring aspects of melancholia (pathology and sound critique). Similarly, my critical analysis of Kincaid nuances Clifton Spargo's "ethics of melancholia," which foregrounds the ethical import of dissent from normative mourning. In many respects, Spargo does not take account of the implications of melancholic attachments to lost objects and eclipses the pathological vicissitudes of melancholia (whether in Freud or Abraham and Torok) that culminate in the cannibalistic incorporation of the other rather than in the ethical sustenance of the relational differential with him or her.

56. Derrida, *Specters of Marx,* 21.
57. Ibid., 23.
58. Spivak, *Death of a Discipline,* 55.
59. Freud, "Remembering, Repeating and Working-Through," 154, italics mine.
60. Behdad, "*Une Pratique Sauvage,*" 76.
61. See Dori Laub, "Truth and Testimony," 66.
62. Derrida, *Cinders,* 30.
63. Derrida, *The Work of Mourning,* 143.
64. Ibid., 143.
65. See Adorno, *Negative Dialectics,* 371.
66. Agamben, *State of Exception,* 73.
67. Erikson, "Notes on Trauma and Community," 185.
68. Ibid., 198.
69. Butler, *Precarious Life,* xiv.
70. Mourning should proceed from within the horizon of the uncoerced imagination (as if one were doing what comes naturally, yet deliberately and out of complete freewill); otherwise, one would have to accept Emile Durkheim's conclusion that, "One weeps, not simply because he is sad, but because he is forced to weep," cited in Watkin, *On Mourning,* 36. Watkin rightly comments that "grief, in the first instance, does not belong to the individual but to the community, and that second, the emotions 'felt' during the process of mourning are not the spontaneous outpourgrings of authentic affective pain, but communally sanctioned and controlled requirements to protect that community at that time" (36).

2. Horizons of Desire

1. In "Trauma, Absence, Loss," Dominick LaCapra argues that the conversion of absence into loss is part and parcel of historicizing, identifying and mourning phantoms of the past: "Specific phantoms that possess the self or the community can be laid to rest through mourning only when they are specified and named as historically lost others" (712–13). Conversely, LaCapra cautions that the unwitting conflation of absence and loss might result in the conversion of historical and specifiable losses into transhistorical and structural absences, thus blocking the road to fulfilling the task of mourning.
2. See, for instance, David Lloyd, "The Memory of Hunger," Seamus Deane, *Strange Country: Modernity and Nationhood in Irish Writing since 1790,* and, particularly, Declan Kiberd, *Inventing Ireland: The Literature of the Modern Nation.*

3. To a large extent, I agree with LaCapra that concepts such as mourning, repression, and working-through "undercut the binary opposition between the individual and society, and their application to individual or collective phenomena is a matter of informed argument and research." See *History and Memory after Auschwitz,* 43.

4. I do not differentiate categorically between "affects" and "emotions" even though I believe that the former pertains to the public expression of mourning and the latter to the private experience of grief. For more on the differences between affects and emotions, see Jonathan Flatley's recent excellent study, *Affective Mapping: Melancholia and the Politics of Modernism.*

5. Freud, "Mourning and Melancholia," 253.

6. Ibid.

7. Ibid.

8. Ibid.

9. See Torok, "The Illness of Mourning and the Fantasy of the Exquisite Corpse."

10. Freud, "Mourning and Melancholia," 258.

11. Staten, *Eros in Mourning,* 22.

12. Ibid., xi: "As soon as desire is something felt by a mortal being for a mortal being," Staten writes, "eros (as desire-in-general) will always be to some degree agitated by the anticipation of loss—an anticipation that operates even with regard to what is not yet possessed."

13. Ibid., 7.

14. I borrow this felicitous concept from Hayden White, *Tropics of Discourse,* 87.

15. Joyce, *Dubliners,* 37.

16. Torchiana, *Backgrounds for Joyce's Dubliners,* 70, italics mine.

17. Norris, *Suspicious Readings of Joyce's "Dubliners,"* 58. See also Tanja Vesala-Varttala's *Sympathy and Joyce's "Dubliners": Ethical Probing of Reading, Narrative, and Textuality,* a study that foregrounds "sympathy" as an ethics of reading *Dubliners.*

18. Paul de Man, "Autobiography as De-Facement," 78.

19. I have no intention to intervene in debates that have to do with the topography of prosopopoeia in relation to other tropes. Rather, I seek to explore the analytical potential (textual and psychic) of de Man's conceptualization of prosopopoeia and locate it in close proximity to narrative mourning. For a study of the controversies and debates surrounding the taxonomy of tropes, see James Paxson wide-ranging study, *The Poetics of Personification.*

20. Joyce, *Dubliners,* 36.

21. Ibid., 39.

22. Ibid., 191.

23. Ibid., 40.

24. Ibid., 221. Let's recall here how Stephen defines a ghost in *Ulysses:* "One who has faded into impalpability through death, through absence, through changes of manners" (240). If death is only a change of manners, then absence and impalpability become a form of life by other means, life through death; a ghost becomes nothing less than a living entity whose manners of coming and going are just a bit out of the ordinary.

25. Freud, "Mourning and Melancholia," 253, italics mine.

26. Joyce, *Dubliners,* 41.

27. Ibid., 210.

28. Riffaterre, "Prosopopoeia," 108.

29. Joyce, *Dubliners,* 212.

30. Ibid., 221, italics mine.

31. In *Ulysses,* Joyce's scrupulous meanness in his treatment of Dubliners becomes derisive: "sorrow for the dead is," he points out, "the only husband from whom they refuse to be divorced" (273). Ultimately, Joyce's treatment of sorrow is an allegory of the embattled national situation: it is as if Dubliners and the Irish in a more general sense are so drunk with sorrow, with the past,

and with the nightmare of history to be able to think and act straight and achieve national self-determination. For Joyce, then, "Ireland sober is Ireland free" (402). On national allegory, see Jameson, "Third-World Literature in the Era of Multinational Capitalism." On Joyce and national self-determination, see the fine collection of essays edited by Derek Attridge and Marjorie Howes, *Semicolonial Joyce.* By and large, any reflection on the question of nationalism in relation to mourning should confront the question of writing itself. It is as if writing were for Joyce the only answer or retaliation to an otherwise totally disarming *incapacity to mourn:* while Joyce himself falls short of accomplishing the task of mourning (him being an exiled fetishist of "dear dirty Dublin" and a faithless devotee to Catholicism), he nonetheless transforms that incapacity to mourn into an occasion for writing. "We'll paralyse Europe," screams Myles Crawford euphorically, urging Stephen to write "Something with a bite in it" (171) and to give to the English the "whole bloody history" on a "hot plate," in which case the incapacity to mourn becomes a "*strong* weakness" (*Ulysses,* 70, italics mine).

32. For a consideration of the material and historical origins of Eveline's predicament, see especially Norris, *Spurious Readings* (53–67). Foregrounding the immigration policies in the context of turn-of-the-century Ireland, Norris persuasively suggests that "The story functions both as a gesture of understanding the feeling of peril that might make a young woman unable to go through with an elopement or, conversely, a reversed tribute to the courage required by one [like Nora Barnacle who eloped with Joyce] who did" (67).

33. Joyce, *Dubliners,* 112.

34. Herring, *Joyce's Uncertainty Principle,* 69, italics mine.

35. Staten, *Eros in Mourning,* xi.

36. Joyce, *Dubliners,* 108.

37. Ibid., 115.

38. Ibid., 117.

39. Ingersoll, "Melancholy and Mourning in *Dubliners,*" 88.

40. Joyce, *Dubliners,* 116, 117.

41. Ibid., 116.

42. Ibid., 117.

43. Ibid., 204.

44. Ibid.

45. Epicurus, "Epicurus to Menoeceus," 30–31.

46. Lucretius, "On the Nature of Things," 131.

47. Ibid., Nietzsche, *Unfashionable Observations,* 89, 140

48. Ibid., 163, original italics.

49. Barbie Zelizer, *Remembering to Forget,* 202.

50. Joyce, *Dubliners,* 219.

51. Santner, *Stranded Objects,* 3.

52. Ferenczi, *Final Contributions,* 316.

53. See Alexander and Margarette Mitscherlich, *The Inability to Mourn: Principles of Collective Behavior.* As used by the Mitscherliches, "the inability to mourn" is not at all analogous with Freud's notion of melancholia. Quite the contrary, it refers indeed to instances in which melancholia is called for by the situation but is—lest it should result in narcissistic mortifications—called off by the individual's system of defenses. In this sense, the inability to mourn should not be understood as the expression of an unbroken attachment to a lost love-object (Freud), but rather as the deliberate and sustained burning of bridges with things past (the Mitscherliches). In the context of this chapter, I use the inability to mourn in its Freudian sense in relation to Gretta, but I adhere to the Mitscherlichian ex-appropriation of the term in relation to Gabriel.

54. Joyce, *Dubliners,* 220.

55. Ibid., 223, 222.

56. Ibid.
57. Derrida, *Specters,* 50.
58. Ibid., 54.
59. Joyce, *Dubliners,* 222.
60. Eide, *Ethical Joyce,* 4.
61. Joyce, *Dubliners,* 222–23.
62. Ibid., 112.
63. Ibid., 223.
64. Winnicott, "Fear of Breakdown," 93.
65. Ibid.
66. Ibid., 90, 91.
67. Joyce, *Dubliners,* 223.
68. Shakespeare, *Hamlet,* 5.2. 151.
69. Nancy, "L'Intrus," 7.
70. Freud, "On Transience," 306.
71. Beckett, *Three Novels,* 7.
72. Frey, *Interruptions,* 75.
73. Joyce, *Dubliners,* 223.
74. Nancy, "L'Intrus," 7.
75. Joyce, *Dubliners,* 223.
76. Paul de Man, "Autobiography," 81.
77. Joyce, *Dubliners* 224; Frey, *Interruptions,* 76.
78. Nancy, "L'Intrus," 7.
79. Frey, *Interruptions,* 75.
80. Butler, *Precarious,* 21.
81. Staten, *Eros in Mourning,* xii.
82. Ibid., 108.
83. Joyce, *Dubliners,* 111.
84. Ibid., 116, italics mine.
85. Derrida, *Work of Mourning,* 11.
86. Joyce, *Dubliners,* 116.
87. Ibid., 117.
88. Baccolini, "She Had Become a Memory," 154; Knapp, "Joyce's 'A Painful Case,'" 45. In "The Most Intimate of Creations: Symptoms as Memorials to One's Lonely Suffering," Peter Shabad shows how this desire for otherness is in fact a desire for a "credibly empathic witness" that would confer "the dignity of recognition . . . to a person's experience of lonely suffering" (210). It is in this sense that I understand Duffy's loneliness at the end of the story as symptomatic not of a return to an earlier state, but as a desire for an empathic witness and potentially a mourner. I call this desire the desire for "otomourning," the desire for the ear and the tears of the other—the desire, in short, to be mourned.
89. Žižek, "Melancholy and the Act," 658.
90. Derrida, *The Ear of the Other,* 53.
91. Joyce, *Dubliners,* 116.
92. Staten, *Eros in Mourning,* xiii.

3. The Vicissitudes of Melancholia

1. See Ellmann, *James Joyce,* 243–53.
2. Joyce , *Dubliners,* 223. Earlier in the story, Gabriel states to Miss Ivors that "Irish is not

[his] language" and that he is "sick of [his] own country, sick of it" (189). For Ellmann, Gabriel's journey westward "suggests a concession, a relinquishment, and Gabriel is conceding and relinquishing a good deal—his sense of the importance of civilized thinking, of continental tastes, of all those tepid but nice distinctions on which he had prided himself" (*James Joyce,* 249).

3. Joyce, "A Letter to Grant Richards," 262.
4. Freud, *The Ego and the Id,* 368.
5. Freud, "Mourning and Melancholia," 254.
6. Ibid., 257–58.
7. Freud, *The Ego and the Id,* 369.
8. Ibid., 368, 394.
9. Freud, *Beyond the Pleasure Principle,* 302.
10. Ibid.
11. Joyce, *Dubliners,* 109–10.
12. Freud, *Beyond the Pleasure Principle,* 303.
13. Ibid., 299, italics original.
14. Staten, *Eros in Mourning,* 5
15. Joyce, *Dubliners,* 9, original italics.
16. Ibid., 9.
17. Torchiana, *Backgrounds for Joyce's "Dubliners,"* 29.
18. Joyce, *Dubliners,* 17, italics mine.
19. Ibid., 9.
20. LaCapra, "Trauma, absence, Loss," 698.
21. Joyce, *Dubliners,* 17.
22. Ibid., 13; LaCapra, "Trauma, Absence, Loss," 717.
23. Freud, *The Ego and the Id,* 390.
24. Ibid., 393.
25. Joyce, *Dubliners,* 16.
26. Ibid., 17, italics mine.
27. Ibid., 18, italics mine.
28. Joyce, "An Early Version of 'The Sisters,'" 243.
29. Joyce, *Dubliners,* 18.
30. Freud, *The Ego and the Id,* 395.
31. Ibid., 394, italics mine.
32. Joyce, *Dubliners,* 18.
33. Butler, *Psychic Life of Power,* 191–92.
34. Freud, *The Ego and the Id,* 395.
35. Joyce, *Dubliners,* 110.
36. Ibid., 109, 111.
37. Ferenczi, *Final Contributions,* 316, italics mine.
38. Torok, "The Illness of Mourning," 113.
39. Rand, trans. and ed., *The Shell and the Kernel,* 80.
40. See Freud, "Remembering, Repeating, Working-Through."
41. Joyce, *Dubliners,* 112–13.
42. Ibid., 109.
43. Torok, "The Illness of Mourning," 114, italics mine.
44. See Freud, "Mourning and Melancholia," 258.
45. Torok, "The Illness of Mourning," 114.
46. Joyce, *Dubliners,* 111.
47. Ibid., 110, italics mine.
48. Ibid., 112.

49. Staten, *Eros in Mourning,* 10.
50. Joyce, *Dubliners,* 112.
51. Freud, *The Ego and the Id,* 398.
52. Ibid., 373–74, italics mine.
53. Ibid., 376.
54. Freud, "The Economic Problem of Masochism," 425, original italics.
55. Butler, *Psychic,* 148.
56. Freud, *The Ego and the Id,* 396, italics mine.
57. Joyce, *Dubliners,* 114, 115.
58. Freud, "Economic Problem of Masochism," 425.
59. Freud, *The Ego and the Id,* 400.
60. Joyce, *Dubliners,* 114.
61. Butler, *Psychic,* 162.
62. In *Symbolic Loss,* Peter Homans studies the origins and ramifications of the decline of mourning practices in the West, and in fin de siècle Britain and the United States in particular. Homans distinguishes between grief (the emotional turmoil and pain triggered by the loss of a love-object) and mourning (the cultural and symbolic containment of grief by communitywide solidarity) and traces the decline of mourning practices back to, among other factors, the modernization of social life and the rise of psychoanalysis, as well as the breakup and dispersal of community into the carefully discriminated spheres of the private and the public. Withdrawing into the recesses of the individual psyche, mourning has become a role without an actor. With no visible community to fall upon, the burden of mourning has (as in Sinico's case) fallen on the individual and therefore given rise to what Homans calls, in a very suggestive phrase, "mourning without mourning practices" (9). While in agreement with Homans about the decline of mourning practices in present-day consumerist culture, Alessia Ricciardi ascribes the devaluation of the concept of mourning rather to the general ahistoricity promoted by postmodernity and inaugurated by Lacan's revisionism of Freud's provincial concept of loss in terms of the universal concept of lack—a concept that, in the final analysis, winnows down historically specific experiences of loss into undifferentiated, transhistorical, and somewhat, by default, instances of lack. Regardless of its originating causes, what is left of our mourning practices is not always extended to all members of the *umma* or society, let alone to the entire global community: not infrequently, mourning, as Butler argues in *Precarious Life,* is deferentially allocated, extended to some and denied to others depending on racial differentials or, as is the case with Sinico, on the cognizance and legitimacy of the loss itself. Signifying mourning therefore becomes in no small measure a sociopolitical and human as well as humane undertaking as the following chapter on Jamaica Kincaid's postcolonial writings seeks to demonstrate.

4. Kincaid's Claim

1. In the formulation of this question, I am indebted to Shane Weller, whose article, "Nothing to Be Said: On the Inexpressible in Modern Philosophy and Literature," disentangles in a compelling and lucid manner the ramifications of the following question: "Who (or what) would speak were there nothing to be said?" (91).

2. Spivak, *Outside,* 60. For Spivak catachresis is a concept-metaphor whose claim to universality is undercut by the absence of a one-to-one correspondence between the concept (as a master-word) and the referent (as referring to a specific woman, subject, history, etc.). It might be tempting to think in the spirit of deconstruction of all languages as structured by catachreses, and this is to a certain extent an inevitable condition of being in language, but I am inter-

ested here in the claims to singularity and, above all, in the psychoaffective structures that produce and sustain such claims.

3. Lyotard, *Differend,* 8.
4. Derrida, *Post Card,* 321.
5. Heidegger, *Being and Time,* 208.
6. Freud, "Remembering, Repeating and Working-Through," 148, italics mine.
7. Ibid., 148–49.
8. See Freud, "Mourning and Melancholia," 251.
9. Freud, "Remembering, Repeating and Working-Through," 147.
10. Ibid., 148.
11. Ibid., 151.
12. Ibid., 150, italics original.
13. Ibid., 153.
14. See Gana, "Remembering Forbidding Mourning."
15. Freud, "Remembering, Repeating and Working-Through," 154.
16. Ibid., 148. Presumably the past draws attention to itself, and thus whoever is drawn to it might eventually "lose the name of action" by giving in to "the pale cast of thought" (*Hamlet* 3.1.82). Not only that, but the past is not so much at the service of life as it is at its disservice, not so much fruitful as it is troublesome, and not so much necessary for life as it is parasitical on it. By and large, Nietzsche surmises that one can readily live happily in bestial oblivion rather than perish miserably in the voracious shrine of memory: "it is possible to live almost without memory, indeed, to live happily, as the animals show us; but without forgetting, it is utterly impossible to live at all" (*Unfashionable Observations,* 89). By and large, although Nietzsche and Freud putatively agree that forgetting, regardless of whether it is re-creative or repetitive, facilitates the passage to action, they diverge sharply on the diagnosis, treatment, and location itself of the illness. And while Nietzsche prescribes forgetting as a curative pill to an otherwise overwhelmingly paralyzing and unhealthy remembering, Freud prescribes the outright and direct opposite—remembering—as a therapeutic measure against neurotic and regressive forgetting.
17. Ibid., 153. The analyst has to turn the compulsion to repeat into a "motive for remembering" (154) or into an "impulsion to remember" (151).
18. In "Present Pasts: Media, Politics, Amnesia," Andreas Huyssen suggests that "we now need productive remembering more than productive forgetting." He adds that Nietzsche's second *Untimely Meditation* "may be as untimely as ever" (37). Variations around the Freudian theme of curative remembering can be found in several recent studies of the Holocaust, apartheid, or of postcolonialism. Taking Freud as their starting point, some of these studies (LaCapra/Caruth) carry on within the same Freudian framework while others wish explicitly to depart from the therapeutics of remembering toward either a survival-based approach (Lloyd/Rinaldo Walcott), or a strategic and pedagogically minded one (Simon). On further inspection, it is worth noting that Nietzsche himself remains—in contradistinction with his own theoretical brand of productive forgetting, and somewhat to Freud's credit—ambivalent rather than decided about the absolute relevance of forgetting. In the foreword to the second of his *Unfashionable Observations,* Nietzsche confesses, "I have sought to depict a feeling that has often tormented me; I am taking my revenge on it by *exposing it to public scrutiny*" (85, italics mine). Here we can sense a tension between what Nietzsche calls for and what he actually practices.
19. Ricoeur, *La Mémoire, l'Histoire, l'Oubli,* 96. In *History and Memory after Auschwitz,* LaCapra coins a neologism, "re-petitioning" to subvert the hold of repetition-compulsion (45). While LaCapra's analyses are lucid overall, especially when it comes to distinctions between structural lack and historical loss, they could have benefited from further attention to Freud's own problematization of the concept of mourning, especially in *The Ego and the Id* and beyond.
20. Ibid., 83–97.
21. Roger I. Simon, Sharon Rosenberg, and Claudia Eppert, eds., *Between Hope and Despair,* 2.

22. Reading Simon, Rosenberg, and Eppert, one gets the impression that remembering is an entirely volitional activity in which a return *of* memory is scarcely distinguishable from a return *to* memory. Indeed, the writers use "of"/"to" loosely, as the following excerpt from their text might illustrate: "Implicated in this remembrance [as a difficult return] is a learning to live with loss, a learning to learn with a *return of* a memory that inevitably instantiates loss and thus bears no ultimate consolation, a learning to live with a disquieting remembrance. On these terms, the memorial impulse *to turn to* and *return* traumatic history is an *assignment* [original italics], not simply a matter of choice" (4, italics mine). Clearly, what this deliberate assignment does not allow for is an enlightening distinction between the volitional *returns to* memory, and the free-floating and involuntary *returns of* memory. Memories of the "return of" category take on a life of their own, and become, potentially, actantial agents capable of destabilizing, disrupting and jeopardizing individual and collective ties that might be built around the imperative to remember. In addition, the ostensibly pedagogical veneer of what is to be remembered fails to account for the oftentimes polarized and politicized pedagogies of (national) remembering in systems of education across the globe.

23. Ricoeur, *La Mémoire, l'Histoire, l'Oubli,* 561.

24. Žižek, "Melancholy and the Act," 695; Butler, *Psychic,* 162.

25. Habiby, *The Secret Life of Saeed: The Pessoptimist.*

26. Walcott, "What the Twilight Says," 5.

27. Shakespeare, *Hamlet,* 3.2.92.

28. Ibid., 1.5.53.

29. Deleuze, *Difference and Repetition,* 105, italics mine.

30. Instead of seeing repetition as an effect of repression, as the Freud of up to *Beyond the Pleasure Principle* does, Deleuze pushes Freud's still hesitant findings to an edge: repression is an effect of repetition, and not the contrary. In other words, repetition is no longer an unconscious enactment of the repressed and forgotten, but, rather, a quite self-conscious reproduction of the yet-to-be repressed once it has been repeated. Thus, repetition becomes catalytic for repression, while repression remains the ineluctable aftermath for repetition (to go on repeating itself). In a word, repression in the Deleuzian sense is called upon only to *clean the Augean stable of repetition.* For an elaborate examination of this conjecture, as well as for a move beyond cyclical repetition toward a horizontal and quasi-labyrinthine conception of repetition—of the same, as much as of the different—see Deleuze, *Difference and Repetition* (96–122). No wonder, then, that the concept of repetition discussed herein should not be confused with the Nietzschean doctrine of "Eternal Return" scattered through his writings, especially *Thus Spake Zarathustra* and *The Gay Science.* If one can speak of a compulsion to repeat the (gruesome) *same* from a Freudian perspective, one might speak of a will to repeat the *different* (i.e., the potentially better, too) from a Nietzschean point of view. As Deleuze elaborately demonstrates in his *Nietzsche et la Philosophie,* eternal recurrence is more of a *selective* theory of *becoming* and *affirmation* of *being* through *transmutation, will to power,* and *active* force than a regressive and passive harking back and reiteration of the same operating under a *reagent* force, a force that might haul one to the abyss. In this respect, one might find Nietzsche to have been anticipated by Kierkegaard. Throughout *Repetition,* Kierkegaard hungers and despairs for the repetition of selected existential experiences, and sees the real challenge ahead of modern philosophy as residing in the will to repeat rather than in the will to recollect as the Greeks might have thought. But while selection of the experiences to be repeated remains for Kierkegaard the starting point from which repetition will proceed, for Nietzsche, cognizant of Darwin, selection becomes the driving force, and the will to repeat is ultimately a will toward *transvaluation* and *transmutation* (*Nietzsche et la Philosophie,* 81; *Repetition,* 125–231). Almost the same account of Nietzsche can be found in a compact way in Foucault's essay, "Nietzsche, Genealogy, History." Foucault coins the term "counter-memory" to oppose "the endlessly repeated play of dominations" (150)—a practice that Donald Bouchard rightly characterizes, in his preface to *Language, Counter-Memory, Practice,* as that

of "vigilant repetitions" (9). It is worth noting, in conclusion, that Heidegger elects, in a quasi-Kierkegaardian spirit, repetition (*Wiederholung*) as the vehicle for entertaining an *authentic* relationship with the *past.* Loosely speaking, repetition becomes, for Heidegger, not only a liberator of the pastness of the past but also a potentially liberating force for *Dasein* from the clutches of *forgetfulness,* which is nothing less than the mode of an *inauthentic* relationship with the past perpetrated and perpetuated by the "they" in their vulgar and "everyday" mode of existence. See *Being and Time,* especially paragraphs 67 and 74.

31. Shakespeare, *Hamlet,* 2.1.56.

32. I agree here with Ranjana Khanna's view in *Dark Continents* that "psychoanalysis itself is a colonial discipline" (x). In many ways, Khanna's reactivation of the well-known Fanonian contention about the complicity between the practice of psychoanalysis in the colonies and the larger ideological scope of colonialism is worth examining at some length in a different project.

33. Fanon, *The Wretched of the Earth,* 303.

34. Ibid., 207.

35. Benjamin, "Critique of Violence," 280; Fanon, *The Wretched of the Earth,* 38.

36. Benjamin, "Critique of Violence," 277.

37. See Spivak, *Death of a Discipline,* 72.

38. Fanon, *The Wretched of the Earth,* 39.

39. Ibid., 37. Fanon further argues that "it is precisely at the moment [the native] realizes his humanity that he begins to sharpen the weapons with which to secure its victory" (43).

40. Here I am alluding to Jameson's succinct remark (which is itself an allusion to Deleuze and Guattari's *Anti-Oedipus*) that, "[w]hen a psychic structure is objectively determined by economic and political relationships, it cannot be dealt with by means of purely psychological therapies; yet it equally cannot be dealt with by means of purely objective transformations of the economic and political situation itself, since the habits remain and exercise a baleful and crippling residual effect." See "Third-World Literature in the Era of Multinational Capitalism," 76.

41. Fanon, *The Wretched of the Earth,* 56.

42. Ibid., 84.

43. Ibid., 54.

44. Ibid.

45. Ibid., 55.

46. Ibid., 55.

47. Ibid., 56. Fanon's remark here is reminiscent of the kind of indifference, jubilant self-contentment, and vindictive mockery with which the Ibo natives (and the elders of Mbanta) in Chinua Achebe's *Things Fall Apart* first cheered the settlers/missionaries and sold them a plot of land from the "Evil Forest" (literally, the garbage bin at the outskirts of the village, in which whatever is not condoned by the religion of Umuofia is disposed of, including men who killed themselves, twins, and *ogbanje,* or wicked children) on which to build their shrine, believing all along that they were sending the missionaries to their fate, that the Evil Forest would finish them off, and that the gods would finally find ample opportunity to exact their vengeance against them: "They offered them as much of the Evil Forest as they care to take. And to their greatest amazement the missionaries thanked them and burst into song" (107).

48. Ibid., 56.

49. Ibid., 57, italics mine.

50. Ibid., 56, 58, 304.

51. In "On the Irremovable Strangeness of Being Different," Bhabha addresses Fanon's strategic conceptualization of violence in the reparative project of decolonization; however, he exaggerates the so-called "proximity" at the heart of the otherwise "irremovable strangeness" of difference between colonizer and colonized. While it is arguably true, as Edward Said insists, that the histories of the colonizer and colonized overlap and their territories intertwine—lending thus credence to what Bhabha calls the "historical relationality, the interstitial in-between

that defines and divides them into antagonistic subjects"—nothing could be gained by watering down or attenuating the historical ferocity of the colonial encounter, about which the Fanonian text is patently clear. "The anxious struggle for the historical consciousness of freedom that eschews transcendence—or a higher unity—*derives from violence,*" Bhabha contends, "*an ethics that takes responsibility for the other* in the transformation of the 'thing'" (38, italics mine). If Fanon gives up, as Sartre himself observes, on the colonial other, on Europe, and on its models of development and progress, Bhabha sees in the violence with which Fanon wants to root out the colonizer an "ethics that takes responsibility for the other." Bhabha's is an overinterpretation, as alienating from as alienated with the Fanonian text it seeks to illuminate. Bhabha's text betrays a twisted form of resistance to Fanon's vindication of violence. One cannot fail to note that at the core of the admiration the postcolonial critic has for Fanon is in fact an embarrassment at the fact that Fanon furnishes him with an unsettling position which he feels obligated to abridge. After citing excerpts from page 295 of *The Wretched of the Earth,* and specifically Fanon's heavily metaphoric sentence—"You must therefore weigh as heavily as you can upon the body of your torturer in order that his soul, lost in some byway, may finally find once more [its universal dimension]"—Bhabha asks, "Is this plot of proximity a vindication of violence?" His answer is: "I do not believe so" (39). In Bhabha's citation, the phrase "its universal dimension," which I added between brackets, is omitted in order for him to resolve *forcefully* the anxiety that Fanon's text leaves unresolved into the Levinasian reassuring oasis: "This is a freedom that does not demand *universal frames* or synchronous knowledges but that will allow the silence to inscribe the raveling and unraveling between the psychic body and its political weight" (39, italics mine). Undoubtedly, Bhabha weighs all too heavily the body of Levinas onto that of Fanon in order for him to gesture toward an ethics without transcendence (which in Levinas's more idiosyncratic term is called "excendence," a transcendence of transcendence, a concept that Bhabha does not use anyway), which is, in my view, a far cry from the Fanonian text. When Fanon explicitly asserts that "The colonized man finds his freedom in and through violence" (*Wretched,* 86), I would like to ask again, could anything be gained by isolating phrases and sentences marked by a fringe of open texture in such a way as to excise their excess and contend that Fanon does not vindicate violence? Is it not far more beneficial to *work through* Fanon's vindication of productive violence rather than *disavow* it? On the other hand, postcolonial critics who acknowledge Fanon's vindication of revolutionary violence seem to me too distracted by the scandalizing nature of Fanon's thesis to return to Fanon's text and engage with its internal tensions and nuances. For instance, Robert Young devotes, in his ambitious introduction to postcolonialism, *Postcolonialism,* most of his commentary on Fanon to discussing the polemics—whether inimical (Hannah Arendt) or sympathetic (Serequeberhan and Sartre)—surrounding Fanon's thesis. The few instances in which Young touches on the abstract dimension of Fanon's theory could have immensely benefited from a more undistracted textual analysis.

52. Fanon, *The Wretched of the Earth,* 58–59.

53. Ibid., 306, Fanon notes, "There are no more disputes and no longer any insignificant details which entail the death of a man. There are no longer explosive outburst of rage because my wife's forehead or her left shoulder were seen by my neighbor. The national conflict seems to have canalized all anger, and nationalized all affective or emotional movements."

54. At the very end of *The Wretched of the Earth,* Fanon overturns Freud's conception of pathological and autodestructive melancholia and states that the French psychiatrists in Algeria "were accustomed when dealing with a patient subject to melancholia to fear that he would commit suicide. Now the melancholic Algerian takes to killing. The illness of the moral consciousness, which is always accompanied by auto-accusation and auto-destructive tendencies, took on in the case of Algerians hetero-destructive forms. The melancholic Algerian does not commit suicide. He kills" (299).

55. Ranjana Khanna's *Dark Continents* is in part an attempt to remedy this lack of theorization of the passage from Freud's pathological to Fanon's resistant or militant melancholia

through her concept of "critical melancholia," which she sees as a symptom of colonialism and an energetic response to it (x).

56. Fanon, *The Wretched of the Earth,* 253.

57. Derrida, *Specters,* 21, italics mine.

58. Joyce, *Ulysses,* 251.

59. It is worth noting that in the "Scylla and Charybdis" episode in *Ulysses,* in which he presents his algebraic theory about *Hamlet,* Stephen protests vehemently the chilling sequence of homicides committed en route to undoing the first homicide—old Hamlet's murder.

60. Kincaid, *My Garden (Book),* 122; *A Small Place,* 32, italics mine.

61. See Abraham and Torok, *The Shell and the Kernel.*

62. Rather than "blaming the victims"—a tendency in postcolonialism of which V. S. Naipaul is the most notorious practitioner and Edward Said the most notable critic—Kincaid lodges a complaint against the British colonial powers whose bad governance was absorbed and reproduced by the newly liberated Antiguans: "Have you ever wondered to yourself why it is that all people like me seem to have learned from you is how to imprison and murder each other, how to govern badly, and how to take the wealth of our country and place it in Swiss bank accounts? Have you ever wondered why it is that all we seem to have learned from you is how to corrupt our societies and to be tyrants? You will have to accept that this is mostly your fault. Let me just show you how you looked to us. You came. You took things that were not yours, and you did not even, for appearances' sake, ask first" (*A Small Place,* 34–35). While Kincaid seems to puncture, or perhaps accentuate, the gravity of the scenario (whereby Antiguans internalize, mime, or compulsively reproduce colonial oppression) by a prickling irony, a dramatic relief of sorts, Suzanne Gauch complains that all Kincaid seems to be interested in is a retroactive request for a mere ritual of politeness, effecting thus a "startling reduction of racism [and all colonial indignities] to a question of bad manners" ("*A Small Place:* Some Perspectives on the Ordinary," 913). While *A Small Place* was not accepted for publication in the *New Yorker* because of its "distorted anger" (Simmons, *Jamaica Kincaid,* 136), Gauch, strangely and ironically enough, finds an underpinning strain in Kincaid toward dissolving weighty questions of racism into banal occurrences or mere aspects of everydayness.

63. Weller provides a concise account of this prolific theme in "Nothing to Be Said."

64. Glissant, *Caribbean Discourse,* 62, italics mine.

65. Ibid., 64.

66. Ibid., 161, italics mine.

67. Glissant, *Caribbean Discourse,* 63, 168.

68. Kincaid, *Annie John,* 107.

69. See Derrida, "The Laws of Reflection," 23. Derrida argues that the aim of reflection is that "it reveals to understanding what goes past understanding." Perhaps this is the motor force—the instigating challenge—that explains Kincaid's fascination with *what happened:* not that the "locus of referentiality" (Caruth's notion) is visible—it is not—but that it continues to be invisible. "Transporting the invisible into the visible, this reflection does not," in the words of Derrida, "proceed from the visible, rather it passes through understanding." In other words, the specificity of reflection is that it produces the very object of its reflection in the process of its unfolding; it "does not *reproduce* the visible, it *produces* it." It produces the visible, yet the visible remains caught within the pull of reflection; the visible is always what will have been visible once its production-reflection is over—disregarding, of course, the regenerative and reiterative nature of the cycle of production-reflection.

70. Lyotard, *The Differend,* 9, 8.

71. Ibid., 13.

72. Kincaid, "In History," 153.

73. See White, *Tropics,* 87. Accordingly, the postcolonial subject can be seen to charge certain events "with a meaning so intense that, whether real or merely imagined, they continue to

shape both his perceptions and his responses to the world long after they should have become 'past history.'"

74. See Butler, *Bodies that Matter,* 38; Savoy, Embarrassments."

75. *What happened* is thus, if we are to adopt Spivak's words, "given over to a future that is not just a future present but always a future anterior. It never will be, but always will have been," which is "the most practical assurance in view of which one works on" (Spivak, *Outside,* 22). I might have given the impression that this is only a question of hermeneutic temporality, but, really, at the heart of this hermeneutic temporality is nothing less than what Judith Butler calls the "tropological inauguration" of the object (Butler, *Psychic,* 3).

76. Freud, "Mourning and Melancholia," 253–54, original italics.

76. Freud, "Mourning and Melancholia," 253–54, original italics.

77. Ibid., 254, italics mine.

78. Yeats, "Among School Children," 325.

79. There is no gainsaying the fact that for Kincaid the impossibility of naming the object originates in the fear of losing it. For more on this, see Baudrillard on the impossible exchange in *Passwords:* "But as soon as something is named, coded, enciphered, we are back to the circuit of exchange again" (74).

80. Paul de Man, "Epistemology of Metaphor," 19.

81. Ibid.

82. In *Caribbean Discourse,* Glissant articulates with remarkable clarity the correlation between the hermeneutic task of sensemaking and the discontinuous but integrative process of mourning: "The rupture of the slave trade, then the experience of slavery, introduces between blind belief and clear consciousness a gap that we have never finished filling. The absence of representation, of echo, of any sign, makes this emptiness forever yawn under our feet. Along with our realization of the process of exploitation (along with any action we take), we must articulate the unexpressed while moving *beyond* it" (201, italics mine). Is it not a trait of reflection—of understanding, memory, and thought in general—to become entangled in the cobwebs of the object of its reflection? Glissant's remark, of course, sends us back to the introductory chapter and to Joyce's categorical imperative—"Get out of mourning first"—and refuels the question of whether mourning is prerequisite to understanding, correlative to understanding, or anterior to it. Must not all of these—like creation day—happen all at once?

83. Benjamin, "Theses on the Philosophy of History," 262, 257.

84. Ibid., 263.

85. Glissant, *Caribbean Discourse,* 201.

86. Nichanian, "Catastrophic Mourning," 105, original italics.

87. "Should it be an idea" is, in my view, an intertextual allusion to Conrad's *Heart of Darkness,* in which the "idea" that Conrad evokes remains despite his adjectival prolixity shrouded in mystery: "The conquest of the earth, which mostly means the taking it away from those who have a different complexion or slightly flatter noses than ourselves, is not a pretty thing when you look into it too much. What *redeems* it is an *idea.* An idea at the back of it, not a sentimental pretence but an idea; and an unselfish *belief* in the idea—something you can set up, and bow down before, and offer a sacrifice to . . ." (10, italics mine). No one who has read and been marked by this passage has failed to be impressed and mystified by Conrad's recondite belaboring of the "idea." One is, in particular, very struck by the unsettling inscription of this idea in terms of its characteristics—or, shall I say catachrestics?—that is, in terms of the narrative of negative dialectics into which Conrad molds it: an idea, *not* a sentimental pretense; an unselfish *belief* in the idea, *not* an idea as such; an unselfish belief *but* one that can nevertheless be set up—unselfish *but* by design; unselfish *but* you should bow down before it; unselfish *but* to which you should offer sacrifice. The play of negative dialectics follows its course, unsettling any hermeneutic closure and leaving open the doors for new interpretive entrepreneurship. It is impossible here to do justice to Conrad's rhetorical moves, or to deal with the plethora of *hesitant,* yet still prolif-

erating interpretations that this passage alone has provoked, but I would like to suggest that the idea that undergirds the conquest of the earth is nothing but the sense that one can either get away with it or be redeemed from it by virtue of having believed in the idea of redemption itself. At the horizon of the conquest of the earth, there is the horizon of redemption. This interpretation of the "idea" seems to me very much in tune with Kincaid's own thinking. In *A Small Place,* for instance, she argues that "[p]eople who think about these things [i.e., heaven/hell; reward/punishment] believe that every bad deed, even every bad thought, carries with it its own retribution. So do you see the queer thing about people like me? Sometimes *we hold your retribution*" (27, italics mine). It is possible to refer to Kincaid's strategy as a "poetics of occlosure," a kind of seesaw, chiastic flutter between a textual and intrinsic strain toward closure and an extrinsic, somewhat overlordly interdiction or occlusion of closure (see my "Beyond the Pale," 326). Such a poetic strategy is clearly a function of heteromelancholia, of the psychoaffective tendency to inflict mourning on those who committed the crimes of colonialism—or on their current affiliative, not necessarily filial, descendants. Poetic occlosure is at the core of the narrative structure of the Kincaidian text, especially in *A Small Place;* its function is to open up the colonial other to mourning and to guilt, and to deny him or her the sense of closure and the promise of redemption correlative with the willing sensation of grief that the reader might have entertained/assumed at the outset of the act of reading. This is, of course, an urgently political task, especially since the former colonizer is suffering a colonial hangover, as Gilroy demonstrates in *Postcolonial Melancholia.*

88. Nichanian, "Catastrophic Mourning," 111.

89. White, *Tropics,* 91. The figure of the "open wound" is very much a "historical wound," a "mix of history and memory," whose "truth is not always verifiable by historians"; see Attwood, Chakrabarty, and Lomnitz, "The Public Life of History" (2).

90. Darmesteter, *La Vie des Mots,* 63.

91. Derrida, *Specters,* 21, original italics. The metaphor of the "open wound" in Kincaid is similar to the notion of "haunting" in Derrida insofar as "haunting is historical, to be sure, but it is not *dated,* it is never docilely given a date in the chain of presents, day after day, according to the instituted order of a calendar" (4, original italics).

92. Kristeva, *Intimate Revolt,* 189.

93. Miller, "The Figure in the Carpet," 176; Savoy, "Embarrassments," 234; Spivak, *Outside,* 29.

94. Kincaid, "In History," 166.

95. Ibid., 153.

96. Ibid., 156.

97. See Simmons, *Jamaica Kincaid,* and Ferguson, "A Lot of Memory."

98. See, for instance, the Mitscherliches, *The Inability to Mourn,* and Eric Santner, *Stranded Objects.*

99. Kazanjian and Nichanian, "Between Genocide and Catastrophe," 129.

100. Ibid., 134, italics mine.

101. Kincaid, *Autobiography,* 3.

102. Most of Kincaid's critics agree on the ambivalent daughter-mother relationship in Kincaid's work. This ambivalence is, most critics also unanimously agree, a staging of Kincaid's haunting indebtedness to her mother and her unfinished revolt against her; it is, in other words, the staging in fiction of the stirring into awareness of a love-hate relationship between Kincaid and her mother before and after her self-willed exile in the United States. I will discuss the specific twist of this relationship in *The Autobiography of My Mother;* for more on its representation in earlier novels, see, among others, Alison Donnell's "When Daughter's Defy: Jamaica Kincaid's Fiction," Diane Simmons's *Jamaica Kincaid,* and Moira Ferguson's *Jamaica Kincaid: Where the Land Meets the Body.*

103. Gilmore, *The Limits of Autobiography,* 96.

104. Paravisini-Gebert, *Jamaica Kincaid,* 149.
105. Ibid., 149.
106. Kincaid, *Annie John,* 43, italics mine.
107. Ibid., 43–44.
108. See Cudjoe's interview with Kincaid, "Jamaica Kincaid and the Modernist Project," 401; Kincaid, *Annie John,* 45.
109. Holcomb, "Travels of a Transnational Slut," 301.
110. Kincaid, *At the Bottom of the River,* 3–4.
111. Kincaid, *Autobiography,* 171, 100.
112. Holcomb and Holcomb, "'I MADE HIM,'" 975.
113. Kincaid, *Autobiography,* 32.
114. See Ferguson's interview with Kincaid, "A Lot of Memory," 177.
115. Paravisini-Gebert, *Jamaica Kincaid,* 144.
116. Donnell, "When Writing the Other Is Being True to the Self," 123.
117. Ibid., 124.
118. Ibid., 129, 127.
119. Ibid., 129.
120. Ibid., 130.
121. Ibid., 133, italics mine.
122. Kincaid, *Autobiography,* 3.
123. Ibid., 199, italics mine.
124. Ibid., 225, italics mine.
125. Freud, "Mourning and Melancholia," 257.
126. See Frye, *Anatomy of Criticism,* 281.
127. Derrida, *Specters,* 54, original italics.
128. Kincaid, *Autobiography,* 210.
129. Ibid., 202.
130. Parker, "Metaphor and Catachresis," 73.

5. Ineluctable Modality

1. Gilmore, *Limits of Autobiography,* 1–2.
2. For more on this, see my essay, "Beyond the Pale."
3. See Derrida, "A Discussion with J. D."
4. See Hart, *The Concept of Law.*
5. For more on this, see my essay, "Donne Undone."
6. Frey, *Interruptions,* 75, italics original.
7. White, *Tropics of Discourse,* 83.
8. See Brooks, *Reading for the Plot.*
9. Freud, *Civilization and its Discontents,* 256.
10. Freud, "Constructions in Analysis," 258–57, original italics.
11. Freud, "Screen Memories," 322, italics original.
12. On the literary aspects of Freud's writings, see Philips, "Making the Case."
13. Since her arrival to the United States in the late sixties, Kincaid must have been sensitive to the stakes involved in ransacking family history and in exposing family secrets by putting them to the use (and, allegedly, the abuse) of her art. Indeed, her family did not tarry to find out about and to inveigh against her early pieces even though Kincaid had already changed her name from "Elaine Potter Richardson" into "Jamaica Kincaid." In a recent conversation with Brittnay Buckner, she states, "Literally, I am a bastard. My parents were not married. I take the

bastard view. I don't feel I owe any honor to the group of people I come from. Not because I hate them or anything, but it's just that when I am writing, I am such a singular beast that I refuse to take in any worldly consideration for the people I'm from" (464). My aim is to engage the ethical stakes involved in writing about family matters, especially that such a form of writing is triumphantly celebrated by Kincaid herself as a form of self-redemption and rescue. Writing becomes the ladder of salvation of an otherwise runaway and endangered life. While this kind of approach to writing has been taken for granted by a number of feminists since Helen Cixous's feminist manifesto, "The Laugh of the Medusa," its ethico-political implications remain largely unaccounted for. Kezia Page theorizes Kincaid's memoir as a form of "literary remittance," reenacting asymmetrical power relations between the United States and the Third World (40), or, more precisely, between Kincaid's Vermont and Devon's Antigua. For Page, "the intrusive nature of Kincaid's nonfiction [is] fueled by her distance, and a kind of absence of respect for familial privacy for the family she had not visited for more than twenty years" (45).

14. Rushdy, "Rememory," 303.
15. Lukacher, *Primal Scenes,* 35.
16. Ibid., 36.
17. Kincaid, *My Brother,* 12.
18. Ibid., 6.
19. Ibid., 12.
20. Kincaid, *At the Bottom of the River,* 4.
21. Derrida, *Monolingualism,* 20, italics original.
22. Kincaid, *My Brother,* 130.
23. Ibid., 131.
24. Kincaid, *My Brother,* 108.
25. For an account of the failure of countertransference and the potential interminability of analysis, see Freud's "Analysis Terminable and Interminable." For an account of Freud's obsessive returns to the Wolf Man case history, see Abraham and Torok, *The Wolf Man's Magic Word: A Cryptonymy,* as well as Muriel Gardiner, *The Wolf-Man by the Wolf-Man,* which contains a collection of the memoirs of the Wolf Man.
26. Kincaid is not unaware of the expiatory function of narrative. In *The Autobiography of My Mother,* she contends that "to describe your own transgressions is to forgive yourself for them; to confess your bad deeds is also at once to forgive yourself, and so silence becomes the only form of self-punishment" (60). Silence becomes here the *conditio sine qua non* of self-punishment for wrongdoing. Breaking the silence is not only tantamount to opening up a space for performing mourning and expiation, but also for the repetition of those transgressions.
27. Brophy, "Angels in Antigua," 267.
28. Kincaid, *My Brother,* 134.
29. Caruth, *Unclaimed Experience,* 5.
30. See Freud, "Moses and Monotheism."
31. Ricoeur, *La Mémoire, l'Histoire, l'Oubli,* 650.
32. In her interview with Brad Goldfarb, Kincaid points out that while it was her mother who had precisely stirred the book-burning episode into her consciousness again, she had not realized its magnitude and tormenting effects until she began writing about it: "Yeah. It's a brutal scene, isn't it? You know, I'd completely forgotten that incident, and then something she said around the time of my brother's death made me remember it. But it must have been a source of enormous shame that made me suppress it, and when I remembered it and began to write about it, I found it very painful. But I wanted to write it." In *Unclaimed Experience,* Caruth suggests that the traumatic experience is devastating, not at the moment of its occurrence, but precisely at the moment of "*waking from it,*" that is, at the moment of realizing that one has survived it "*without knowing it.*" It is at this stage, this "waking into consciousness," Caruth goes on to

add, that reliving the experience of trauma becomes an "attempt *to claim one's own survival* . . . to assume one's survival as one's own" (64, original italics). Kincaid's decision to write about an experience that is not only traumatic but also shameful might therefore be understood as an affirmative decision—a claim to/of survivance or survival.

33. Caruth, *Unclaimed Experience,* 17, italics mine.

34. Brophy, "Angels in Antigua," 274.

35. See Frey, *Interruptions,* 39.

36. Ferguson, "A Lot of Memory," 176.

37. Kincaid, *My Brother,* 99–100, italics mine.

38. Cudjoe, "Jamaica Kincaid and the Modernist Project," 407.

39. Kincaid, *My Brother,* 196, italics mine.

40. Kristeva, *Black Sun,* 6.

41. See Derrida, *Monolingualism,* 7.

42. Ferguson, "A Lot of Memory," 171.

43. According to Soto-Crespo, "The hybridity of mourning enables Kincaid to relive these connections [with her brother, with her burned books, as well as with her "small place"] because by mourning her brother she mourns also a larger cultural condition" ("Death and the Diaspora Writer," 370). In the fleshing out of his own concept of "hybrid mourning" to the history of colonialism, Soto-Crespo finds himself overtly involved in the specific tensions, delays, tactics, politics, and lacunae that jeopardize the otherwise connective force of mourning. A good deal of what passes for mourning in Soto-Crespo's reading of Kincaid does fall under the heading of melancholia and is within a hairbreadth of morphing into tension, renunciation, or suspension of the vaunted cross-cultural connections it is said to effect.

44. Bernard, "Countermemory and Return," 130.

45. Some of the passages in *My Brother* are as tasteless for the narrator as much as for the reader. An example is when Devon exposes his penis to his sister: "I stood looking at him for a long time before he realized I was there. And then when he did, he suddenly threw the sheets away from himself, tore his pajama bottoms away from his waist, revealing his penis, and then he grabbed his penis in his hand and held it up . . . and he said in a voice that was full of deep panic and deep fear, 'Jamaica, look at this, just look at this.'" The intrusiveness of this scene cannot be overstated. What is perhaps ethically problematic is, as Kezia Page contends, that her brother (whose physical deterioration and pain are portrayed to the reader in their intricacies from the outset) "does not have the option of anonymity" (44).

46. Lyotard, *Differend,* xv, original italics.

47. Auden, "In Memory of Sigmund Freud," 54–55. See also Ramazani, "When There Are So Many We Shall Have To Mourn."

48. Derrida, *Writing and Difference,* 9.

49. Derrida, *Work of Mourning,*143, italics original. Further citations from this work will be given by page number in text.

50. Lyotard, *Differend,* 10.

51. Derrida, *Work of Mourning,* 55.

52. Lyotard, *Differend,* 9.

53. Crimp, "Melancholia and Moralism," 200.

54. Ben Jelloun, *The Last Friend,* 154.

55. Ibid.

56. Ibid.

57. Ibid., 158.

58. Ibid., 157. See also *The Politics of Friendship,* where Derrida builds on, among others, Aristotle, Montaigne, Nietzsche, and Blake to disentangle friendship's entanglement with enmity (271–306).

59. Ibid., 172.
60. Ibid., 154.
61. Ibid., 171.
62. Ibid., 155.
63. Joyce, *Ulysses,* 128.
64. Ben Jelloun, *The Last Friend,* 177.
65. Ibid., 177–78.
66. Ibid., 182. For the original French version, see Ben Jelloun, *Le dernier ami,* 248.
67. Ibid., 1.

6. Formless Form

1. Jay, *Refractions of Violence,* 3, original italics.
2. Ibid., 3.
3. Hardt and Negri, *Multitude,* 12–13.
4. Foucault, *"Society Must be Defended,"* 50.
5. See Appadurai, *Fear of Small Numbers,* 15.
6. Nancy, *Being Singular Plural,* 178.
7. See Agamben, *State of Exception,* 73.
8. Di Orio and Vegso, "The Politics of War," 5. I am aware of the pitfalls of politics, whether in K. Von Clausewitz's aphoristic parlance ("war is the continuation of politics by other means"), or in Foucault's insightful reversal of the Clausewitzian axiom ("politics is the continuation of war by other means"), see Foucault, *Society,* 15–16. While it remains true that (world) politics is a function of power-relations—and might ultimately do nothing but sanction and reproduce the power asymmetries that characterize warfare—it is more than ever crucial nowadays to reconfigure and reinscribe the role of politics, of foreign policy or of world politics and diplomacy in a continuum with peace and not war. In short, diplomacy, along with a commitment to fostering global literacy and economic prosperity, is what needs to be reinvigorated not in spite of the endemic cooptability and appropriative liability of politics but, precisely, because of it. This is all the more incumbent a task at a time when nuclear proliferation might usher in a new global cold war between polycentric spheres or constellations of nuclear power and strategic influence. There is nothing to be gained now I believe from the emerging consensus on the Left that the distinction between war and peace has been unsettled nor from the claim that that distinction has never existed in the first place but was "one of liberalism's major myths," see Mark Neocleous, "War as peace, peace as pacification." My sense is that the distinction between war and peace is sufficiently blurred already and need not be blurred any further; the more practical task at present is to *criticize* war and violence as they arise all the while *critiquing* the systemic conditions from which they arise.
9. The subtitle of Vali Nasr's *The Shia Revival*—"How Conflicts Within Islam Will Shape the Future"—clearly foregrounds the so-called Sunni-versus-Shiite contest for dominance, also understood as "the battle of Islamic fundamentalisms" (147). Deliberately ignoring the contest for corporate profiteering and imperial domination in Iraq, Nasr ventures the following conclusion: "the character of the region will be decided in the crucible of [Shia] revival and the Sunni response to it" (22). Nasr unbendingly defuses the historical and clearly imperial character of violence in the Middle East and index it in a primarily transhistorical lexicon, one that has to do more with the dualistic structure of Islam—and the perpetual duels between Sunna and Shia Muslims and between radicals and moderates—rather than with Empire's primary instincts: the scramble for oil and global dominance!

10. One might feel justified in pathologizing these licensed displacements: they seem to serve and act as mere defense mechanisms whereby the censorship of Euro-American and Zionist implications in the state of turmoil in the Arab world is stubbornly maintained. They seem to have a certain irresistible "truthiness" about them, to borrow Stephen Colbert's neologism; they are simultaneously pathological and instrumental in their *orientalizing* (in the Saidian sense) "gut feeling" (Colbert) about, for instance, the genetic tendency of Arabs and Muslims toward violence, see Colbert, "Truthiness."

11. Tatum, *The Mourner's Song,* xi.

12. Klein, *The Shock Doctrine,* 6.

13. Mahmoud Mamdani goes as far as to suggest that, "Since the French Revolution, violence has come to be seen as the midwife of history," *Good Muslim, Bad Muslim,* 3. While this might be the case, I think a sweeping statement of this sort ought to be nuanced lest it should lend credence to Condoleezza Rice's cynical comparison of the 2006 devastating Israeli bombing of Lebanon to the "birth pangs of a new middle east," quoted in *The War on Lebanon,* 109.

14. The modernist studies include in particular Ramazani, *Poetry of Mourning;* Ricciardi, *The Ends of Mourning;* Spargo, *The Ethics of Mourning;* Rae, *Modernism and Mourning;* Moglen, *Mourning Modernity;* Flatley, *Affective Mapping;* the postcolonial studies include in particular Durrant, *Postcolonial Narratives and the Work of Mourning;* Khanna, *Dark Continents;* Gilroy; *Postcolonial Melancholia.* For a good overview, see Rae, "Modernist Mourning."

15. In a lecture titled "Sociology and the Novelist," Elias Khoury maintains that "the Lebanese civil war novel was born with the birth of the war itself and, as such, it evolved into a unique social and literary phenomenon," see Khoury, "Sociology and the Novelist," *AUB Bulletin Today* 5.5.

16. Khoury, "The Memory of the City," 139.

17. Ibid.

18. Peter Homans, introduction to *Symbolic Loss,* edited by Peter Homans, 9.

19. As Sune Haugbolle argues, "The state-sponsored amnesia in Lebanon can hardly be described as structural or mechanical forgetting. On the contrary, there is evidence that officialdom in Lebanon is at pain with the memory and that they try to suppress it. There is no state-sanctioned memorial, apart from a few scrappy attempts, just as there is no war museum. Project plans for a war monument in the central Martyr's Square in Beirut are being discussed, and a nearby Garden of Forgiveness has been scheduled, but even if these plans materialize, they will not change the fact that the Lebanese state has no coherent official discourse to offer on the one historical event that constitutes the basis for the present regime," see Haugbolle, "Public and Private Memory of the Lebanese Civil War," 197–98.

20. Khoury, *Abwāb al-madīna,* 6; *City Gates,* translated by Paula Haydar, 3; *Gates of the City,* translated by Paula Haydar, 3.

21. Meyer, *The Experimental Arabic Novel,* 160.

22. See Khoury, *Zaman al-ʾIḥtilāl,* 253, translation mine.

23. Meyer, *The Experimental Arabic Novel,* 167–68.

24. Khoury, "The Unfolding of Modern Fiction and Arab Memory," 5, 8.

25. Shklovsky, "Art as Technique," 16.

26. Ibid.

27. Spivak, *Death of a Discipline,* 72.

28. See Shklovsky, "Art as Technique," 19.

29. Laub, "An Event without a Witness," *Testimony,* edited by Shoshana Felman and Dori Laub, 80.

30. Ibid., 81, original italics.

31. Khoury, *Little Mountain,* 4.

32. Hoffman, *Lost in Translation,* 278.

33. Khoury, *City Gates,* 15, 21.

34. Caruth, *Unclaimed Experience,* 6.
35. Khoury, *City Gates,* 3.
36. Caruth, *Unclaimed Experience,* 5.
37. Alphen, "Symptoms of Discursivity," in *Acts of Memory,* edited by Mieke Bal, Jonathan Crewe and Leo Spitzer, 33.
38. Khoury, *City Gates,* 4.
39. Brooks, *Reading for the Plot,* 109.
40. Frey, *Interruptions,* 76.
41. Ibid., 75.
42. Ibid., 76.
43. Caruth, *Unclaimed Experience,* 18; Alphen, "Symptoms of Discursivity," 33.
44. Brooks, *Reading for the Plot,* 123.
45. Alphen, "Symptoms of Discursivity," 27; Van der Kolk and McFarlane, "The Black Hole of Trauma," 488.
46. Alphen, "Symptoms of Discursivity," 27.
47. Ibid.
48. Leys, *Trauma: A Genealogy,* 2.
49. Hillis Miller, "The Problematic of Ending in Narrative," 4.
50. Frey, *Interruptions,* 23.
51. Khoury, *City Gates,* 95–96. Further citations in text.
52. The search for the suitcase could also be associated with the search for the city itself and for the homeland (*al-waṭan*), both of which have gone missing amid the civil war ravages. In his long documentary poem, *Madīḥ al-Ẓill al-ʿālī,* or *In Praise of the High Shadow,* Mahmoud Darwish wrote: "*waṭanī ḥaqība* / My homeland is a suitcase / *ḥaqībatī waṭanī* / My suitcase is my homeland," see Darwish, *Madīḥ al-Ẓill al-ʿālī,* 55. At the time Khoury was writing *City Gates,* he must have been in close contact with Mahmoud Darwish who was also in Beirut at the time of the Lebanese civil war and became an official exile after the Sabra and Shatila massacre of 1982 and the departure of Palestinians to Tunisia.
53. Khoury, *City Gates,* 25. Further citations in text.
54. Said, "After Mahfouz," 322.
55. Lyotard, *The Postmodern Condition,* 81.
56. Alphen, "Symptoms of Discursivity," 26.
57. Khoury, "Politics and Culture in Lebanon."
58. Al-Nowaihi, "Committed Postmodernity," 388.
59. Khoury, *City Gates,* 19. Further citations in text.
60. Shabad, "The Most Intimate of Creations," 200. Further references in text.
61. Erikson, "Notes on Trauma and Community," 186.
62. Ricoeur, *The Course of Recognition,* 248–49.
63. Khoury, *City Gates,* 13.
64. Ibid., 71.
65. See Lacan, *The Four Fundamental Concepts of Psychoanalysis,* 3–9.
66. Erikson, "Notes on Trauma and Community," 198.
67. Ibid., 194, original italics.
68. Felski, *Uses of Literature,* 30.

CODA

1. In *Postcolonial Narrative and the Work of Mourning,* Sam Durrant poignantly argues, in reference to Coetzee's early works, that "the novel consists not in the factual recovery *of* history,

nor yet in the psychological recovery *from* history, but rather in the insistence on remaining inconsolable *before* history," 24, original italics. In *Mourning, Modernism, Postmodernism,* the latest example of studies that advocate inconsolability, Tammy Clewell baptizes the tendency in modernist and postmodernist narratives to orchestrate an "internal resistance to consolation" as one of "ongoing mourning," 3.

2. Derrida, *The Work of Mourning,* 142.
3. Santner, *Stranded Objects,* 29.
4. I am alluding specifically here to Judith Butler's essay, "Agencies of Style for a Liminal Subject," 36, in which she states the following: "We have doubtless failed to reconcile the political and the psychoanalytic on the question of agency, but perhaps we have cleared the way to ask another sort of question, one that brings the question of style together with the urgency of survival: how do we read the agency of the subject when its demand for cultural and psychic and political survival makes itself known as style?"
5. Butler, *Precarious Life,* xii.
6. Ibid., xiv
7. Freud, "On Narcissism: An Introduction," 82
8. Butler, *Precarious Life,* xiii.

Bibliography

Abraham, Nicolas. "Notes on the Phantom: A Complement to Freud's Metapsychology." *Critical Inquiry* 13 (1987): 287–92.

Abraham, Nicolas, and Maria Torok. *The Shell and the Kernel: Renewals of Psychoanalysis.* Edited and translated by Nicholas T. Rand. Chicago: University of Chicago Press, 1994.

———. *The Wolf Man's Magic Word: A Cryptonymy.* Translated by Nicholas T. Rand. Minneapolis: University of Minnesota Press, 1986.

Achebe, Chinua. *Things Fall Apart.* Portsmouth, NH: Heinemann, 1986.

Adorno, Theodor W. "Commitment." In *Aesthetics and Politics,* edited by Ronald Taylor, 177–95. New York: Verso, 1980.

———. "Cultural Criticism and Society." In *Prisms* by Theodor W Adorno, 17–34. Translated by Samuel and Shierry Weber. Cambridge: The MIT Press, 1988.

———. *Negative Dialectics.* New York: Continuum, 1973.

Agamben, Giorgio. *State of Exception.* Translated by Kevin Attell. Chicago: University of Chicago Press, 2005.

Al-Nowaihi, Magda M. "Committed Postmodernity: Muḥammad Barrāda's *The Game of Forgetting.*" In *Tradition, Modernity, and Postmodernity in Arabic Literature,* edited by Kamal Abdel-Malek and Wael Hallaq, 367–88. Boston: Brill, 2000.

Alphen, Ernst van . "Symptoms of Discursivity: Experience, Memory, Trauma." In *Acts of Memory: Cultural Recall in the Present,* edited by Mieke Bal, Jonathan Crewe and Leo Spitzer, 24–38. Hanover and London: University Press of New England, 1999.

Appadurai, Arjun. *Fear of Small Numbers: An Essay on the Geography of Anger.* Durham, NC: Duke University Press, 2006.

Attridge, Derek, and Marjorie Howes, eds. *Semicolonial Joyce.* New York: Cambridge University Press, 2000.

Attwood, Bain, Dipesh Chakrabarty, and Claudio Lomnitz. "The Public Life of History." *Public Culture* 20.1 (2008): 1–4.

Auden, W. H. "In Memory of Sigmund Freud." In *Selected Poetry of W. H. Auden,* edited by W. H. Auden, 54–58. New York: Vintage, 1971.

Baccolini, Raffaella. "'She Had Become a Memory': Women as Memory in James Joyce's *Dubliners.*" In *ReJoycing: New Readings of Dubliners,* edited by Rosa M. Bollettieri Bosinelli and Harold F. Mosher Jr., 145–64. Lexington: University of Kentucky Press, 1998.

Baudrillard, Jean. *Passwords.* Translated by Chris Turner. New York: Verso, 2003.

Beckett, Samuel. *Three Novels: Molly, Malone Dies, The Unnamable.* New York: Grove Press, 1958.

———. *Waiting for Godot.* New York: Grove Press, 1954.

Behdad, Ali. "*Une Pratique Sauvage:* Postcolonial Belatedness and Cultural Politics." In *The Pre-Occupation of Postcolonial Studies,* edited by Fawzia Afzal-Khan and Kalpana Seshadri-Crooks, 71–85. Durham, NC: Duke University Press, 2000.

Benjamin, Walter. "Critique of Violence." In *Reflections: Essays, Aphorisms, Autobiographical Writing,* edited and with an introduction by Peter Demetz, 277–300. Translated by Edmund Jephcott. New York: Schocken Books, 1986.

———. "Theses on the Philosophy of History." In *Illuminations: Essays and Reflections,* edited and with an introduction by Hannah Arendt, 253–64. Translated by Harry Zohn. New York: Schocken Books, 1969.

Ben Jelloun, Tahar. *Le dernier Ami.* Paris: Seuil, 2004.

———. *The Last Friend.* Translated by Kevin Michel Capé and Hazel Rowley. New York: The New Press, 2006.

Bernard, Louise. "Countermemory and Return: Reclamation of the (Postmodern) Self in Jamaica Kincaid's *The Autobiography of My Mother* and *My Brother.*" *MFS* 48.1 (2002): 13–138.

Bhabha, Homi. "On the Irremovable Strangeness of Being Different." *PMLA* 113.1 (1998): 34–39.

Birbalsingh, Frank. "Jamaica Kincaid: From Antigua to America." In *Frontiers of Caribbean Literatures in English,* edited by Frank Birbalsingh, 138–51. New York: St. Martin's Press, 1996.

Bloom, Harold. *A Map of Misreading.* Oxford: Oxford University Press, 2003.

Borch-Jacobsen, Mikkel. "The Oedipus Problem in Freud and Lacan." Translated by Douglas Brick. *Critical Inquiry* 20 (Winter 1994): 267–82.

Bouchard, Donald F. Preface to *Language, Counter-Memory, Practice,* by Michel Foucault. Edited by Donald F. Bouchard, translated by Donald F. Bouchard and Sherry Simon. Ithaca: Cornell University Press, 1977.

Bowlby, John. *Loss.* Vol. 3 of *Attachment and Loss.* Forward by Daniel N. Stern. New York: Basic Books, 1980.

Brooks, Peter. *Reading for the Plot: Design and Intention in Narrative.* Cambridge, MA: Harvard University Press, 1984.

Brophy, Sarah. "Angels in Antigua: The Diasporic of Melancholy in Jamaica Kincaid's *My Brother.*" *PMLA* 117.2 (2002): 265–77.

Brush, Stephen G. *The Temperature of History: Phases of Science and Culture in the Nineteenth Century.* New York: Burt Franklin, 1978.

Buckner, Brittnay. "Singular Beast: A Conversation with Jamaica Kincaid." *Callaloo* 31.2 (2008): 461–69.

Butler, Judith. "Agencies of Style for a Liminal Subject." In *Without Guarantees: In Honor of Stuart Hall,* edited by Paul Gilroy, Lawrence Grossberg and Angela McRobbie, 30–37. New York: Verso, 2000.

———. *Bodies That Matter.* London: Routledge, 1993.

———. *Gender Trouble: Feminism and the Subversion of Identity.* London: Routledge, 2006.

———. *Precarious Life: The Powers of Mourning and Violence.* New York: Verso, 2004.

———. *The Psychic Life of Power: Theories in Subjection.* Stanford, CA: Stanford University Press, 1997.

Caruth, Cathy. "Trauma and Experience." Introduction to *Trauma: Explorations in Memory,* edited by Cathy Caruth, 3–12. Baltimore: Johns Hopkins University Press, 1995.

———. *Unclaimed Experience: Trauma, Narrative, and History.* Baltimore: Johns Hopkins University Press, 1996.

Cheng, Ann Anlin. *The Melancholy of Race: Psychoanalysis, Assimilation, and Hidden Grief.* New York: Oxford, 2001.

Cixous, Hélène. "The Laugh of the Medusa." In *Critical Theory Since 1965,* edited by Hazard Adams and Leroy Searle, 309–21. Tallahassee: Florida State University Press, 1992.

Clewell, Tammy. *Mourning, Modernism, Postmodernism.* New York: Palgrave Macmillan, 2009.

Colbert, Stephen. "Truthiness." http://en.wikipedia.org/wiki/Truthiness.

Conrad, Joseph. *Heart of Darkness.* Edited by Robert Kimbrough. New York: Norton, 1988.

Crimp, Douglas. "Melancholia and Moralism." In *Loss: The Politics of Mourning,* edited by David L. Eng and David Kazanjian, 188–202. Berkeley: University of California Press, 2003.

Cudjoe, Selwyn R. "Jamaica Kincaid and the Modernist Project: An Interview." *Callaloo* 12.2/39 (1989): 396–411.

Darmesteter, Arsène. *La Vie des Mots.* Paris: Éditions Champ Libre, 1979.

Darwish, Mahmoud. *Madīḥ al-Ẓill al-ʿālī* [*In Praise of the High Shadow*]. Beirut: Dār al-ʿawda, 1983.

Deane, Seamus. *Strange Country: Modernity and Nationhood in Irish Writing since 1790.* Oxford: Clarendon, 1997.

Deleuze, Gilles. *Bergsonism.* Translated by Hugh Tomlinson. New York: Zone Books, 1988.

———. *Difference and Repetition.* Translated by Paul Patton, 70–128. New York: Columbia University Press, 1994.

———. *Nietzsche et la Philosophie.* Paris: Press Universitaire de France, 1973.

De Man, Paul. "Anthropomorphism and Trope in the Lyric." In *The Rhetoric of Romanticism,* edited by Paul de Man, 239–62. New York: Columbia University Press, 1984.

———. "Autobiography as De-Facement." In *The Rhetoric of Romanticism,* edited by Paul de Man, 67–82. New York: Columbia University Press, 1984.

———. "The Epistemology of Metaphor." In *On Metaphor,* edited by Sheldon Sacks, 11–28. Chicago: University of Chicago Press, 1979.

Derrida, Jacques. *Cinders.* Translated by Ned Lukacher. Lincoln: University of Nebraska Press, 1991.

———. "A Discussion with Jacques Derrida." *Theory and Event* 5.1 (2001), http://muse.jhu.edu/journals/theory_and_event/v005/5.1derrida.html.

———. "Force of Law: The 'Mystical Foundation of Authority.'" In *Deconstruction and the Possibility of Justice,* edited by Drucilla Cornell, Michel Rosenfeld and David Gray Carlson, 3–67. New York: Routledge, 1992.

———. *The Ear of the Other: Otobiography, Transference, Translation.* Edited by Christie McDonald. Translated by Peggy Kamuf. Lincoln: University of Nebraska Press, 1985.

———. "The Laws of Reflection: Nelson Mandela, in Admiration." In *For Nelson Mandela,* edited by Jacques Derrida and Mustapha Tlili, 13–42. Translated by Mary Ann Caws and Isabelle Lorenz. New York: Henry Holt, 1987.

———. "Let us not Forget—Psychoanalysis." *Oxford Literary Review* 12.1–2 (1990): 3–7.

———. *Mémoires for Paul de Man.* Translated by Cecile Lindsay, Jonathan Culler, and Eduardo Cadava. New York: Columbia University Press, 1986.

———. *Monolingualism of the Other; or, The Prosthesis of Origin.* Translated by Patrick Mensah. Stanford, CA: Stanford University Press, 1998.

———. *The Politics of Friendship.* Translated by George Collins. New York: Verso, 1997.

———. *The Post Card: From Socrates and Beyond.* Translated by Alan Bass. Chicago: University of Chicago Press, 1987.

———. *Resistances of Psychoanalysis.* Translated by Peggy Kamuf, Pascale-Anne Brault and Michael Naas. Stanford, CA: Stanford University Press, 1998.

———. *Specters of Marx: The State of the Debt, the Work of Mourning, and the New International.* Translated by Peggy Kamuf. Introduction by Bernd Magnus and Stephen Cullenberg. New York: Routledge, 1994.

———. *The Work of Mourning.* Edited by Pascale-Anne Brault and Michael Naas. Chicago: University of Chicago Press, 2001.

———. *Writing and Difference.* Translated, with an introduction and additional notes by Alan Bass. Chicago: University of Chicago Press. 1978.

Di Orio, Alexei and Roland Vegso. "The Politics of War," *umbr(a)* (2004): 5.

Donnell, Alison. "When Daughter's Defy: Jamaica Kincaid's Fiction." *Women: A Cultural Review* 4.1 (1993): 18–26.

———. "When Writing the Other Is Being True to the Self: Jamaica Kincaid's *The Autobiography of My Mother.*" In *Women's Lives into Print: The Theory, Practice and Writing of Feminist Auto/Biography,* edited by Pauline Polkey, 123–36. New York: St. Martin's Press, 1999.

Durrant, Sam. *Postcolonial Narrative and the Work of Mourning: J. M. Coetzee, Wilson Harris, and Toni Morrison.* New York: State University of New York, 2003.

Eco, Umberto. *Interpretation and Overinterpretation.* Edited by Stefan Collini. Cambridge: Cambridge University Press, 1992.

Eide, Marian. *Ethical Joyce.* Cambridge: Cambridge University Press, 2009.

Eliot, T. S. *The Complete Poems and Plays: 1909–1950.* New York: Harcourt, 1971.

Ellmann, Richard. *James Joyce.* Rev. ed. New York: Oxford University Press, 1983.

Eng, David L. and David Kazanjian, eds. *Loss: The Politics of Mourning.* Berkeley: University of California Press, 2003.

Epicurus. "Epicurus to Menoeceus." In *The Stoic and Epicurean Philosophers,* edited by Whitney Jennings Oates, 30–33. Translated by C. Bailey. New York: Random House, 1940.

Erikson, Kai. "Notes on Trauma and Community." In *Trauma: Explorations in Memory,* edited by Cathy Caruth, 183–99. Baltimore: Johns Hopkins University Press, 1995.

Fabian, Johannes. *Time and the Other: How Anthropology Makes its Objects.* New York: Columbia University Press, 1983.

Fanon, Frantz. *The Wretched of the Earth.* Preface by Jean-Paul Sartre. Translated by Constance Farrington. New York: Grove Press, 1968.

Felski, Rita. *Uses of Literature.* Malden, MA: Blackwell Publishing, 2008.

Ferenczi, Sándor. *Final Contributions to the Problems and Methods of Psychoanalysis.* Edited by Michael Balint. New York: Brunner/Mazel, 1980.

Ferguson, Moira. *Jamaica Kincaid: Where the Land Meets the Body.* Charlottesville: University Press of Virginia, 1994.

———. "A Lot of Memory: An Interview with Jamaica Kincaid." *The Kenyon Review* 16.1 (Winter 1994): 163–88.

Flatley, Jonathan. *Affective Mapping: Melancholia and the Politics of Modernism.* Cambridge: Harvard University Press, 2008.

Foucault, Michel. "Nietzsche, Genealogy, History." In *Language, Counter-Memory, Practice,* by Michel Foucault, edited by Donald F. Bouchard, 139–64. Translated by Donald F. Bouchard and Sherry Simon. Ithaca: Cornell University Press, 1977.

———. *Remarks on Marx: Conversations with Duccio Trombadori.* Translated by James Golstein and James Cascaito. New York: Semiotext(e), 1991.

———. *"Society Must be Defended": Lectures at the Collège de France 1975–1976,* edited by Mauro Bertani and Alessandro Fontana. Translated by David Macey. New York: Picador, 2003.

Freud, Sigmund. "Analysis Terminable and Interminable." In *The Standard Edition of the Complete Psychological Works of Sigmund Freud,* edited and translated by James Strachey, 5: 211–53. London: Hogarth, 1937.

———. *Beyond the Pleasure Principle.* In *On Metapsychology,* edited by Angela Richards, 269–339. Vol. 11 in Penguin Library Freud, gen. ed. and trans. James Strachey. London: Penguin, 1991.

———. *Case Histories II,* compiled and edited by Angela Richards, 225–366. Vol. 9 in Penguin Library Freud, gen. ed. and trans. James Strachey. London: Penguin, 1991.

———. *Civilization and its Discontents.* In *Civilization, Society and Religion,* edited by Albert Dickson, 243–340. Vol. 12 in Penguin Library Freud, gen. ed. and trans. James Strachey. London: Penguin, 1991.

———. *Civilization, Society and Religion,* edited by Albert Dickson. Vol. 12 in Penguin Library Freud, gen. ed. and trans. James Strachey. London: Penguin, 1991.

———. "Constructions in Analysis." In *The Standard Edition of the Complete Psychological Works of Sigmund Freud,* 5: 257–69.

———. "The Economic Problem of Masochism." In *On Metapsychology,* edited by Angela Richards, 409–426.

———. *The Ego and the Id.* In *On Metapsychology,* edited by Angela Richards, 340–401.

———. "From the History of an Infantile Neurosis." In *Case Histories II,* edited by Angela Richards, 225–366. Vol. 9 in Penguin Library Freud, gen. ed. and trans. James Strachey. London: Penguin, 1991.

———. *Group Psychology and the Analysis of the Ego.* In *Civilization, Society and Religion,* edited by Albert Dickson, 91–178.

———. "Inhibitions, Symptoms and Anxiety." In *On Psychopathology,* edited by Albert Dickson, 227–333. Vol. 10 in Penguin Library Freud, gen. ed. and trans. James Strachey. London: Penguin, 1993.

———. "Moses and Monotheism." In *The Origins of Religion,* edited by Albert Dickonson, 237–386. Vol. 13 in Penguin Library Freud, gen. ed. and trans. James Strachey. London: Penguin, 1990.

———. "Mourning and Melancholia." In *On Metapsychology,* edited by Angela Richards, 245–69.

———. *On Metapsychology: The Theory of Psychoanalysis.* Edited by Angela Richards. Vol. 11 in Penguin Library Freud, gen. ed. and trans. James Strachey. London: Penguin, 1991.

———. "On Narcissism: An Introduction." In *On Metapsychology,* edited by Angela Richards, 59–97.

———. "On Transience." In *Art and Literature,* edited by Albert Dickson, 283–290. Vol. 14 in Penguin Library Freud, gen. ed. and trans. James Strachey. London: Penguin, 1990.

———. "Remembering, Repeating and Working-Through." In *The Standard Edition,* ed. and trans. James Strachey, 12: 147–56. London: The Hogarth Press, 1968.

———. "Screen Memories." In *The Standard Edition,* ed. and trans. James Strachey, 5: 301–22.

———. *The Standard Edition of the Complete Psychological Works of Sigmund Freud.* Edited and translated by James Strachey. 25 vols. London: The Hogarth Press, 1953–74.

———. "Thoughts on War and Death." In *Civilization, Society and Religion,* edited by Albert Dickson, 57–89.

Frey, Hans-Jost. *Interruptions.* Translated by Georgia Albert. New York: SUNY Press, 1996.

Frye, Northrop. *Anatomy of Criticism.* Princeton: Princeton University Press, 1973.

Gana, Nouri. "Beyond the Pale: Toward an Exemplary Relationship between the Judge and the Literary Critic." *Law and Literature* 15.3 (2003): 313–43.

———. "Donne Undone: The Journey of Psychic Re-integration in Wilson Harris's *Palace of the Peacock.*" *Ariel* 32.1 (2001): 153–70.

———. "Remembering Forbidding Mourning: Repetition, Indifference, Melanxiety, Hamlet" *Mosaic* 37.2 (June 2004): 59–78.

———. "War, Poetry, Mourning: Darwish, Adonis, Iraq," *Public Culture* 22.1 (2010): 33–65.

Gardiner, Muriel. *The Wolf-Man by the Wolf-Man.* New York: Basic Books, 1971.

Gauch, Suzanne. "*A Small Place:* Some Perspectives on the Ordinary." *Callaloo* 25.3 (2002): 910–19.

Gilmore, Leigh. *The Limits of Autobiography: Trauma and Testimony.* Ithaca: Cornell University Press, 2001.

Gilroy, Paul. *Postcolonial Melancholia.* New York: Columbia University Press, 2004.

Glissant, Edouard. *Caribbean Discourse: Selected Essays.* Translated and with an introduction by J. Michael Dash. Charlottesville: University Press of Virginia, 1989.

Goldfarb, Brad. "Writing = Life" Interview with Writer Jamaica Kincaid." In *A Closer Look: The Writer's Reader,* edited by Sidney I. Dobrin and Anis S. Bawarshi, 359–64. New York: McGraw-Hill, 2003.

Gordon, John. "Dubliners and the Art of Losing." *Studies in Short Fiction* 32.3 (1995): 343–52.

Greenberg, Jay R., and Stephen A. Mitchell. *Object Relations in Psychoanalytic Theory.* Cambridge, MA: Harvard University Press, 1983.

Habiby, Emile. *The Secret Life of Saeed: The Pessoptimist.* Northampton, MA: Interlink Books, 2001.

Hardt, Michael and Antonio Negri. *Multitude: War and Democracy in the Age of Empire.* New York: Penguin, 2004.

Harpham, Geoffrey Galt. "The Business of Mourning." *Southern Review* 32.3 (1996): 537–55.

Hart, H. L. A. *The Concept of Law.* Oxford: Clarendon Press, 1961.

Hassan, Ihab. "From Postmodernism to Postmodernity: The Local/Global Context." *Philosophy and Literature* 51.1 (2001): 1–13.

Haugbolle, Sune. "Public and Private Memory of the Lebanese Civil War." *Comparative Studies of South Asia, Africa and the Middle East* 25.1 (2005): 191–203.

Heidegger, Martin. *Being and Time.* Translated by John Macquarie and Edward Robinson. New York: HarperSanFrancisco, 1962.

Herring, Philip F. *Joyce's Uncertainty Principle.* Princeton: Princeton University Press, 1987.

Hoffman, Eva. *Lost in Translation: A Life in a New Language.* New York: Dutton, 1989.

Holcomb, Gary E. "Travels of a Transnational Slut: Sexual Migration in Kincaid's *Lucy.*" *Critique* 44.3 (2003): 295–312.

Holcomb, Gary E. and Kimberly S. Holcomb. "'I MADE HIM': Sadomasochism in Kincaid's *The Autobiography of My Mother.*" *Callaloo* 25.3 (2002): 969–76.

Holst-Warhaft, Gail. *The Cue for Passion: Grief and its Political Uses.* Cambridge, MA: Harvard University Press, 2000.

Homans, Peter. Introduction to *Symbolic Loss,* edited by Peter Homans, 1–40.

———, ed., *Symbolic Loss: The Ambiguity of Mourning and Memory at Century's End.* Charlottesville: University of Virginia Press, 2000.

Hovsepian, Nubar, ed., *The War on Lebanon: A Reader.* Northampton, MA: Olive Branch Press, 2008.

Huyssen, Andreas. "Present Pasts: Media, Politics, Amnesia." *Public Culture* 12.1 (2000): 21–38.

Ingersoll, Earl G. "Melancholy and Mourning in *Dubliners.*" *Q/W/E/R/T/Y: Arts, Littératures & Civilisations du Monde Anglophone 10* (2000): 85–90.

James, Henry. *The Turn of the Screw.* Edited by Peter G. Beidler. New York: Bedford, 1995.

Jameson, Fredric. "Third-World Literature in the Era of Multinational Capitalism." *Social Text* 15 (Fall 1986): 65–88.

Jay, Martin. "The Apocalyptic Imagination and the Inability to Mourn." In *Force Fields: Between Intellectual History and Cultural Critique,* edited by Martin Jay, 84–98. New York: Routledge, 1993.

———. *Refractions of Violence.* New York: Routledge, 2003.

Joyce, James. *Dubliners.* Edited by Robert Scholes in consultation with Richard Ellmann. New York: Viking Press, 1967.

———. "An Early Version of 'The Sisters.'" In *Dubliners,* 237–46.

———. *Exiles.* London: New English Library, 1952.

———. "A Letter to Grant Richards, May 5, 1906." In *Dubliners,* 260–64.

———. *Ulysses.* Edited by Declan Kiberd. New York: Penguin, 1992.

Khanna, Ranjana. *Dark Continents: Psychoanalysis and Colonialism.* Durham, NC: Duke University Press, 2003

Kazanjian, David, and Marc Nichanian. "Between Genocide and Catastrophe." In *Loss: The Politics of Mourning,* edited by David L. Eng and David Kazanjian, 125–47.

Khoury, Elias. *Abwāb al-Madīna.* Beirut: Dar al-Adāb, 1981.

———. *City Gates.* Translated by Paula Haydar. New York: Picador, 2007.

———. *Gates of the City.* Translated by Paula Haydar. Minneapolis: University of Minnesota Press, 1993.

———. *Little Mountain.*Translated by Maia Tabet. Minneapolis: University of Minnesota Press, 1989.

———. "The Memory of the City," *Grand Street* 54 (Autumn 1995): 137–42.

———. "Politics and Culture in Lebanon: Interview with Elias Khoury," http://www.lcpslebanon.org/pub/breview/br5/khourybr5.html

———. "Sociology and the Novelist," *AUB Bulletin Today* 5.5 (August 2004), http://staff.aub.edu.lb/~webbultn/v5n6/28.html.

———. "The Unfolding of Modern Fiction and Arab Memory." *The Journal of the Midwest Modern Language Association* 23.1 (1990): 1–8.

———. *Zaman al-ʾIḥtilāl* [Colonial Time]. Beirut: Muʾassasat al-Abḥāth al-Arabiyya, 1985.

Kiberd, Declan. *Inventing Ireland: The Literature of the Modern Nation.* Cambridge, MA: Harvard University Press, 1996.

Kierkegaard, Søren. *Repetition.* In *Fear and Trembling/Repetition,* by Søren, Kierkegaard. Translated by Howard V. Hong and Edna H. Hong. Princeton: Princeton University Press, 1983.

Kincaid, Jamaica. *Annie John.* New York: Plume, 1986.

———. *At the Bottom of the River.* New York: Plume, 1992.

———. *The Autobiography of My Mother.* New York: Farrar, Straus and Giroux, 1996.

———. "In History." In *My Garden (Book),*153–66.

———. *Lucy.* New York: Plume, 1991.

———. *Mr. Potter.* New York: Farrar, Straus and Giroux, 2002.

———. *My Brother.* New York: Farrar, 1997.

———. *My Garden (Book).* New York: Farrar, Straus and Giroux, 1999.

———. *A Small Place.* New York: Plume, 1988.

Klein, Naomi. *The Shock Doctrine: The Rise of Disaster Capitalism.* New York: Metropolitan Books, 2007.

Knapp, Bettina L. "Joyce's 'A Painful Case': The Train and an Epiphanic Experience." *Études Irlandaises* 13.2 (1988): 45–60.

Kristeva, Julia. *Black Sun: Depression and Melancholia.* Translated by Leon S. Roudier. New York: Columbia University Press, 1989.

———. *Intimate Revolt: The Powers and Limits of Psychoanalysis.* Translated by Jeanine Herman. New York: Columbia University Press, 2002.

———. *The Sense and Non-Sense of Revolt: The Powers and Limits of Psychoanalysis.* Translated by Jeanine Herman. New York: Columbia University Press, 2000.

Lacan, Jacques. "Desire and the Interpretation of Desire in *Hamlet.*" Edited by Jacques-Alain Miller. Translated by James Hulbert. *Yale French Studies* 55/56 (1977): 11–52.

———. *Écrit: A Selection.* Translated by Alan Sheridan. New York: Norton, 1977.

———. *The Four Fundamental Concepts of Psychoanalysis.* Translated by Alan Sheridan. New York: Norton, 1977.

LaCapra, Dominick. *History and Memory after Auschwitz.* Ithaca: Cornell University Press, 1998.

———. "Trauma, Absence, Loss." *Critical Inquiry* 25 (1999): 696–727.

Laub, Dori. "An Event without a Witness: Truth, Testimony and Survival." In *Testimony: Crises of Witnessing in Literature, Psychoanalysis and History,* edited by Shoshana Felman and Dori Laub. New York: Routledge, 1992. 75–92.

———. "Truth and Testimony: The Process and the Struggle." In *Trauma: Explorations in Memory,* edited by Cathy Caruth, 61–75. Baltimore: Johns Hopkins University Press, 1995.

Leys, Ruth. *Trauma: A Genealogy.* Chicago: Chicago University Press, 2000.

Lloyd, David. "Colonial Trauma/Postcolonial recovery?" *Interventions: International Journal of Postcolonial Studies* 2.2 (2000): 212–28.

———. The Memory of Hunger." In *Loss: The Politics of Mourning,* edited by David L. Eng and David Kazanjian, 205–28.

Lucretius. "On the Nature of Things." In *The Stoic and Epicurean Philosophers,* edited by Whitney Jennings Oates, 69–219. Translated by H. A. J. Munro. New York: Modern Library, 1957.

Lukacher, Ned. *Primal Scenes: Literature, Philosophy, Psychoanalysis.* Ithaca: Cornell University Press, 1986.

Lyotard, Jean-François. *The Differend: Phrases in Dispute.* Translated by Georges Van Den Abbeele. Minneapolis: University of Minnesota Press, 1988.

———. *Political Writings.* Translated by Bill Readings and Kevin Paul Geiman. Minneapolis: University of Minnesota Press, 1993.

———. *The Postmodern Condition.* Translated by Geoff Bennington and Brian Massumi. Minneapolis: University of Minnesota Press, 1984.

Mamdani, Mahmoud. *Good Muslim, Bad Muslim: America, the Cold War, and the Roots of Terror.* New York: Pantheon Books, 2004.

Memmi, Albert. *The Colonizer and the Colonized.* Translated by Howard Greenfeld. Introduction by Jean Paul Sartre. London: Earthscan Publications, 1990.

Meyer, Stefan G. *The Experimental Arabic Novel: Postcolonial Literary Modernism in the Levant.* Albany: State University of New York, 2001.

Miller, J. Hillis. "The Critic as Host." In *Deconstruction and Criticism,* edited by Harold Bloom, Paul de Man, and Jacques Derrida, 217–53. New York: Seabury, 1979.

———. "The Figure in the Carpet." In *Modern Literary Theory: A Reader,* edited by Philip Rice and Patricia Waugh, 172–85. London: Arnold, 1989.

———. "The Problematic of Ending in Narrative," *Nineteenth-Century Fiction* 33.1 (1978): 3–7.

Mitscherlich, Alxander, and Margarette Mitscherlich. *The Inability to Mourn: Principles of Collective Behavior.* Translated by Beverley R. Placzek and Robert Jay Lifton. New York: Grove Press, 1975.

Moglen, Seth. *Mourning Modernity: Literary Modernism and the Injuries of American Capitalism.* Stanford, CA: Stanford University Press, 2007.

Nancy, Jean-Luc. *Being Singular Plural.* Translated by Robert D. Richardson and Anne E. O'Byrne. Stanford, CA: Stanford University Press, 2000.

———. "L'Intrus." *New Centennial Review* 2.3 (2002): 1–14.

Nasr, Vali. *The Shia Revival: How Conflicts Within Islam Will Shape the Future.* New York: Norton, 2007.

Neocleous, Mark. "War as peace, peace as pacification." *Radical Philosophy,* http://www.radicalphilosophy.com/default.asp?channel_id=2369&editorial_id=28991.

Nichanian, Marc. "Catastrophic Mourning." In *Loss: The Politics of Mourning,* edited by David L. Eng and David Kazanjian, 99–124.

Nietzsche, Friedrich. *The Gay Science.* Translated by Walter Kaufmann. New York: Vintage, 1974.

———. *Thus Spake Zarathustra: A Book for All and None.* Translated by Thomas Common. New York: Russell & Russell, 1964.

———. *Unfashionable Observations.* Translated by Richard Gray. Stanford, CA: Stanford University Press, 1995.

Norris, Margot. *Suspicious Readings of Joyce's "Dubliners."* Philadelphia: Pennsylvania University Press, 2003.

Page, Kezia. "'What if He Did not Have a Sister [Who Lived in the United States]?' Jamaica Kincaid's *My Brother* as Remittance Text." *Small Axe* 21 (2006): 37–53.

Paravisini-Gebert, Lizabeth. *Jamaica Kincaid: A Critical Companion.* Westport, CT: Greenwood Press, 1999.

Parker, Patricia. "Metaphor and Catachresis." In *The Ends of Rhetoric: History, Theory, Practice,* edited by John Bender and David E. Wellbery, 60–73. Stanford, CA: Stanford University Press, 1990.

Paxson, James J. *The Poetics of Personification.* Cambridge: Cambridge University Press, 1994.

Philips, Adam. "Making the Case: Freud's Literary Engagements." *Profession* (2003): 10–20.

Rae, Patricia. "Modernist Mourning." Introduction to *Modernism and Mourning,* edited by Patricia Rae, 13–49.

———. *Modernism and Mourning,* ed. Lewisburg: Bucknell University Press, 2007.

Ragland-Sullivan, Ellie. *Jacques Lacan and the Philosophy of Psychoanalysis.* Urbana: University of Illinois Press, 1986.

Ramazani, Jahan. *Poetry of Mourning: The Modern Elegy from Hardy to Heaney.* Chicago: University of Chicago Press, 1994.

———. "When There Are So Many We Shall Have to Mourn." Afterword to *Modernist Mourning,* edited by Patricia Rae, 286–95.

Rand, Nicholas, trans. and ed. *The Shell and the Kernel: Renewals of Psychoanalysis,* by Nicolas Abraham and Maria Torok. Chicago: University of Chicago Press, 1994.

Ricciardi, Alessia. *The Ends of Mourning: Psychoanalysis, Literature, Film.* Stanford, CA: Stanford University Press, 2003.

Ricoeur, Paul. *The Course of Recognition.* Translated by David Pellauer. Cambridge, MA: Harvard University Press, 2005.

———. *La Mémoire, l'Histoire, l'Oubli.* Paris: Édition Seuil, 2000.

———. "What is a Text? Explanation and Understanding." In *Twentieth Century Literary Theory: An Introductory Anthology,* edited by Vassilis Lambropoulos and David Neal Miller, 331–49. Albany: State University of New York Press, 1987.

Riffaterre, Michel. "Prosopopoeia." *Yale French Studies* 69 (1985): 107–23.

Rushdie, Salman. *Imaginary Homelands.* London: Penguin, 1991.

Rushdy, Ashraf H. A. "'Rememory': Primal Scenes and Constructions in Toni Morrison's Novels." *Contemporary Literature* 31. 3 (1990): 300–23.

Sacks, Peter. *The English Elegy: Studies in Genre from Spencer to Yeats.* Baltimore: Johns Hopkins University Press, 1985.

Said, Edward. "After Mahfouz." In *Reflections on Exile and Other Essays* by Edward Said, 317–326. Cambridge, MA: Harvard, 2003.

Santner, Eric. *Stranded Objects: Mourning, Memory, and Film in Postwar Germany.* Ithaca: Cornell University Press, 1990.

Sarkar, Bhaskar. *Mourning the Nation: Indian Cinema in the Wake of Partition.* Durham, NC: Duke University Press, 2009.

Savoy, Eric. "Embarrassments: Figure in the Closet." *The Henry James Review* 20 (1999): 227–36.

———. "Necro-filia, or Hawthorne's Melancholia." *English Studies in Canada* 27 (2001): 459–80.

Shabad, Peter. "The Most Intimate of Creations: Symptoms as Memorials to One's Lonely Suffering." In *Symbolic Loss: The Ambiguity of Mourning and Memory at Century's End,* edited by Peter Homans, 197–212. Charlottesville: University Press of Virginia, 2000.

Shakespeare, William. *Hamlet.* Edited by Susanne L. Wofford. Boston: Bedford Books, 1994.

Shklovsky, Viktor. "Art as Technique." In *Literary Theory: An Anthology,* edited by Julie Rivkin and Michael Ryan, 15–21. Oxford: Blackwell Publishers, 2004.

Simmons, Diane. *Jamaica Kincaid.* New York: Twayne, 1994.

Simon, Roger I. "The Paradoxical Practice of Zakhor: Memories of 'What Has Never Been My Fault or My Deed.'" In *Between Hope and Despair,* edited by Simon et al., 9–25.

Simon, Roger I., Sharon Rosenberg, and Claudia Eppert, eds. *Between Hope and Despair: Pedagogy and the Remembrance of Historical Trauma.* New York: Rowman & Littlefield, 2000.

———. "Between Hope and Despair: The Pedagogical Encounter of Historical Remembrance." In *Between Hope and Despair,* edited by Simon et al., 1–8.

Smythe, Karen E. *Figuring Grief: Gallant, Munro, and the Poetics of Elegy.* Montreal: McGill-Queen's University Press, 1992.

Soto-Crespo, Ramón E. "Death and the Diaspora Writer: Hybridity and Mourning in the Work of Jamaica Kincaid." *Contemporary Literature* 43.2 (2002): 342–76.

Spargo, R. Clifton. *The Ethics of Mourning: Grief and Responsibility in Elegiac Literature.* Baltimore: Johns Hopkins University Press, 2004.

Spivak, Gayatri Chakravorty. *Death of a Discipline.* New York: Columbia University Press, 2003.

———. *Outside in the Teaching Machine.* New York: Routledge, 1993.

Staten, Henry. "The Bride Stripped Bare, or Lacan *avec* Plato." In *Eros in Mourning,* by Henry Staten, 166–85.

———. *Eros in Mourning.* Baltimore: The Johns Hopkins University Press, 1995.

Tatum, James. *The Mourner's Song: War and Remembrance form the Iliad to Vietnam.* Chicago: University of Chicago Press, 2003.

Thiongo, Ngugi wa. "Borders and Bridges: Seeking Connections between Things." In *The Pre-Occupation of Postcolonial Studies,* edited by Fawzia Afzal-Khan and Kalpana Seshadri-Crooks, 119–25. Durham, NC: Duke University Press, 2000.

Torchiana, Donald T. *Backgrounds for Joyce's "Dubliners."* Boston : Allen & Unwin, 1986.

Torok, Maria. "The Illness of Mourning and the Fantasy of the Exquisite Corpse." In *The Shell and the Kernel: Renewals of Psychoanalysis,* by Nicolas Abraham and Maria Torok. Edited and translated by Nicholas T. Rand, 107–24. Chicago: University of Chicago Press, 1994.

Van der Kolk, Bessel A. and Alexander C. McFarlane. "The Black Hole of Trauma." In *Literary Theory: An Anthology,* edited by Julie Rivkin and Michael Ryan, 487–502. Oxford: Blackwell Publishers, 2004.

Vesala-Varttala, Tanja. *Sympathy and Joyce's Dubliners: Ethical Probing of Reading, Narrative, and Textuality.* Tampere, Finland: Tampere University Press, 1999.

Walcott, Derek. "What the Twilight Says: An Overture." In *Dream on Monkey Mountain and Other Plays,* edited by Derek Walcott, 1–40. New York: Farrar, Straus and Giroux, 1970.

Walcott, Rinaldo. "Pedagogy and Trauma: The Middle Passage, Slavery, and the Problem of Creolization." In *Between Hope and Despair,* edited by Simon et al., 135–51.

Watkin, William. *On Mourning: Theories of Loss in Modern Literature.* Edinburgh: Edinburgh University Press, 2004.

Weller, Shane. "Nothing to Be Said: On the Inexpressible in Modern Philosophy and Literature." *Angelaki* 8.1 (2003): 91–108.

White, Hayden. *Tropics of Discourse: Essays in Cultural Criticism.* Baltimore: Johns Hopkins University Press, 1978.

Winnicott, D. W. "Fear of Breakdown." In *Psycho-Analytic Explorations,* by D. W. Winnicott. Edited by Claire Winnicott, Ray Shepherd, and Madeleine Davis, 87–95. Cambridge, MA: Harvard University Press, 1989.

Yeats, W. B. "Among School Children." In *Yeats's Poems,* edited by Norman Jeffares, 323–325. London: Papermac, 1989.

Young, Robert J. C. *Postcolonialism.* Oxford: Blackwell, 2001.

Zelizer, Barbie. *Remembering to Forget: Holocaust Memory Through the Camera Eye.* Chicago: University of Chicago Press, 1998.

Žižek, Slavoj. "Melancholy and the Act." *Critical Inquiry* 26 (Summer 2000): 657–81.

———. *Violence: Six Sideways Reflections.* New York: Picador, 2008.

Index

www.ingramcontent.com/pod-product-compliance
Lightning Source LLC
Chambersburg PA
CBHW071356100726
47908CB00004B/1004

* 9 7 8 1 6 1 1 4 8 5 7 8 3 *